IRIS MURDOCH

A WRITER AT WAR

IRIS
MURDOCH
A WRITER
AT WAR

Letters & Diaries 1939-45

EDITED & INTRODUCED BY

PETER J CONRADI

First published in 2010 by

Short Books
3A Exmouth House
Pine Street
EC1R 0JH

10 9 8 7 6 5 4 3

A CIP catalogue record for this book is available from the British Library.

ISBN 978-1-906021-22-1

Printed in Great Britain by Clays, Suffolk

Cover design: Emily Fox

For Aurea and Rebecca, with appreciation

CONTENTS

GENERAL INTRODUCTION
& CAST-LISTS

DAME IRIS MURDOCH, world-renowned novelist and philosopher was born in Dublin on 15 July 1919 and died in Oxford on 8 February 1999. Two years later, this death was re-enacted by Dame Judi Dench playing old, demented Iris in the film *Iris* while a young, promiscuous Iris was brought to life by Kate Winslet. Directed by Sir Richard Eyre, this film was shot on a small budget in a few weeks, and presented a moving love story. Part of the interest, as in Greek tragedy, was in watching the wasting of brilliance and greatness, and the endurance of love. It also dealt bravely and harrowingly with Dame Iris's decline and death from Alzheimers.

Made from two of John Bayley's memoirs[1] with good intent and heart, the universality, rather than the particularity, of this film was witty and poignant. None the less the film seemed to this observer, who acted as consultant, problematic. It was as if a film

---

[1] *Iris: A Memoir* – in USA *Elegy for Iris* (1998); and *Iris and The Friends* – in USA *Iris and Her Friends* (1999). The terms of his contracts precluded either Prof Bayley or the IM estate from any 'cut' or interest in this film and John Bayley indeed did not profit.

about Nietzsche told us that he lost his wits from tertiary syphilis, had a big moustache, was rude to Wagner, and was looked after by his sister, but never that he wrote *The Birth of Tragedy*. That the film contained not one word Murdoch ever wrote nor much accurate rendition of any she said seemed no accident. Nor did the fact that neither actress, reportedly, bothered to read any works by Dame Iris.

After this film came out, to a deal of publicity, I found myself at an exhibition of paintings by Dame Iris's friend Harry Weinberger. Here were two elderly ladies examining a beautiful gouache portrait, one asking: 'I recognise that face – whose is it?' and being answered, 'Oh you know, *that's that writer who went mad*'.

Dame Iris, in life so august, remote and intensely private, was in death unwittingly reduced to two opposed stereotypes: in vulgar language bonking (younger Iris) or bonkers (elderly Iris). If you're American: screwing or screwy. Both sensational-isms reduced her to gross physicality, by-passing and demean-ing the one thing about her that was truly remarkable – the freedom of her mind. And anyone doubting the ripple-effect of such publicity might have been sobered on 2 July 2007 by a *Daily Telegraph* headline. That paper's Arts and Media Editor reported the acquisition by the Iris Murdoch Centre at Kingston University of a blameless letter-run to a young gay American suf-fering from AIDS, letters written towards the end of Dame Iris's life, full of a very affectionate and transparently sexless interest in helping him.[2] This headline read: *Even Alzheimers Could Not Quell her Lust*. That married both sensationalisms.

Included in this present volume is a 1943 letter from Frank

<hr />

[2] For a full and frank account of another such friendship between Murdoch and a different younger student, see *With Love and Rage : a Memoir of Iris Murdoch* by David Morgan, published by Kingston University Press in 2009.

Thompson warning the young Murdoch about how violently misogynistic most men secretly are. Frank was a prescient friend and she was right to mourn his murder at age 23 and to miss his wise counsel thereafter. The same week that Frank died, Keith Douglas, another war poet, was killed during the D-day campaign in Normandy. One of his best-known poems bears the ironic title *Simplify Me When I'm Dead*. The simplification of Iris Murdoch has been impressive. She, whose life-work fervently championed the complexity of the inner life, has had a simplified afterlife.

Such portrayal leaves untouched everything that keeps seven of her greatest novels – *Under the Net, The Bell, The Flight from the Enchanter, A Severed Head, A Fairly Honourable Defeat, The Black Prince* and *The Sea, The Sea* – compelling and mysterious. And her philosophy – *The Sovereignty of Good* in particular – also remains luminous and urgent. Her own passionately imaginative inner life stayed private. Philippa Foot (née Bosanquet), her closest friend over sixty years, compared Murdoch's secrecy to that of a cat.[3] She remains in some ways hard to focus.

One task of the present book is therefore to reclaim the living writer as she begins her adult life. The journal and these letters show her, by contrast, as a person vividly alive and fascinated by her world, trying to make sense of it by writing it down, seeking to be in charge of her own destiny. That she was disturbed by a troubled love-life does not prevent her being a role-model for young women today. Such experiences, which mark the growing-up of most of us, were to feed her strenuous moral philosophy and her fiction alike. And in these writings she walks and talks and lives once more.

She possessed a formidably strong will-to-power. In love and in learning, she had an urgent desire to succeed and a fear of

---

[3] Conversation with the editor, 1997.

failing. In 1988, finding some writings dating from this period, she noted accurately in her journal that 'There is a kind of intensity, even rage, about that time when I had no notion what the future held'.[4] In the flat they shared from 1943 Philippa once quipped that Murdoch probably had a diary-note reading '*Memo: to make my mark*'.

To her contemporaries a golden girl for whom the waters parted, she was indeed ambitious and resilient. Six weeks before he was murdered early in June 1944, Frank Thompson (Part Two) writes her his last letter, comforting her over her unhappy, simultaneous affairs with two rival lovers. He expressed his confidence that, despite all heartache, 'you have springs within you that will never fail'. Indeed Murdoch herself, during the worst time, recorded independently to David Hicks (Part Three) that 'I feel, even at the lowest moment, such endless vitality inside me'.[5] Hicks, who got engaged to her in November 1945 and jilted her in January 1946 wrote similarly to reassure her, after their 'madcap' tale was done, that 'you do remain a whole person, with your ability to spring intact'.

She wrote often of feeling joyously 'intoxicated': by discovering Henry James's *The Wings of the Dove* (Oct 44) by Existentialism (May 45), with simply being alive (Sep 45), and with the challenges of postwar adult liberty (Jan 46). She had, in Freudian language, abundant ego-strength. An early letter to Hicks (April 42) while still at Oxford declared '*a certain invincibility at present – intensely alive, physically & intellectually – ready to learn anything, do anything*' (my emphasis).

'Ready to learn anything' is right. She was indeed curious about the world and everything and everybody it contains, with a passionate and omnivorous intellectual hunger. From school

---

[4] Journal comment by IM on re-reading her 1943/4 writings/diaries, 21 Dec 1988.

and Oxford she knew French, Latin and Greek. In 1942/3 she added some German and Russian and soon afterwards arrived at the Turkish Embassy demanding to be taught Turkish – in order, mysteriously, to improve her post-war job prospects. There are passages in these letters here about the excitements of discovering Aeschylus, Rilke, Kafka, Shakespeare, Henry James, TS Eliot, James Joyce, Dostoievsky and many more. There are discussions concerning how she can 'learn to be a writer'... And she is emotionally brave and adventurous.

Iris Murdoch after 1946 came to see human life as a pilgrimage away from self-centred illusion towards other-centredness and her philosophy championed the 'inner life' as the *locus* of the spiritual. Her richly inventive novels are, accordingly, numinous adventure-stories with cultured English moral pilgrims as protagonists. They have been admired by writers as different as A.S. Byatt, John Updike – 'a marvellous creative spirit, a comfort and a stimulant, both' – and Norman Mailer.[6] These fictions feed off Shakespeare and Dostoievsky alike, and their comi-tragic plots, often apparently fantastical, pale in comparison with the complications of her own early life.

It should not surprise us that the intellectually precocious and emotionally immature 20 year-old who wrote The Magpie Journal (Part One here) and the early letters to Frank and David (Parts Two and Three) had plenty of painful growing up to do. In 1940 her letters are often self-conscious and occasionally precious; five years later they are grown-up. Another interest of the letter-runs is what they convey of the process of reaching adulthood during a world war, when everything was unexpected and strange and an Oxford student could find herself digging up Portmeadow for cabbages, threading camouflage meshing

---

[6] See Norman Mailer *The Spooky Art* (2003) passim, John Updike, Letter to the editor, Jan 2002.

for tanks in the Worcester Provost's drawing room and taking care of poor evacuee children from the East End, who dressed in multiple layers of underclothing held together with pins, and sometimes had contagious impetigo; all this in addition to her regular duties of study.[7]

A note about the provenance of these letter-runs. Frank and Iris's extant correspondence is in closed collection in the Bodleian Library.[8] In November 1965 she noted in her journal, 'I looked for Frank's letters today and couldn't find them; upset by this... there were such a lot.' It is certain that what survives in the Bodleian is not the whole of their correspondence: some has been lost. In November 1945 while in London with David Hicks she went through the letters Frank Thompson had written her and chose a few to send to his surviving younger brother the historian E.P. Thompson, who duly published some carefully chosen extracts of letters from Frank (only) the following year in his and his mother Theodosia's *There is a Spirit in Europe: A Memoir of Frank Thompson* (Gollancz) commemorating Frank's life through his writings. In the case of some of his later letters, these extracts alone have survived, and where that is the case, three dots indicating missing text (...) confirms that the text is truncated. I am very grateful to Dorothy Thompson, to Prof John Bayley and to the Bodleian Library for permission to publish all that survives.

As for the letters in Part Three, Murdoch's side of the correspondence is – with the exception of the last page of a letter written 10 October 1945 – virtually complete. These were acquired by the Bodleian Library (as part of a separate collection from the Thompson papers) a few years ago and are as yet uncatalogued. I

---

[7] Philippa Foot's recollection, October 2008

[8] A few are originals; others are photocopies.

am grateful for all John Bayley's encouragement and permission to use copyright materials; to Kingston University's Iris Murdoch Centre for their generous assistance – the prefix KU in Part Three footnotes refer to items held in Kingston's archive – to Simon Kusseff; to Priscilla Martin for help with Latin and Greek, Olga Berezhovska for Russian, Bernard Jantet for French, and to Tamsin Osler who carefully transcribed all the letters. Jane Jantet and Prue Conradi researched Hugh Vaughan James's post-war life. Hannah Sandford at the London Library, David Brown at the Oxford Examination Schools, Pauline Adams at Somerville and Andrew Mussell at Lincoln College helped track the academic careers of Oxford friends. Francis King recalled David Hicks as a colleague, and Tom Hicks and Julia Lysaght as a father.

■■■

Magpies Cast-list

David Henry Arthur **Alexander**, reading Classics at Hertford College 1936-40.

Denys Andrew **Becher**, reading Modern Languages (French and German) at St Edmund Hall 1938 (shortened degree, conferred 1947).

Tony **Cotton** – no exact match – [a John Anthony Cotton goes up to Lincoln College in 1944].

Moira **Dunbar**, reading Geography as an Oxford Home Student (now St Anne's College) 1936-39.

Tom Hugh **Fletcher**, reading English at St Catherine's College 1937 – (shortened degree, conferred 1948).

Hugh Vaughan **James**, reading physiology at St Edmund Hall 1935-39. Passed the exams for the degree of Bachelor of Medicine and Bachelor of Surgery in 1949.

Ruth **Kingsbury**, reading English Literature at Lady Margaret Hall 1936-40.

Stanley Victor **Peskett**, reading English Literature at
St Edmund Hall 1936-39.

Frances Mary **Podmore** [later, Rutherford], reading English Literature
as an Oxford Home Student (now St Anne's College) 1937-40.

Cecil Robert Burnet **Quentin**, reading English Literature at
St Edmund Hall 1936 – degree conferred: 1945.

Kirsteen **Rowntree** [later, Aldridge]. Either Anna Griselda Beaumont
Rowntree, reading PPE at Somerville, 1940-42; or Kirsteen Maie Tait
reading Literae Humaniores at Somerville College, 1939-41.

Charles Henry **Southwood**, reading PPE at Merton College 1938-
conferred 1948.

Joyce Marianne **Taylor** – St Hilda's – achieved Class II exam results in
Classics, 1937; then listed in 1940 as a College scholar in French.

Jack Harry Walter **Trotman**, reading Military History at
Lincoln College 1938-40.

Joan Margaret Wynyard **Yeaxlee** [later, Browne], reading
English Literature at St Hugh's 1934-37, degree conferred 1944.

Cast-list From Parts 2&3

Alastine **Bell** [later, Lehmann], reading History at Lady Margaret Hall,
1938-39; see also Pt 3 n 12.

Ronald **Bellamy** – Queen's College, 1936-38, Classics, 1938, followed
by Class I exam results in PPE, shortened examination, in 1945.

Hugh Armstrong **Clegg** – reading Classics at Magdalen in 1939.

Henry Joseph **Collins** – reading PPE at Queen's College,
1936 -39.

Jack **Dawes** from Bradford, reading Latin and Greek at Queen's
College, 1937-39.

Noel **Eldridge**, reading History at Balliol, 1937-40; see also Pt 2 n 33.

Michael (MRD) **Foot**, reading History at New College
(1938-39 and 1945-47); see also Pt 1 n 18.

Philippa **Foot** (née Bosanquet), reading PPE at Somerville, 1939-42, later Oxford philosopher, see Pt 3, passim.

Henry **Fowler** – either Henry Knyvett Fowler – St John's, 1936-40; or Henry Richmond Harold Fowler – Worcester, 1935-40.

Denis **Healey** – Balliol reading Mods and Greats from 1936-40; see also Pt 3 n 17.

Graham Semyon **Hill**, reading Modern History at Christ Church, 1935-38.

Colin Henry **Judd** – Queen's College, 1937- ? then 1945.

Lucy **Klatschko**, reading Modern Languages at Somerville, 1936-39; see also Pt 3 n 15.

George **Lehmann**, reading Modern Languages at Queens College, 1939-41 and 1944-45; see also Pt 3 n 36.

Hal **Lidderdale**, reading Greats at Magdalen, 1936-40, see also Pt 2 n 11.

Leonie **Marsh** (later: Platt), at Somerville 1938-40, see also intro to Pt 2.

Noel **Martin**, reading Greats at Corpus, 1937-40; see also Pt 2 n 13.

Thomas Wood **Oliver**, reading Modern Languages at Oriel, 1937-38, then 1946.

Leo **Pliatzky**, reading Greats at Corpus, 1937-40; see also Pt 2 n 10.

Robert Dixon **Morrison** – Christ Church, 1927-.

Lionel **Munby**, reading Modern History at Hertford, 1936-40.

Stuart **Schultz**, reading Modern History at Corpus Christi,1936-9.

Peter **Shinnie**, reading Oriental Studies at Christ Church, 1934-38; see also Pt 3 n 9.

Carol **Stewart**, [later, Graham-Harrison] reading PPE at Somerville, 1936-39; see also Pt 3 n 16.

Pat **Thompson** – 1928 matriculation. First degree achieved 1933. MA achieved 1938. Full name Revd. Patrick John Thompson.

John **Willett**, reading PPE at Christ Church 1936-39; see also Pt 2, n 27.

I

COUNTDOWN TO A WAR
Introduction

IN THE SUMMER of 1939 scatty, likeable Tom Fletcher from
Ruskin College, Oxford, who lived on Magpie Lane, organised a
dozen students into a group reminiscent of J.B. Priestley's *Good
Companions* to tour the Cotswolds for a fortnight, perform-
ing mainly set-piece ballads and songs set by Geoffrey Bush
and Jonathan Mayne[1] and short dramatic or comic interludes
– *Tam Lin*, *The Lay of the Heads*, *Auld Witch Wife*, *Binnorie*, *Greensleeves*, *Clydewater*, the mediaeval 'Play of the Weather', *Donna Lombarda*. Since they were to capitalise on 'the fascination
Oxford holds for the general public',[2] they were enacting the role
of 'care-free students', as much as the various roles within the
sketches.

By 16 August, when the tour started, the drum-beat of
approaching war was very clear. The players debated vigor-

---

[1] G. Bush, *An Unsentimental Education* (London, 1990), pp 111, 127.

[2] Fletcher wrote of his plan to create the Magpie Players in *Cherwell*, 13 May 1939, LVI
no 3, pp 50-51.

ously whether, in view of the international situation, they should perform 'Soldiers coming', Auden's alarming ballad about the irruption of anarchic soldierly violence into a quiet farming community. Joyce Taylor, playing the ballad's deserted wife, felt very strongly they should not, and Murdoch agreed. 'With things as they are, it comes far too near to the bone.' There were other reminders. The Magpies gave a free matinee for Basque children, in flight from the Spanish war, in their camp near Aston Bampton. And the tour donated its proceeds to a University Appeal Fund profiting Jewish refugees from Germany (Earl Baldwin Fund), casualties of the Sino-Japanese war (China Relief), and victims of the Spanish civil war (National Joint Spanish Relief).

The fact that it is by Murdoch contributes much of the interest of this 100-page journal concerning the tour. She gets herself and her fellow-Magpies very immediately and strongly onto the page, and shows remarkable talents for close observation and for turning life into compelling narrative. The handwriting is firm and confident, fluent about what she perceives.[3] Their antics are juvenile – she had the previous month reached, after all, only 20 – but her eye is keen. It is an interesting record of a unique historical moment.

Around 1988 Murdoch carefully edited her 1939 Magpie Journal, and her excisions are noted in the published text below. That Murdoch preserved and edited this, while destroying other journals from the 1940s, is striking. Where an excision on the verso causes loss of copy she regards as important on the recto, she

---

[3] Four ex-Magpies – Denys Becher, Moira Dunbar, Frances Podmore and Ruth Kingsbury (who did not act, but sewed) – each endorsed the accuracy of Murdoch's account – for example her description of Denys Becher as 'like some unutterably wronged and troubled lad out of A.E. Housman.' Dunbar wrote that 'one always felt he needed a nanny' and Becher, who laughed as he read the Journal, vouchsafes how young he then was.

writes in her 1988 hand – still the heroine of her own narrative – the missing 1938 text. It is by definition impossible to know what has been removed but likely that survivors, including her husband, are thus protected, while her own story is streamlined and sanitised. Something about the timing of this interlude continued to matter to her. Fifty years later she liked still to recite the words of the ballad *Tam Lin* as also to sing *The Lark in the Clear Air*. The coming war gave that fortnight its special edge of joy.

World wars have a way of starting in summer, a season that can shed retrospective glamour, as Philip Larkin famously showed in his poem MCMXIV. Here, as in an old silent movie, he evokes the long lines of light-hearted volunteers in August 1914, the bric-à-brac of their daily, class-ridden lives, all unknowing of the terrible future. His poem ends poignantly:

> Never such innocence,
> Never before or since,
> As changed itself to past
> Without a word – the men
> Leaving the gardens tidy,
> The thousands of marriages
> Lasting a little while longer:
> Never such innocence again.

This recalls the mood of the Magpie Journal, often self-conscious about the coming war and all it may entail. Here was another confluence of dramatic international events with a pastoral world, elegised as it nears its end.[4] The mismatch between trivial

---

[4] Dunbar wrote from Canada 25/6/98 'The Magpie players left a lasting impression on me, largely because of the dramatic changes that followed. It was a delightful climax to the never-never period of the 1930s' and on 24/5/99 that 'an amusing way to spend the summer…came to represent a sort of fairy-tale close to the care-free prewar period, detached even from the reality of our own lives at the time.'

private and dramatic public events is well-caught in the journal. It was – partly – in defence of privacy, safety and the long little-ness of ordinary life that war, after all, was fought in the first place, and the tone of the second war, after the high rhetoric of the first, was to be resolutely undramatic.

For the first week, spent largely in rehearsal, war merits no mention. On 22 August Fox Photos turn up and take 200 pictures for *Picture Post*. That journal never ran its piece on The Magpie Players – and some of these photographs when I found them through Hulton-Getty in 1998 appeared never even to have been developed, the world's attention soon having more compelling subject-matter. One snap shows a notably attractive Iris prettily sewing, another wolfing food, a third as an emblematic 'Fairy-tale princess'.[5]

The rumours started on Wednesday 23 August, the day the Ribbentrop-Molotov Pact, known also as the German–Soviet Non-aggression Pact, was signed. The two countries renounced warfare and each pledged neutrality if the other were attacked by a third party. In effect it signalled that war was now only days away. That morning Joanne Yeaxlee, who co-directed, and who played Queen of the Fairies to Murdoch's Janet in *Tam Lin*, com-plains of the political situation and Murdoch notes that 'the pa-pers seem scared. And I suppose a grave crisis is on but I can't seem to feel any emotion about it whatsoever. This is a such a strange, new, different, existence I'm leading & so entirely cut-off from the world.'

The following day, notwithstanding that she has little idea what is happening, Murdoch with the arrogance of youth deplores the 'unnecessary fuss' being made over the pact. As a loyal Commu-nist she is unwilling to countenance the possibility that Stalin and

---

[5] For three of these photographs, see Peter J Conradi: *Iris Murdoch: A Life* (2001), henceforth *Life*.

Hitler signed the pact cynically, preparatory to their imminent simultaneous invasions of Poland and their division of the spoils. So on the 28th she reflects, 'Curious how many intelligent people are getting the Soviet Union wrong over this business'.

Magpie attention, she acknowledges, is focused more on the tour than on the international crisis. The players start to have double vision. Murdoch notes 'trouble over Danzig' where Hitler was exaggerating anti-German feeling in order to whip up anti-Polish hysteria and justify invasion. Since so many people seem very upset, she marvels that 'it must be a great storm to ripple these placid waters'. Frances Podmore, a Magpie absent on other business, sends them a telegram asking whether they intend continuing the tour? They wire back: 'Magpies carry on' and put the crisis out of their minds. Although Tom Fletcher and attractive Hugh Vaughan James are moved, 'We have so many urgent little problems of our own, that we have no time to look up & see the gathering clouds'. Most declare that they care 'not two tin tacks' for the international situation: and Tom asks whether there could be any better way of spending the eve of war. The Magpie performance at Filkins village hall on the late afternoon of the 24th is interrupted by a speech over the wireless by pro-appeasement foreign secretary Lord Halifax, who had by then started to appreciate the gravity of the situation.

Low points on the tour are Buscot Park where the chauffeur-driven rich make a frosty audience, and soon after, unsettled, roughneck Northleach where the rainy market square is filled by recruiting bills and adjurations to young men to join the Territorials and defend their home while the hall they are to perform in is stacked with gas masks, inducing panic in the townspeople who imagine slaughter and sudden death. The performance is abandoned when all the lights in the town go out: Air Raid precautions?

By 28 August Murdoch receives a worried letter from her parents that prompts her to wonder whether 'maybe things are worse than I'd thought'. Even the Communist *Daily Worker* is sounding desperate; and MRD Foot, who has just been called up, writes to make Murdoch his 'literary executor, with instructions what to publish should Anything Happen to him'. Murdoch wonders if this is the end of everything at last? 'If it is, I am having a very grand finale'. At Chipping Camden on 30 August she lies across one of the graves and thinks how quiet it would be to be dead. The Territorials are called up.

Before they disband, the Magpies visit another refugee camp on Friday 1 September, the Brüderhof – a radical Protestant group in Gloucestershire who had fled Nazi Germany in 1936. This pacifist commune, on England's declaring war, moved to Paraguay rather than risk internment. They were full of foreboding when the Magpies visited them – and the Magpies were invited not to perform. This rendez vous, absent from her journal and certainly excised, was remembered by other surviving Magpies and by Murdoch alike who referred to it in a letter.[6]

As for the fact that the tour was scheduled to end on the precise day war was to break out, one Magpie, Moira Dunbar wrote later that this coincidence 'would have been called overdrawn and impossible in a work of fiction'.[7] At the time Tom Fletcher promised 'After the war, the Magpies will tour again. But' he added, 'our show will be frightfully pre-war, I'm afraid.' The epoch Murdoch

---

[6] The letter mentioning the visit to the Brüderhof is to Harry Weinberger, undated. One supposition would be that she cut details of her liaison with Hugh Vaughan James, with whom she had long lost touch and so was probably unaware that he died in 1974, and that this excision lost us the Brüderhof visit too. Ruth Kingsbury wrote to John Bayley 1/3/1999 that she was sure this place (i.e. the Brüderhof commune) and its aims featured in Murdoch's *The Bell* (1957) because 'Iris was very impressed by what she saw in the time available'.

[7] Letter to the Editor, (henceforth LTE)

described to Frank Thompson as 'the playtime of the '30s, when we were all conscience-ridden spectators'[8] was coming to its end.

Against the advice of the troupe Murdoch made her way home to London on Sunday 3 September, Hugh warning, 'Do you realise there's a pretty good chance of London being bombed to-night? Don't be a little fool!' It was in expectation of massive bombing followed by invasion that the London Parks had been dug up with great trenches, barrage balloons floated from tall buildings and the biggest mass movement of people in the history of the UK had begun. A quarter of a million evacuees left London each day from Friday 1 September onwards. Each child was separated from its parents, and often from its siblings, labelled like a piece of luggage bearing name, address and relevant information such as 'bed-wetter'. Such was the London to which Murdoch returned, early in the small hours of the first day of war.

■■■

An only child – much indulged – head-girl and a star at both her schools, young Iris Murdoch was famous for Irishness, politics, acting and brilliance, in that order. Although her claim to have lived in Dublin for the first two years of her life is unreliable, Irishness was still her proud stock-in-trade. *Cherwell* had recently published her satirical 'The Irish – Are they Human?' and for sixty years Denis Healey believed that she came to Oxford direct from Dublin. In the Magpie Journal, her first surviving extended prose narrative, she tries out fanciful oaths for an Irish Protestant – 'Mother-of-God' and 'Holy Mother' – and muses to herself

---

[8] IM to FT Nov 12 1943.

of the company 'They're a wonderful collection to be sure, & it's devilish fond I am of them'. (This is not her sole affectation: she spells – and was for decades archaically to spell – show, as 'shew'). No accident that her first published novel – *Under the Net* (1954) – would have an Irish narrator.

She was also well-known for being, together with Healey, one of thirty open members of the Communist Party (CP), and, when she writes in this journal of Hugh Vaughan James only being 'in' for a few months, she means that like herself, Frank Thompson and David Hicks, James belonged to the CP. Her feeling for Hugh is enhanced by the fact that both are in the Party. Her politics at the time were so famously solemn that Healey recalled Murdoch as a 'latter-day Joan of Arc'. But she was able to turn down the intensity on occasion, capable of simple fun.

Her success with the Magpies meant that Frances Podmore invited her the following June to play the Chorus in TS Eliot's *Murder in the Cathedral* in Christ Church, a successful role in a remarkable performance many recalled long afterwards.[9] And it is curious to learn that Murdoch furthered the career, without necessarily ever learning this, of the one Magpie who wanted to be a professional actress. She quietly persuades Tom Fletcher to allow her to give up a coveted part in *Clydewater* to a weeping Joan Yeaxlee,[10] whose career depends upon the tour as she wants a job as an actress with a repertory company. Yeaxlee did indeed become a professional of sorts, albeit remembered by Moira

---

[9] IM refers to the production in a letter to David Hicks, 10 April 1940. It was performed out of doors in College; there was a multiple chorus; and it was the first time that women undergraduates were permitted to act alongside the men. Until this time, in order to protect undergraduate morals, women parts in College plays were performed by dons' wives; and in University plays by West End actresses hired for the occasion. In 1999 Professor Hugh Lloyd-Jones and painter Milein Cosman, among others, recalled IM's performance in *Murder in the Cathedral*.

[10] 'Joan' only in the Journal: second name supplied by Moira Dunbar.

Dunbar as more engaged in management and production.

Theatre, as an image of life, mattered to Murdoch always. Important scenes in her first novel *Under the Net* happen in a Hammersmith theatre; a key scene connected with the discovery of love in her late novel *The Green Knight* happens in a derelict theatre south of the river. She nurtured ambitions as a playwright, wrote two plays that were put on, and saw two of her novels adapted successfully for the stage. Her greatest novel, which won the Booker in 1978, *The Sea, The Sea*, has a theatre-director for narrator, and actors and actresses for all its main characters. Tom Fletcher is not the original for the director in that book, who stems from Canetti, but the Magpie Players' journal has an interest for the many who admire that novel: she knew amateur theatre at first-hand.

Wherever the Magpies toured, their final chorus was a show-stopping reprise of Wendell Woods Hall's immensely successful 1923 vaudeville song, advertised as the Song with a Thousand Laughs, 'It Aint Gonna Rain No Mo'. This was no doubt accompanied by banjo or ukelele and kazoo, and sung by the whole cast front-of-stage with hands fluttering in a minstrel cake-walk:

Now I hope it's not mis-leading
For I've tried to make it plain
That even tho your skies are dark,
It aint a-gonna rain
O it aint gonna rain no mo, no mo
It aint gonna rain no mo
But how in the world can the old folks tell?
It aint a-gonna rain no mo.

However it *was* going to rain, and the dark skies did not lie. First of all, though all the Magpies survived, many Oxford friends did not, including two admirers of Murdoch's, Frank

Thompson and Noel Edridge, whose deaths in 1944 she recounts in Part Three of this book.

And apart from having friends killed, war meant, at the very least, the inconvenience of having six crucial years of your youth stolen from you. Many Magpies, as the cast-list shows, had their degree compressed into two years: or interrupted, some being called up, or leaving for war-work, returning to complete their degrees after it was all over.

War also meant that some surviving friends changed beyond recognition. It is very hard to relate Murdoch's picture of attractive Hugh Vaughan James, so extroverted, funny, and in every sense larger-than-life, doing Cossack dancing on the running-board of a speeding motor car, to the withdrawn and depressive figure he cut after the duration. Dr H.V. James worked post-war as a GP around Norwich, where he was remembered as a good practitioner who didn't suffer fools gladly and could be stern with those coming to surgery with mere colds. His outgoing and popular wife Zeta died of breast cancer in her fifties in 1973: her funeral service was held in Norwich Cathedral. Very cut up after her death, he talked about it to no one, becoming increasingly isolated. They had no children. His part-time work as a clinical assistant in the Diabetic department in the Norfolk and Norwich Hospital made it easy for him to get hold of insulin. In February 1974 he dissembled to his colleagues that he was going away for the weekend. In reality he went home, took an overdose, and committed suicide.

As for the Magpies' only begetter, Tom Fletcher kept in touch with Murdoch during a life largely spent teaching abroad. He turned up in Oxford shortly before his death, around 1991, ebullient as ever, offering to put on a one-man performance of Bellman's Ballads. So John Bayley, after loaning him some cash, secured him St Catherine's College theatre for the night. Apart from Iris, John and the then Master and his wife, no one else came. Fletcher had attracted an audience of precisely four. Unperturbed by the big, empty space, he recited his ballads happily. The picture is both touching and funny, an appropriate coda to a strange interlude over half a century before, during the countdown to a world war.

The Magpie Players, August 1939

August 1939

...[*pp excised by IM*] came with cases full of wonderful props. Jack Trotman, distracted with armsfull of presscuttings & publicity stunts. Kirstie Rowntree to help with the scene painting. And finally Denis Beecher, who had hitch-hiked from Cornwall, looking more than ever like some unutterably wronged and tragic lad out of A.E. Housman.

Greetings and chaos in the big stone-paved room behind the theatre. Then our two cars conveyed us back to Hill Foot for supper. Found Joyce Taylor of St Hilda's had come and installed herself. Had supper, all painfully jocular round the big table in the common room. Some Dutch girls, hiking, arrived to stay the night. Limited our converse to smiles. Tom seems very different here from at Oxford. Here he is exuberantly in his element, a little king – and he is no constitutional monarch either. Moreover he can talk. During supper he came out with amazing volleys of witticisms, some of them quite passable. Victor talks well too, but is more annoying. He lacks Tom's innocent faun-like spontaneity. After supper and hilarious washing up, Denis, Jack, Joyce, Kirstie and myself walked up to the Blade Bone and played darts.

A nice little Inn, oozing with local colour. Must make its further acquaintance. Got back to find that Ruth Kingsbury had arrived. We were very glad to see each other and had a long talk. She has gone down now and intends to write (God help her) and is now out for Experience. Is going to become a Barmaid. Good luck to her then, for she is a sweet lass. (When I first came onto Cherwell she made some quite gratuitous and very complimentary remarks about my poetry. I was instantly enslaved!)

Am sharing room with Joan, which is excellent. We are luxurious compared to the others, in that we have a private room, complete with dressing table, washstand & Improving Textes. One bed is a Goosefeather Bed. My romantic spirit forthwith inclined me to sleep therein in spite of Joan's warnings – now I understand why the lady in the song preferred a cold open field. That was the hottest night of my life. That bed was as hot as flaming cinders on the flagstones of hell. I slept toward dawn – and then was wakened by cocks crowing. Realised this is the first time that I have lived on a genuine farm. Thought poetically about the Bird of Dawning – then 5 o/c struck & confirmed the cocks. (I never really believed it till now.) Then the cows passed under the window – giving tongue. Lay and laughed silently, hoping I wouldn't wake Joan. All sorts of strange birds sing. I sleep, & get up at 7.45 to accompaniment of more cows.

August 17th, Thursday

Walked before breakfast. After breakfast went in Moira's car[1] to the theatre. Read through a few parts sang various songs to Tom,

---

[1] The car was an Austen 10: 'how it coped with a full load of people plus a trailer I don't know, but it never complained' (LTE 14/8/98)

IM and Joan Yeaxlee, courtesy John Bayley

and finally retired into a remote field with my recorder and practised hard.

Denis has a superb Dolmetsch recorder which he plays very
well. Looked on in taciturn envy. Denis is to play Tam Lin to my
Janet (I think) and he certainly looked very elfin as he lay on the
other side of the field learning his part. He is a strangely remote
creature.

The day wore on, as they say, and every half hour or so Tom
would say 'just another letter, and then we'll fix the casting' and
we'd all drift away, and come rushing back to find Tom in the
middle of something else.

Kirstie was the only person who employed herself really well, &
made a good start on the backcloth for Green Bushes. I wandered
from field to field in the sun, playing folk tunes on my recorder,
& watching the men hay-making in the distance. (Seems late for
hay, but I'm sure it was.) At noon the air was hazy & heavy and
the bluebottles invincible, but towards evening it was much pleas-
anter. No lunch seemed forthcoming & I thought it might be bad
taste to enquire, so tightened my belt and played 'Spanish Ladies'.

About 5 o/c Denis & I, both simultaneously remembering that we hadn't eaten, devoured lumps of sugar, which seemed to be the only edible on the premises, & felt better. At last about 6 Tom called us all together & we tried out the parts. We sat on the lawn between the theatre & the lake, and the sun was very golden on the water & in the trees. Felt incredibly sleepy, but soon woke up when I had to sing. I am singing the part of the maiden in 'The Keys of Canterbury' with Denis opposite me, bless his heart. Also I have the part of Evir in 'The Lay of the Heads', and the 'Auld Witch Wife' in 'Broomfield Hill', and (O joyous thought) Janet in Tam Lin to Denis's Tom.

Tom Fletcher I think is acting Conal in the 'Lay of the Heads'. The 'auditions' were most amusing. Moira as a 'guidwife' is magnificent, and Tom as the Demon Lover is positively shattering. There was a terrific echo across that lawn & when he got to the bit about 'the mountains of hell' he nearly broke a window in the theatre. We half killed ourselves laughing. Then we all went in and learnt the tune of 'Binnorie' – Tom is toying with the idea of giving me the part of the Elder Sister as Joan has so much to do. She looks the villainess alright & I the Innocent Maid I fear, but she has a lot of other things to do. However, we shall see.

I'd love the part, but am very well satisfied with what I have. Tom is also toying with a notion of giving me 'Greensleeves' as a solo. I'm wild to have it, but of course treated the suggestion quite carelessly.

David Alexander arrived today complete with Scots accent and red hair. Altogether the cast is exceedingly varied. When Hugh Vaughan James arrives we shall be as heterogeneous a collection of freaks as one would wish to meet anywhere. I hope Hugh comes. He will be a link between Labour Club Oxford and Theatrical Oxford. Also it will be fascinating to watch everyone reacting to him. Several of us haven't met him yet!

Came back and had a long, sleepy & voraciously devoured

dinner, enlivened by fairytales from Tom. I went for a walk alone afterwards & listened for the silence, but it wasn't there. Only a lot of crickets & owls & far-off dogs. Reached the end of the lane, got to thinking of the Demon Lover & decided to turn back. Quite alarmed when a big moth touched my hand. Very blue sky with Mars deep red on the horizon.

August 18th, Friday

Mother of God preserve me from the simple sewing machine. That seems to be the dominating thought for the day – but there were other things. Slept excellently – Joan insisted on taking turns with the goosefeather which struck me as noble. Went down to the theatre early & learnt most of my parts. Discovered two magnificent horses, one black & one dapple grey in a near field. Ransacked the dressing rooms for sugar stores, but of course couldn't find them. Tom asked me what I was looking for, but I didn't like to admit I wanted to feed Magpie sugar to horses. Dissembled. Was just setting off for a remote hilltop with my recorder when a strange figure loomed up the lane. Hugh Vaughan James with all the dust of Kerry on him & the same old devil in his extraordinarily blue eyes. He was very tired – hadn't slept the last 2 nights & had hitch-hiked all the way from West Ireland (cars & a tramp steamer!) Said he just wanted to sleep. So I left him to it & found a field with a convenient stone wall in it where I sat and played 'Greensleeves' to the cows. Then went & explored the local church. Uninspiring – but pleasantly quiet. Went back to the theatre for an excellent lunch of lettuce & bread & cheese.

Then the sewing machine arrived. Apparently, it worked. We scoffed at its owner's lugubrious warnings, & started gaily off – but as it turned out she knew its little ways after all. In no time a fair green silken robe for me as Evir had been made, & Joan and I were exultant. Then we started on Joan's frock for 'Binnorie' –

& then the trouble began. First a needle broke. Then the bobbin wouldn't wind. Then the threads wouldn't connect. Then another needle broke & we had to put in a bent and rusty one. Then the tension went wrong. And finally – for no conceivable or observable reason, it simply would not sew. Ye gods. I had it most of the time, as Joan was cutting out. I took it out into the sun & swore at it. I beseeched it. I twiddled every knob I could see. I prayed for it, & did everything except kick it into the lake. (Tho' it was a near thing at times) Hugh was very sympathetic, and tried (unsuccess-fully) to straighten out the needle with a hammer. Ruth prodded its guts with a screwdriver, and nearly wept over it. I was beyond weeping. Eventually gave it up and handsewed in silent fury.

Got back to the hostel wildly hungry & wolfed supper. Tom & Denys (sic correxit ipse[2]) were away in Newbury, but Hugh was an endless source of amusement. After an hour's sleep he was a giant refreshed (not so much of a metaphor either) and full of his inimitable self. He has a good habit of laughing at his own jokes. . After supper walked about the garden & talked with Hugh about Ireland & this & that. He has the Irish brogue to perfection. Far better than mine. In Kerry they thought he was from Cork, & in Cork they accused him of coming from Ulster (God forgive them). However he did himself in the eye in Valencia when he used his brogue on a trampship captain he was asking a lift of – for the man wouldn't take him for fear he was a member of an IRA! And no wonder, for Hugh with a several days beard, as at present, is no tame sight, nor like anything out of the common rooms of Balliol. He resembles rather a Viking chieftain or some Ancient Celtic Hero. Hope he retains said beard. <u>That'll</u> startle the citizens of Stow-on-the-Wold!

Jack & Hugh went off in a car to pick up Hugh's tent, for

---

[2] 'Thus he corrected himself' i.e. the spelling of his first name.

the Hostel Warden is doubtful of Russell's hospitable capacities towards campers. Oil lamps are lit and look very well from outside. Dark blue skies, & these yellow lamps shining on the oak inside. Joan sits on the steps and plays patience. Hugh tells me an infallible test for a princess – put a pea under 12 feather beds, & if she feels it she's genuine.[3] Meant to try for 8 1/3 % of royal blood with my feather bed tonight, but couldn't find a pea. Thought Joan's grapefruit probably wouldn't prove anything conclusive.

Sat up with all the Magpies in the common room waiting for Tom & Denys & Moira. About 10.30 two cyclists turned up, having scoured the countryside looking for the place. In a bad temper, they were. The others ignored them when they discovered they weren't Tom & co. But Hugh went out & looked after them. I searched for the Warden but she was in bed. However they left in disgust some half hour later when they'd seen the hayloft where they were meant to sleep. Grocers born & bred as Hugh remarked. At about 11.15 Tom & the other two rolled up, tired but trimphant having apparently been half way round England & done some amazing publicity. Were hustled off to bed by us & a furious warden.

August 19th, Saturday

A devastating day. Sewing at the theatre with the crack of dawn. (Vaguely, as Denys would say. About five [?illeg] thirty that is.) Rehearsed Broomfield Hill most of morning. Joan is good but a trifle too fantastic. She is by way of being a female Massine and

---

[3] IM had evidently not then read Hans Christian Andersen's little fable 'The Princess and the Pea' in which the authenticity of a princess is vouchsafed for by her ability to sense a pea through twenty mattresses and twenty feather beds. 'Nobody but a real princess could have such a delicate skin.'

would fit well on a ballet stage. She is perhaps too sophisticated for some of these ballads. Victor as the knight is far too bloody supercilious. He makes me quite wild. So I preserve my witchly silence & give him the evil eye. A fine little ballad it is, though, & with harp accompaniment should be most effective.

After lunch I sewed, and practised, & about 2.45 we began rehearsing 'Tam Lin'. Tom says, & he's right, that this is both the most difficult & also the loveliest of all the ballads we are doing. I thank my propitious stars for the part of Janet. Denys as Tam Lin is perfect – wild & intense & unearthly. And Joan as 'Queen o' Fairies' is beautifully malignant. We foiled each other very well & Tom is exultant. But mon dieu the end is difficult & will need rehearsing. We were plagued to-day by Hugh Vaughan James who kept on popping up at most dramatic moments & making wisecracks. When I had just got myself magnificently into the part & cried 'But how shall I you ken, Tam Lin – How shall I borrow you Among a pack o' uncouth knights the like I never saw?' Hugh chirped gaily to Denys, 'Why not tattoo yourself?' which was too much for our weak exhausted nerves & we collapsed in helpless mirth. We went on rehearsing till about 5 & then staggered out for some tea. After which I sewed Joan's dress for 'Binnorie' for an hour, by which time we were all set for supper. And after supper, down to the theatre again to sew Victor's dress for Broomfield Hill, & make rude criticisms of Tom's indifferent Irish accent & worse Irish jigs in 'The Spanishe Ladye'.

It is Saturday & the Hostel is full, so all our lads have been turned out to sleep in a bell tent. Joan and I contemplate the morning mists & are glad of our goosefeather bed.

Hugh, as I anticipated, has enslaved all the company. All the day Hugh may be seen somewhere on the premises either telling a story or singing a song with an admiring group of satellites about him. Tom is wonderful, & stands no end of fooling from

Hugh (tho' who wouldn't indeed?) & is incredibly patient and good-tempered. Joan is incredibly industrious but a shade less good-tempered about it.

Cecil Quentin arrived to-day on the heels of a rather sour letter, & successfully missed Jack who went to meet him at Reading (an hour late, be it admitted). I'm afraid I view with considerable satisfaction the prospect of Cecil having to sleep in a damp bell tent. I see their light palely glinting out in the murky wilderness. O for an errant cow to trouble Cecil's sleep!

Denys's oboe arrived to-day & he wandered about the gardens with his vague look playing Handel & Mozart. He plays excellently & the instrument has a heart-breakingly lovely tone to it. Debussy on an oboe must be incredibly wonderful. I like Denys. He is so exceedingly young & spontaneous & so completely the artist. He seems moreover to be devoid of vices. In 'Tam Lin' he embraces and kisses me without the least embarrassment, which is good. I was afraid he might be shy. But of course he has done a great deal of acting before.

August 20th, Sunday

We are most prodigiously bitten, all of us & especially myself of course. I have a choice mosquito bite on my leg which Hugh says arouses his professional interest. But needless to say he doesn't propose to do anything useful about it.

Mein Gott. What a day. Some malignant devil – or maybe it was someone's guardian angel, drove me down to the theatre early, skipping breakfast, to get on with the costumes. At first I thought no one was there, & I went up into Victor's 'office' to get the 'Binnorie' dresses. When there, lying against the wall was Joan, sobbing in the most agonising manner. I oughtn't to have been surprised, but I was rather taken aback, so I just patted her shoulder & said 'Joan, Joan', & flew back down the steps again where I bumped into Tom. He was looking as un-concerned as anything, & said cheerfully 'O I've got a nice part for you, Margaret's mother in Clydewater and handed me the script. I said thanks, & then following him into the theatre, 'What have you been doing to Joan?' 'O, why, what's the matter?' (Tom looking as innocent as a newborn faun.) And all the while Joan's sobs were shaking the place. *Mon Dieu*. So Tom and I had a long confabulation in the course of which it appeared that Joan was upset because she was having too much dressmaking & too little acting to do – &, as I know, her career in a sense depends on this tour, as she wants to get a job as an actress with a repertory company. This last part which Tom had carelessly informed her this morning I was to have, was the las[t] straw it seems. Poor kid. So of course I said, look here Tom, I don't care about the part, for heaven's sake let me take over the costumes my future isn't hanging in the balance. So Tom hummed & looked distressed, & finally he talked to a more or less recovered Joan about it, & it was decided that Joan should do the cutting out, & I should carry on from there, & that Joan should have the part in Clydewater. So that is quite satisfactory thank God.

All this was before nine o'clock. It was nearly 11 before the others arrived, as breakfast was late on Sunday. I discovered some very soft biscuits, originally Victor's property, & some stale cheese so didn't starve. Ruth arrived later & helped sew. Ruth is pure gold.

When the others came they rehearsed 'Julius Caesar', and then 'The Play of the Weather' – a mediaeval play 'discovered by Cecil Quentin in the Bodleian', as the programmes impressively but erroneously state. (Hugh was humorous on the subject of 'doing our bit for Bodley'.)

Denys & I rehearsed the difficult parts of Tam Lin in the garden, & afterwards I mended his sandals for him, for which he was pathetically grateful. Had a satisfying lunch of bread & cheese & then sewed huge green sleeves for Tam Lin. Tom has just given me a lovely song, Samuel Daniel's poem 'Love is a sickness...' with melody & accompaniment for flute, oboe & harp by Jon Mayne of Teddy Hall.[4] It has a fine Elizabethan ring & fills me with joy. I practised it with Jack & Denys fairly successfully.

After tea made posters for display in villages. Denys played *La fille aux chevaux de lain*[5] on his oboe – it was wonderful. Kirstie has finished the 'Mowing the Barley' back-cloth which is also wonderful. Charlotte's designs however are all a trifle too yellow-green for my taste.

Chaffed Hugh on the subject of 'laying bare his ignorance'. He replied 'a form of intellectual striptease' – a phrase which has possibilities. Maybe that is what all social intercourse is, only we rarely reach the final stage.

I have revised my ideas of Cecil. Strange how quickly one can change estimations of character. He is not the lofty conceited & utterly snobbish young swine I thought he was at all. He is very keen on the drama, & he is humble enough to want to be liked. Ruth observed that 'he didn't seem quite at home here', and I think she's right. I watched him & Hugh fencing with considerable interest. Hugh had it every time of course, but was kind to his opponent. Cecil eventually retired into a rather awkward silence. I thought of the last time I had seen him, at John Russell's sherry party, & wondered at the contrast.

Cecil is producing the 'Play of the Weather' & making a good job of it. I was dragged in at the last moment to take the nice but hellish difficult part of the little boy. I feel uncomfortably like a little girl all the time, but maybe in shorts I'll feel better.

---

[4] i.e. St Edmund's Hall College.

[5] *Sic.* IM presumably meant *La Fille aux cheveux de lin*: the girl with flaxen hair, famously set to music by Debussy.

At supper to-night Hugh surpassed himself. I don't think we stopped laughing from the beginning of the meal to the end. It wasn't loud healthy belly-filling laughter tho' – we just leaned our heads in our hands & shook in agony, & the creaking of the oil lamp as the table quivered was the only indication of our mirth. Actually it was chiefly nerves – we are all feeling the strain.

After supper Hugh & I wandered out into the 'forecourt' as Victor calls it & Hugh lay flat on the wall, & we indulged in some intellectual striptease. He took up the orthodox Bolshevik position (see Hank Skinner passim) that I should not think in analogies as it was dangerous, & did his best generally to drag me to earth. I refused to be dragged & had the pleasure of tripping Hugh badly just once. But he is excellent fun to argue with, & talks fine sound sense with just the correct dash of nonsense to make it highly palatable. I have discovered a lot of things to-day about our principal characters. They're a wonderful collection, to be sure, & it's devilish fond I am of them.

A fine night of stars, & the men are still sleeping in the bell tent. Talked with Hugh about Marxism and London and jiu-jitsu and life and summer lightning till the Warden drove us to bed at 10.30.

August 21st, Monday

Went down to theatre before breakfast again, but no weeping women this time. Got plenty of sewing done by the time the others had guzzled their eggs & bacon & arrived about 10. Found a ginger biscuit in a bag. Eureka. Sewed Joan's sleeves for 'Broomfield Hill'. She has let herself go on that dress alright. I've never seen so many exquisite but unutilitarian draperies attached to any garment in my life. Rehearsed 'The Keys' with Tom & Denys – very charming it will be I think with recorder accompaniment. Then Denys lured me down to the lake to see the reflection, & having got me onto a highly poetical island with seven trees upon it, whipped out his camera. A bad habit he has. After lunch had a long talk with Hugh. Was startled to hear that he had got a fourth in schools and that he knew practically no women at Oxford. A strange lad indeed. Leaned on a gate and moralised on the countryside. Thought we saw a fox, but decided reluctantly it was merely a cat. Went back and sewed, Hugh & David lying on the grass & talking nonsense the while. Talked shop with David who thinks Greats a pleasant mental exercise but wonders how anyone can take it seriously. A prevalent notion it seems (see Frank[6] passim). Rehearsed Tam Lin again, all goes excellently. Tom is working out the male and female voices very artistically, & with music it should be perfect. Joan wants me to play the girl in 'Green Bushes' & explained at length, but was too tired to take it in. Ruth works indefatigably & smiles. Tomorrow she is hitch-hiking 16 miles to see a friend. Hermes be her speed.

After a chastened dinner we rehearsed the 'Play of the Weather' with Cecil's comments. It's a difficult thing, but C. has the right ideas.[7] He has a fine smile that man, & I owe him apologies for my former bad opinion. Tom overacts but makes on the whole a grand Jupiter Pluvius with top-hat tails, & a red umbrella. Should amuse the sixpennies anyway. Ended rowdily about 10.30 with 'It ain't gonna rain no mo' (theme song) & were driven home with loud complaints from Mrs Brown & spouse. The cars hadn't come yet, so Hugh & I walked in the misty &

---

[6] Frank Thompson (1920-44): see section 2.

[7] In 'The Play of the Weather', written 1533 by John Heywood, the cast petitions Jupiter Pluvius (Jupiter Reliever of Droughts, played by Tom Fletcher) for contradictory weather conditions – dry and clear for the gentleman hunting, temperate for the lady safe-guarding her complexion, sunny for the washerwoman, windy for the little boy played by IM who wishes to fly his kite etc etc.

ominous silence of the roads. Hugh sang Russian gipsy songs & we talked of ghosts & fairies. He has the right ideas on the subject. And anyone could see with half an eye he was second cousin to a giant. (He confessed to Cecil that he turned the scale at 15 stone.)

My mind is getting bit blank and empty like [*sic*]. Couldn't remember my part to-night. Denys is very tired too, & Tom and Joan are certainly feeling the strain. Jack is wonderful & manages all the business side with unobtrusive slickness, & is never out of countenance. He and Hugh are devoted to each other I was interested to observe. Jack of course by way of being a satellite. Charlie Southwood arrived with all his carpentary gadgets & the rostrum. We were glad to see him.

August 22nd, Tuesday

O ye immortal gods. As David said to-night at supper, 'Does anyone seriously think we are putting on a show to-morrow?' Realised that I hadn't ever rehearsed the 'Lay of the Heads' yet – except once when Tom was shaving & I was sewing & we said it over to each other. Also the transport problem is not yet solved, & the car-lorry controversy rages as strongly as ever. But a calm optimism reigns. The gods will provide and 'noe doubt we will be there' as Tam Lin would say. Fox Photos turned up this afternoon to take '200 pictures' for Picture Post. Made a thoro' nuisance of himself he did. The usual rôle of the photographer. All afternoon rehearsals were sabotaged. Tom & I began to rehearse 'The Lay' about 2.30 and went on with countless interruptions till after 4. Just when I would be getting really upset about Cuchulain's death up would pop Fox Photos from behind the hedge & cry 'hold that!' Or else Jack would call Tom away to 'look at the trailer' or a covey of telegrams would come fluttering in.

Had supper early and a long 'dress rehearsal' afterwards,

8-10.30 – even then did only half the programme. I am worried about 'Tam Lin', & fear it won't get across. We did it in costume to-night, with music but without full lighting effects. Cecil says it will be entirely incomprehensible, that it drags & that we'd better cut half of it. Joan assures me that Cecil is nothing to go by, but still. Am inclined to think that the audience will not gather the significance of the herb-picking! Even Denys after 2 rehearsals did not get it till Tom mentioned 'illicit purposes'.[8] 'The Keys' went alright, except that we were at cross purposes with the music. We didn't have to do 'The Lay'. Fear that will be laughed at, as Tom is inclined to overact. He does so love being a bloodthirsty Celtic chieftain, bless his heart, & he lets himself go. He suggests we have Hugh on a bier to represent the body of Cuchulain. Am not sure if I approve of that idea. One twinkle from Hugh's eye would wreck all my high tragedy. 'Clyde-water' produced by Hugh will go very well. It's the funniest thing I've seen for a long time & David is perfect as the high-hearted Hero. Joan & Tom in 'Donna Lombarda' will probably be the most perfect thing in the programme.

Wish Cecil had not messed up the 'Play of the Weather' with too much burlesque. Especially at the end. I think he spoils its curious charm & quaintness by introducing the modern vulgarity to vie with the old. And then when he Bowdlerises for the benefit of the rows of parsons in the five shillings the damage is complete. Long controversy raged as to whether 'tit' or 'bit' had the most dangerous significance when applied to a woman. Decided 'bit' was safer.

A wren flew into the scene-painting room today & Hugh & I caught it in The Spanishe Ladye's silver net, & let it fly out of the

---

[8] Tam Lin, bewitched by the Queen of the Fairies, renders her rival Janet (played by IM) pregnant: Janet by means of herbs tries to procure an abortion.

window. Poor little thing, it was so afraid, & kept hurting itself on the walls.

Hugh found a wild bees nest behind the theatre.

August 23rd, Wednesday

Well, we did put on a show – but only just. We didn't know our lines (some of us), our costumes weren't finished, & held together with pins, parts of the scenery were unpainted, & we had to cut out chunks of the programme because it was under-rehearsed. But we put on a show – & what's more they liked it! The whole day was a glorious nightmare of sewing on clips & fasteners & buttons & bells, & drawing innumerable magpies on innumerable sheets of paper for innumerable purposes. Hugh & I took half an hour off after lunch & walked up to the meadow where the horses were & talked about the Party. I was amazed when he told me he had been in only a few months – & there was I imagining him an Old Bolshevik. Hugh is full of surprises.

He makes a very good dead Cuchulain in the 'Lay of the Heads', and even shewed great enthusiasm for the part!

We were supposed to have a 'Dress & Lighting Rehearsal' at 3.30, but of course it did not materialise. At 3.30 I was just beginning Joan's 'Queen o' fairies' dress, & the bulbs for the spotlights hadn't come! About 5 Joan and Hugh & I went and lay on the grass exhausted & Joan did the Times crossword & moaned about the political situation. The papers seemed scared & I suppose a grave crisis is on – but I can't seem to feel any emotion about it whatsoever. This is such a strange, new, different, existence I'm leading, & so entirely cut off from the world.

About 6 o/c we rehearsed Tam Lin & it was <u>appalling</u>. Denys, of course, nervous creature, went off the deep end, & said O I wish we weren't doing this! But I tried to reassure him, privately thinking he was quite right.

Tom almost lost his temper several times during the afternoon – quite unheard of. But Joan was magnificent & sorted all the costumes out, & was sweet to us when we rushed about & said Joan, where is that cloak? Joan, where are my shoes...

And at 8 o'clock there we were, Joan & Moira & I, singing the theme song & trembling all over. 'Julius Caesar' was on first, & Moira told me afterwards it was terrible. Victor had to be prompted every other line, & she sang her song wrong. Alas. Then we did Tam Lin – and it went wonderfully, never better. And they liked it!

Denys was exultant. (Joyce said afterwards my arm movements were perfect & reminded her of Peggy Ashcroft! I like that girl Joyce, she says the right things.) 'Broomfield Hill' didn't get across so well, tho' Joan's dress was splendid, like a young parachute.

'Clydewa'er' was the hit of the evening tho', with Hugh compèring, & doubled the House up in laughter. Joan gave a fine little introductory speech to the 'Lay of the Heads' & it went down amazingly well. No one laughed! 'The Keys' also went far better than I'd expected. Hugh filled all the sceneshifting intervals with a brilliant & endless stream of songs & patter which the audience loved. First he was American & sang cowboy songs, then he sang in Welsh, then Irish & Scottish songs. The production went moderately smoothly, with only one major blunder, when Joan was left sitting alone in the middle of the stage for 3 minutes in 'Donna Lombarda', while Joyce & I desperately jabbed Denys's costume as full of safety pins as a porcupine is of quills. The 'Play of the Weather' went well, tho' Cecil said it was 'a shaggy performance, just hanging together, with everyone inventing their lines for themselves.' I think some of the audience were shocked at the bawdier parts, tho' the curate in the back row whom we'd fixed on as a test case, laughed heartily thro'out.

Well – that worst part is over. Tomorrow, to pack, & then onto the Road & away. Details, like lorries & portable pianos & car insurance, remain to be settled – but nought shall stay our triumphant flight. On Magpies, on!

Buscot & Filkins.
August 24th, Thursday.

Holy mother! What a long long day. I can hardly believe we left Bucklebury only this morning. Bucklebury seems a thousand miles & years away. Now it will be a miracle if we reach the end of the tour without being arrested, for the number of copyright songs we are singing without permission, & performances we are giving without licences, & cars we are driving without insurances, is really amazing. However we comfort ourselves with the thought that as Jack is 'the actual & responsible manager' of the company he will be one to sojourn in the debtors' prison or face the angry mobs & magistrates. 'Never mind Jack' said Hugh to him, 'we'll come & give you a show when you're incarcerated. We'll do you "The Ballad of Reading Gaol".'

Joan & I meant to get up at 6 this morning & start on the sorting & packing at the theatre before breakfast, but we both slept till 7 much to our annoyance, & it was hardly worthwhile going down, as everyone else was up early too. Had breakfast (first time for several days) and paid the Warden fabulous sums of money for food & bed. Then we packed our clothes and hied us down to the theatre as fast as we cou'd gae. And God! What a time we had packing up. All was chaos & confusion, & Tom rushing about distracted in the midst, falling over everything & contradicting his orders 3 times every minute. The place was full of woeful cries.

'O Tom, where shall we put that confounded thundersheet, there isn't room for it on the trailer!'

'Tom, where did you put your helmet, I must mend it.' 'Oh you blighter, you've packed all your things in my case!' 'String, for heaven's sake, bring some string!' 'SCISSORS!' and so on.

Joan kept wonderfully calm amidst the hurley burley, & went on sorting out the clothes serenely.

We were supposed to leave at 10.45, as we had a matinée at Buscot Park at 2.30, but at 11.30 there was still a lot to be done. Moira and Joyce & Denys went on ahead in Moira's car with some of the stuff, & about 12 Victor set off in the hired car with Kirsteen and Hugh & Joan and Tom & myself. Moira had one trailer, & we left the other one for Jack, who was in Reading on Magpie business, & was due to call for the others before 12. But at 12 there was no sign of him, & we set off leaving Cecil & Charley & David and Tony (Tony Cotton who arrived yesterday) to follow with Jack – and an incredible amount of luggage. Indeed we had plenty ourselves, besides an overload of people. Tom and Victor sat serenely in front, & Hugh took up half the back (15 stone takes up a hell of a lot of room) with K. & J. & me perched precariously amid the 4 large suitcases, two haversacks, & endless swords & butterfly nets which filled the back of the car. The hobby horse with the Magpie Pennon attached protruded thro' the roof & drew cheers from the passers by.

We got to Buscot about 1.10 and ate bread and chocolate. Buscot Park is the residence of Lord Faringdon the Labour Peer, & ye gods but he has done himself well.[9] Acres & acres of fine parkland we drove thro', up the sweeping drive, flanked by noble trees & commanding a gracious prospect, (see Jane Austen passim) past the expansive lake & up between the terraces to the magnificent house, a huge 18th century building in good Oxford stone, quiet & well designed. The Theatre is a building by itself in imitation Greek temple style, divided from the house by a wide swimming pool. And the Theatre! Cool runnels of prose cannot

---

[9] The house dates from 1780: for a virtual tour, including the theatre, see http://www.buscot-park.com.

do justice to that theatre – it needs a fiery fount of Helicon to set forth its virtues – an ode, a sonnet. It is a theatre wonderful beyond words – a scrap of super-cinema come adrift – but no super-cinema, however super, ever had such soft armchairs for seats, such magnificent velvet curtains, such inches-deep Turkish carpets. And the stage! It had every conceivable gadget for light-ing & scenery. Glorious curtains at the back, reversable (mark that) black on one side and grey on the other, & of the softest velvet. Moreover (and this was what stole Victor's heart) there was a telephone in the vestibule! Victor shewed me everything in the proudest manner as if he'd designed it all himself (I believe he discovered the place.) But actually, whoever did design it had one or two bad & untheatrical lapses. For the wings are small, & the changing rooms are below the stage & are reached by a narrow iron staircase on which hurrying is impossible or disastrous. Also, and this was worst of all, there was a space below the stage, so that the slightest whisper in the changing rooms could be heard in the auditorium. But there was hot & cold water laid on! Ye gods & little fishes! The Theatre seats about 70. After the little Manor Theatre at Bucklebury, pleasant but barn-like, this place was paradise, & we crept around it with bated breath & exclama-tions of glee.

However our glee soon began to evaporate. We went to un-pack Moira's trailer & found it full of spots & floods which we didn't need, & that all the scenery & costumes were on Jack's trailer & there was nothing we could 'get on with' while we were waiting. The time crept on. It was nearly 2 o/c and the matinée began at 2.30 – and there we were with nothing ready. We paced the expanses of terrace – all complete save for the peacocks – deplored the noble lord's taste in statues, admired the frescos of 'Lord Faringdon addressing the Labour Party' and 'Lord Faring-don at dinner' etc., which decorated the porticos of the theatre. Hugh and I observed the lilies in the lilyponds and discussed the international situation & consulted our watches – & listened hard for a car. About 2.10 we had a confabulation with Tom. The audience were beginning to arrive & our hearts gradually filled with despair. There was still no sign of Jack. Victor wrote out a dismal notice saying that 'Owing to breakdown in transit the Magpies regretted they would be unable to do a show.' But Tom was all for doing what we could without costumes or scenery. This was eventually decided upon. It was an appalling prospect! There were the noble lords and ladies rolling up in their rollsroy-ces, & we were forced to offer them a rotten impromptu show with half the company absent. We were distracted. It was 2.20. Then Joan, who had climbed a nearby hill to watch, set up a yell – And there, far off down the drive, we saw Jack's car appearing, with the trailer & Charley standing on it waving & shouting. Our horrid imaginations of Jack as a gory mess on some blind corner (he is a terribly reckless driver) vanished, & we rushed to meet them with shouts of triumph. *Mon dieu*, we were glad to see them. We embraced them & shook them & wept over them. The meet-ing of Odysseus's comrades freed from the spell of Circe were nothing to it. We rushed back to the Theatre & hurled the props out of the trailer, & finally started our show only 20 minutes late.

But the audience. The theatre may have been paradise, but the audience was purgatory. There were only about 20 of them, & they were well-bred. God! but they were well-bred. They sat in well-bred silence, & clapped genteelly & unenthusiastically at the end of every item. Compared with the Bucklebury audience, they were as dead as doornails, every confounded aristocratic one of them. Then to add to our misery, the curtains (the beau-tiful velvet curtains) got temperamental & refused to close in every other scene. And to crown my despair, Jack forgot the blackout in the middle of Tam Lin. At least, he didn't forget it, but he forgot to tell us that (for some quite mysterious reason) it

was impossible to black out Lord Faringdon's magnificent lighting. So poor Tam Lin, who should have hied him across the
stage to Miles Cross (behind the centre rostrum) in the blackout,
was left stranded in the wings, & I was left in a melodramatic
attitude on top of Miles Cross, cursing hard under my breath,
trying to look soulful, & whispering 'BLACKOUT, man,
BLACKOUT' from the corner of my mouth. Tom & Joyce, also
shrieked 'BLACKOUT' in piercing whispers from the other
side of the stage, but the yellow flood never wavered its unwink-
ing stare, & eventually Denys had to creep tamely out from the
side of the stage instead of arising dramatically from behind the
rostrum.

And 'Clydewater' fell flat. As flat as pancakes it fell – I had
not conceived it possible. 'The Lay' went well, but all the humorous things missed fire completely. 'The Keys' just came off, but
there was no enthusiasm at all. And finally, for Time, we had to
cut out 'Broomfield Hill' and 'The Play of the Weather', which
was just as well, as the latter would have surely shocked the delicate sensibilities of our hearers. The devil take them, they were
neither flesh nor fowl nor good red herring – we didn't know
where to have them. If they had been less genteel they'd have
liked the broader things, & if they'd been more cultured they'd
have like(d) the ballads – but they were merely gentry & so got
no fun.

Actually it may have been our fault as well, for we got hell
afterwards from Cecil for a dull performance. We were tired – but
still...

We finished about 4.30, & David & Denys & Hugh & I rushed
out & bathed. That <u>was</u> paradise. And then we had tea in the
noble Lord's library with his secretary officiating. And what a
library! It had <u>everything</u> (bound in calf moreover) from Voltaire
to Calderon, from Engels to Browning, from Dorothy Sayers to
Chaucer. Every book, on every subject, that a cultured man could

desire – <u>only,</u> no classics![10] But the man seems to have the right line, as Hugh observed for we saw rows & rows of left book club covers, & not a few volumes of Marx & Engels.

The international situation must be grave indeed. I have not seen a paper for weeks, it seems, & have not the remotest idea what is happening, except that Germany & Russia have signed a non-aggression pact (over which much unnecessary fuss is being made) & that there is more trouble over Danzig. But all the people we meet seem very upset, & it must be a great storm to ripple these placid waters. Moreover we got a wire from Frances this morning asking if we intended to continue the tour. We wired back 'Magpies carry on.' We try not to think of it at all – and find it amazingly easy. We have so many urgent little problems of our own, that we have not time to look up & see the gathering clouds. Hugh, of course, is moved, and so, strangely enough, is Tom. But Denys & Victor & the others care not two tin tacks for the international situation.

After tea we carried on to Filkins, matter of ten miles or so, & occupied the village hall, & a fine little hall it was. We changed into costume, & climbed on a lorry, & had a triumphal procession thro' the neighbouring villages. David played his pipe, Denys shook a tambourine, I flourished the Magpies pennon at the end of a long pole, Tom waved his sword, & we all yelled & shouted & generally publicised ourselves. It was terrific fun. As Tom said, was there any better way of spending the eve of a war? All the inhabitants turned out & laughed & waved to us, & little boys followed us on bicycles & cheered. And we cheered back & cried 'Magpies forever'. We got back to the village hall about 7.30, & got things ready, & the yokels rolled up in their thousands. (About

[10] i.e. no ancient Roman and Greek authors.

50 people came.) And a fine good audience they were – a sweet solace to our wounded hearts after the baleful blues of Buscot Park. They were a trifle hearty & inclined to laugh at some of the serious things, but that was better than insensate stillness. They didn't giggle in 'The Lay' anyhow – Joan silenced them I think with her little preparatory speech. And in the funny items, how they laughed! Hugh was a roaring success. Every time he came on for his scene-changing interludes they yelled the house down with applause & stamped their feet. And over 'Clydewater' they shrieked & wept & cheered – it was magnificent. I heard later that Ronny Fletcher (the Teddy Hall English don who lives hereby) had trained them well with plenty of Gilbert & Sullivan. The only blot on the landscape was Halifax's speech which came in the middle, interrupting the performance.[11]

Another blot was that I had to sing Jon Mayne's song unaccompanied & sang it wrong. Not that that mattered, as I sang it nicely & the audience didn't know the right tune. But Norry McCurry was among the audience, & tho' all he said to me afterwards was 'that song of Jon's must be hard to learn' I think it was a pity all the same. Also I began to feel very queer after the elation of the wild procession. I think it must have been hunger, & as most of us had had practically nothing to eat the day – the noble lord only ran to very slim cucumber sandwiches & none too many either. My nerves were on edge, & I was quite wild with poor Victor for disappearing into the next door pub just when I wanted to practise a song with him. I cursed him roundly. Denys was more nervous than I have ever seen him, & got quite frantic over his costumes. He invariably loses all the nu-

---

[11] Foreign Secretary and architect of appeasement, Lord Halifax failed to realise how close relations had become between Moscow and Berlin until the Molotov-Ribbentrop Pact had already occurred.

merous properties for 'The Keys of Canterbury' & I have to rush round & find them 2 minutes before the curtain. Hugh is on edge too, tho' he conceals it well. He finds it a strain to keep the audience laughing with more or less impromptu nonsense till the scenes are ready. We must get more inter-act songs to relieve him.

A minor contretemps has arisen over 'The Lay'. There is a point towards the end where I say 'by Cuchulain's set my stone, let my cold lips touch his in death' – & then according to Tom's instructions, I kiss the corpse's lips. Actually, I didn't do this in the Bucklebury performance, as I hadn't placed myself right, & the distance across Hugh's broad chest to his lips was far too far to stretch gracefully. However, at Buscot Park I managed things better & was also feeling reckless, so I followed out Tom's instructions to the letter. While tonight at Filkins, I was tired & the audience was dangerously humorous, so I contented myself with touching his cheek. And Hugh forsooth immediately took this as a *casus belli*![12] However I met him after the performance later, when we were all going off, & he kissed my hand & said 'Well, Evir, they liked the Lay after all', so I presume all is well.

We took £7 in the Bucklebury performance, & £4 at Buscot. I'm not sure yet of the Filkins receipts. The bookstall certainly did well & we sold several copies of 'The Play of the Weather'. All the production side went sweetly & smoothly to-night. Charley Southwood is a jewel, & manages the countless combinations of rostra & steps with unfailing memory & good humour. And Jack of course is another jewel. Tony talks loudly behind the scenes & frequently annoys me, but looks after the props most efficiently. My opinion of Victor is going up by leaps & bounds.

---

[12] Latin: justification for war.
[13] Vivian Stark : unidentified.

I think he is pure metal after all in spite of his Vivian-Starkish[13] air & his irritating brand of humour. And this sort of thing certainly tries the metal pretty thoroughly. Hugh, I noticed with pleasure, has the right line on many things besides politics. This afternoon when we were having tea in Faringdon's library (Faringdon, by the way, was up in London looking after the crisis) the company behaved very badly, & talked loudly among themselves about the performance, & didn't say a word to their vicarious host, Captain Bourne, F's secretary. I spotted this & was searching my mind desperately for something to say to the man, when I saw Hugh looking similarly worried, & in a moment he came across the room & engaged Bourne in conversation.

Tonight we sleep soft, oh very soft. All the men have gone out to 'Goodfellows' to be the guests of Sir Stafford Cripps[14] while we women are quartered on the village notables. Joyce & Kirsteen & I are staying in a huge & beautiful old house as guests of a dear lady doctor (good politically too, as I gathered from a brief conversation over the cocoa and biscuits). There are hot baths galore, fine beds with real sheets & eiderdowns, a maid to call us in the morning, & a genuine breakfast. Also no mosquitoes and no bugs. Ye gods! (I discovered towards the end of my stay at the Bucklebury Hostel that I was not the only living thing on that goosefeather mattress.) And huge windows that open! And privacy! Oh wondrous place! Goodnight!

---

[14] Sir Stafford Cripps bought Goodfellows Place near Filkins in 1920, its farm of 410 acres worked by his tenants. Cripps might have had time on his hands: in early 1939 he had been expelled from the Labour Party for his advocacy of a Popular Front with the Communist Party and anti-appeasement Liberals and Conservatives; and it would not be until 1940 that Churchill would appoint him Ambassador to the Soviet Union.

Brightwell.

August 25th Friday.

No bugs, maybe – but moths. I hadn't been in bed 5 minutes before they started bumping round the room & I did draw the line at their walking on my face. So before long I leapt out of bed & slaughtered about a dozen of them. A wicked thing it is, killing soft creatures like moths, & when I thought of sweet Joyce 'catching a moth in a golden net' I felt quite guilty about it.

A maid woke me about 8 o/c with tea and biscuits!

Then I had a long hot bath ....

After a very pleasant breakfast Moira called for us[15] & we returned to the theatre. As we went thro' the village everyone waved & smiled & said 'We did like your show', which was fine hearing. We packed up, & by 11.30 were on the road again bound for Brightwell. We set off together, all 3 cars, with Magpie flags & banners flying. I went as before in Victor's car, with V., Tom, Kirsteen, Joan & Hugh. Tom & Hugh kept up their usual fire of wit on the way. We passed a grocery van marked 'Rant and Tombs Ltd'. 'Touring company doing Hamlet' was Tom's comment. Passed a horse fair at Abingdon & an ordinary fair at Wallingford, where we asked the way of some gipsies. ('We're in the business ourselves' said Hugh.) Tom wanted to visit the Basque children's camp (where we are giving a free matinée on Monday) and this determination & the fact that he seemed unnecessarily shy of saying precisely where and why he was taking us, gave rise to a controversy on the undemocratic organisation of the Magpies, & almost a quarrel between Jack & Tom.

Another controversy which wages strongly at present is that of whether or not in view of the international situation, we should do 'Soldiers coming', Auden's recruiting poem. Joyce, who plays

---

[15] Probably she had spent the night at her mother's house, about one mile away.

the deserted wife, feels very strongly we should not, & I agree with her entirely. With things as they are, it comes far too near to the bone. J. asked me to raise this question with Tom, & I did very strongly on the way to Wallingford. Hugh unexpectedly sided with Tom. The argument ended by Tom saying 'Don't be silly, of course we must do it, & that's that.' But we didn't do it. Tom said not another word, but it wasn't on the programme to-night, & everyone kept quiet.

When we reached Brightwell we found we were hardly expected. <u>Four</u> tickets precisely had been sold, & the village was very far from being Magpie-conscious. So we decided to create a stir. And we did. We hauled up our flags over the village hall, we plastered the post office & the pub & the bus stop with posters. I drew some very fiery drawings of Tam Lin & Broomfield Hill & dashed some bright paint on them to attract attention. And then we got hold of a hay-cart, & processed around the neighbourhood with cymbals & drum. We got our usual tail of little boys, & Hugh stood on the back of the cart and urged them on to shout our slogans. Our progress was triumphal.

Joan & I & most of the men are staying at the Rectory with the Girlings, & I went round in the afternoon to install my things. Joan didn't dare to appear as she had trousers on. The Rector, sweet man, shewed me his huge & lovely garden, his church (generally uninspiring but with a couple of fine Norman arches set in a later building) & Dean Inge's house just behind. The Rectory itself is a fine noble building, partly Elizabethan. Joan and I are sleeping in 'the Bridal Suite' – a <u>huge</u> room with 2 small beds adrift in the middle of it. This is better than Hill Foot!

The audience was so-so. The others pronounced it a good audience, but I felt there were too many giggling small boys. The funny things went down fine. The mirth was almost too raucous & uproarious – but I could feel 'Tam Lin' dragging on them. Tom's latest idea for 'Tam Lin' is that I should leave my girdle behind after I have been seduced. A nice piece of symbolism, but lost I rather fear on Brightwell. 'The Play of the Weather' went down splendidly, tho' we did it worse than ever before. Everyone without exception forgot their part & gagged. Tom put in huge chunks of extemporising, & left out about a page of the script at the end. But the audience laughed like hell – so it was not so bad, though Cecil would have wept over it – fortunately he had left us in the afternoon.

I sang John's song with Victor & Tony at the piano, Victor playing the harp part & Tony the oboe part. The first 'Heigh ho' went wrong, but otherwise all was well. Audience lukewarm – but they loved 'The Keys'.

Tom is full of bright ideas to-day. He outlined to Joan & Joyce & me this morning a beautiful idealistic scheme for dealing with costumes. And we just sat on the floor & laughed at him for about 20 minutes. But really we must take some precautions. Apparently when I was singing 'Love is a sickness' yesterday Denys gave an appalling display of temperament because he couldn't find his tights. Eventually he discovered them, where he had put them himself, rolled up inside a flower pot! Dear Denys – he needs about 10 nursemaids to trail him about. At present he has lost his Dolmetsch recorder & is getting frantic about it...

The stage here is appalling – no wings at all, just wooden steps up, masked by light flimsy orange curtains, & no room at all in front. Charley is disgusted with it. The financial side, too, was not as satisfactory as it might have been. We got only £3.12 altogether, including bookstall. Out alas.

After the show we went down to the Rectory & ate sandwiches & fruit & biscuits – talked & smoked – and staggered ...off...to... bed....

Northleach!

August 26th, Saturday

Christ! What an awful day! It began very pleasantly – a nice late civilised breakfast at the Rectory, then a walk & talk in the garden with the Rector, & a discussion of books in his library. Then we went down to the Hall & cleared up & packed the cars & trailers. We didn't start till pretty late, owing to late rising, & it was nearly one when we left the village to the accompaniment of waves & cheers. We stopped at Abingdon & lunched at the 'Gargoyle'. I economised, but was fed afterwards by Charley on Bath buns. Victor's car was an incredible sight. The hobby horses & banner stuck thro' the roof, placards bedecked the sides, & Hugh's haversack was strapped to the spare wheel, all but obscuring the number plate. In front were Victor & Tom – Tom as often as not opening the roof & standing up to view the countryside – while in the back were Charley & Joan & Hugh & me, woven in and out of each other like a half-inch twill, as Charley put it. Hugh & I sat in the middle, & the other two lay diagonally across us with their feet out of the windows. It was a splendid sight, & drew shouts of mirth & glee from all beholders. After an hour or so Hugh nobly got out & rode dangerously on the running board – at least it wouldn't have been so dangerous if he hadn't insisted on doing Cossack tricks all the way. Then it began to rain & we packed Hugh in again & I sat on his knee.

We reached Northleach in a thunderstorm. And my God it was an exact omen of our luck. The rain came down in sheets from a black sky, & the tall greyish houses of the long dull main street looked very uninspiring and singularly like my conception of a South Wales mining village in a deep depression. No one was about (of course) but we were met at the Cotswold Hall by our 'agent', a fine Anglican curate, an Oxford man, named Maine. And the first thing he said to us was – 'This place is no good. You'd better cancel your show. I haven't sold a single ticket!' And as we came into the hall we saw one reason – the place was stacked with gas masks. Apparently Northleach is scared stiff & in an appalling state of nerves. Never having seen or heard of gas masks before, they are now in a panic & imagining slaughter & sudden death.

We parked the trailers under cover at the 'Wheatsheaf', & then went into the dismal sordid hall, feeling very wet & cold & dispirited, & had a conference. Victor and Hugh and some others were for cancelling the show altogether & just rehearsing, but Tom (needless to say) & Charley and me were for carrying on. We were to have paid £1 for the hire of the hall, but the caretaker generously offered a 'sliding scale'. Tom urged strongly that we should have a publicity drive & do the show. I didn't feel much like a publicity drive, being cold & hungry, & observing the pouring rain, but it seemed a crying shame to give up the show if there was any possibility of drawing an audience. Eventually Victor went out to 'sound the pulse of public opinion'. This he did by going down to the billiard room & asking everyone in general if they would be willing to come to the show if we put it on. There were about 50 people in the room, & they all yelled 'Yes' with one accord. So the show went on.

It was about 5.30 by now & we'd had no tea, but the caretaker's wife was soon wheedled into producing a pot. Then we unpacked the scenery & costumes – and O what a sight they were! All the noble grey screens had run, & looked like maps of northern Scandinavia, & wet trickles of paint polluted every single thing in the trailers. As for the dresses, even those in the depths of trunks and cases were wet, & those on top were soaking! We could have wept. The caretaker's wife lit a fire in the dressing room, & we trailed in dismally & hung our things round it. Then Moira & I made posters & plastered them round the market square in all the spaces not filled by recruiting bills & adjurations to young men to join the Territorials & defend their homes.

By this time it had stopped raining, & Denys who had been sent out by Tom to commandeer a hay-wain or a lorry returned empty handed. But was Tom daunted? No! He decreed a procession on foot – and out we set, a gallant but heavy hearted little band, in costume, with bells & drums & tambourines to apprise the town of our coming. And apprise them we did! Crowds of people turned up at every corner & waved us on. Tom was quite shameless, & rushed from one side of the street to the other, putting his head thro' people's windows, & striding into pubs & shops, crying 'Come and see the Magpie Players! 8 o/c tonight! Best show in England!'

Then when we had got about 1/2 a mile from the hall it began to pour with rain! Denys's Tam Lin costume began to run. Denys said 'I dislike this more than I can say!' Luckily friend Maine's dwelling was hereby, so we all trooped in there and drank his sherry till the rain stopped.

About 8 o/c all the sixpennies were full – & very few expensive seats had been sold. Joan & I sat behind the curtain waiting to begin the theme song & listened to the audience – it sounded dangerous. And my God it was dangerous. There was a great mob of toughs at the back, intent merely on making themselves as obstreperous as possible to the actors. 'Julius Caesar' flopped hard – no one listened, & there was talking the whole time. And 'Tam Lin' was absolute purgatory – the audience just laughed at it, & catcalled. I was mad with rage, & spoke my 'fierce' lines with a most indelicate intensity. I wanted to rush out into the audience and kill a few of them – & consequently I acted badly. Denys was almost in tears too, & the whole ballad was spoilt. Then – the final thorn in my crown of affliction – I had to go out & sing 'Love is a sickness' to that gang of roughnecks. Lots of them got up & marched out, and the rest laughed & jeered, quite unrestrained by loud 'sh's' from the intelligentsia in the 2s 6d seats. I came off

nearly weeping with fury, & was quite uncheered by the sympathy of the cast, who were terribly upset for me, especially Hugh.
(Charley said afterwards he 'felt just like starting a free fight right
now'.)'Edward' and 'Donna Lombarda' were laughed at. 'The
Keys' got a few giggles & a great deal of uninterested talking.
Hugh's cowboy songs got a terrific ovation. But as for 'Clydewater' – they took it seriously!!! Scarcely a laugh till over halfway
through!

We were absolutely flabbergasted – we thought 'Clydewater'
would be a sure hit with this audience – but no, they carried
their perversity to its final conclusion, & just refused to laugh. We
had every possible piece of bad luck. Hugh was terribly cut up
about it, & seemed to imagine it was his fault, as he produced the
thing.

I was dreading the 'Lay of the Heads' & begged Tom not
to do it – but he was determined to, & actually it went down
surprisingly well. 'The Demon Lover' also, with Tom & Joyce,
its first performance went down not too badly, & Tom looked
fiendish with a bare chest with red flames painted on it! I
disagreed entirely with his interpretation of the ballad, & so
did Denys, but we hadn't much time to object, as we had only
one hurried rehearsal in the afternoon, with Denys & me as nar-
rators.

At last, with a sigh of relief, we got to the 'Play of the Weather', the last item on the programme. And then Tom lost his
head. He had been departing farther and farther from the
script in each performance, but now he went off the rails completely. He was nervous of the audience, & determined to raise
laughs at any expense – so he put on a broad Yorkshire accent,
gagged continually, garbled his lines unrecognisably, & completely vulgarised the whole play. (He still didn't know his part
properly, & had the script with him.) Behind the scenes we stood
in silent fury & amazement to hear our charming witty little 'Play

of the Weather' being turned into a farce & a pretty poor farce at that.

It was in the middle of Joan's long speech, when I was just preparing to come on, that the final glorious artistic finish to our eventful evening occurred. All the lights suddenly went out. There was a moment's horrid silence. Then all the people on the stage began to gag desperately, all at once, but were soon drowned by the laughter & yelling & whistling from the audience. It was not unlike the tragic ending of Hugh's tale about Little George's Balloon – 'In the darkness shouts and yells were mingled with electric bells, & shrieks and cries for help and groans And crackling of broken bones.'[16] I rushed across the stage in the dark with some wild notion of finding Charley, & on the way knocked Moira's accordion down from the top of one of the rostra, & nearly snapped my collar bone on it. Then Jack's voice rose above the tumult, explaining that the whole town was in darkness, & no doubt it was something to do with the Air Raid precautions. For a moment we were afraid the audience would panic.

Then Charley & Hugh, our gallant stalwarts, leapt down among them & struck matches, & asked everyone to leave the hall quietly, as there was obviously no hope of finishing the play. They filed noisily out, & we were left in the dark. At last the lights came on again, & revealed a scene closely resembling a battlefield on the following dawn. We sat and laughed. Thank God we could laugh! Then we staggered down to our miserable little dressing room, & ate Moira's greengages & packed up for the night. Everyone behaved magnificently – especially David,

---

[16] cf. Hilaire Belloc's *Cautionary Tales* no 3, George (The boy who played with dangerous toys): 'And in the darkness shrieks and yells Were mingled with electric bells, And falling masonry and groans, And crunching, as of broken bones…'

who almost silenced the louts at the back at one point during his comic act, by appealing to them, or rather rebuking them, in the name of the hospitality of Northleach. But the company was very angry with Tom, even considering the extenuating circumstances, & a strong vote of censure was passed upon him, which he took amazingly meekly.

Then Moira & Joan & I left for our night's lodgings. We are sleeping at an immense Elizabethan manor – with a 'skeleton staff' as our curate called it – and the master away. So here we are, tucked away in one wing of this monstrous, ghostly place, & waited on by a taciturn butler & his wife. And 'Northleach hospitality' received its final blow as far as we were concerned when we arrived & found no food prepared for us! We had had nothing to eat since lunch, & lo now we had to ask specially, & were given some very dry & unappetising biscuits to eat! And we felt like juicy beefsteaks! Furthermore, to add to our misery, our rooms are perfect Victorian period pieces, bristling with horrid restless ornaments, sickly with sentimental pictures of dogs & cats, & putrid with bad hunting prints & photographs of army groups of the 1860s. However, one consolation is that however bad our luck in the rest of the tour, it will shew up magnificently beside to-day. It is like Tom & Charley's method of circumnavigating the shaving question – whereby Tom stands beside Charley, & manages to look quite cleanshaven by contrast, & Charley stands besides Hugh, whose beard by now is long & curling! And really in retrospect it is all damn funny!

Water Eaton Manor.
August 27th, Sunday.
A peaceful day. We left Northleach with mingled relief & imprecations, after the men had been well rooked by a charming

but villainous robber of a Youth Hostel warden. And, as a grand finale, Joyce had her purse stolen. O Northleach, Northleach, we shall pass this way but once! We went to Water Eaton via Shipton-under-Wychwood, & left our big props & the trailers behind there. Water Eaton is a fine Elizabethan manor belonging to Prof. Carr Saunders, the London university population expert.[17] We weren't exactly welcomed with open arms by the professor & his lady. Not exactly. But we found Frances was there – with her two harps – so that compensated for a slight aloofness on the part of the family & a noticeable scarcity of basic nourishment. We wandered the gardens, lay on the grass, & Tom talked vaguely of rehearsing this & that. My opinion of everyone in the company is going up by leaps & bounds – with 2 exceptions. Tom & Jack. Tom really is maddening. He refuses to make up his mind, and when he does make it up, he won't tell anyone. He was well served this afternoon, for as a result of his not divulging what ballads we were going to rehearse, half the company went off in a punt & left him fuming. Actually it was mean of them too to wander off without a word, & I ticked Joyce & Moira off about it when they came back. Frances played her harp in the family chapel & I came & sang softly to it, & happily we passed the day. At 6 we gave a show to the Carr Saunders & aristocratic & arty friends. It was beautiful to do Tam Lin out of doors in such a superb setting, & it went well. Tom wrecked Donna Lombarda by too early an entrance, but on the whole all was delightful.

After the show Hugh & I wandered down to the Cherwell which flows thro' meadows below the house, & sat & watched

---

[17] Sir Alexander Morris Carr-Saunders (1886-1966) English demographer, sociologist, academic administrator and pioneer in analysing population problems and social structures.

the moon rise. A group of white swans sailed silently past. It was a most magical evening. Hugh lay down beside me with his head touching my side, & I sat & looked across the river. Then gradually we gave expression to what had been tacit between us for several days. There is something incredibly tender & gentle about Hugh, for all his terrific strength & bluffness.

I went back late to the house to find Moira & Joan had been waiting for me. They then took Joyce & me in the car to the people we were to stay with in Yarnton. Both Joyce & myself, by some unlucky chance had lost our cases, & were in great distress. However, we survived the night. We were staying with a hearty old couple, good working class stock, but unintelligent. The sort of people who are nice to you when you come canvassing, but who will not buy a copy of the 'Daily Worker' as they 'already get the Herald, thank you very much.'

Shipton-under-Wychwood.
August 28th, Monday.

A very pleasant day this was. Joyce & I had a strenuous breakfast, & were informed by our host that Oxford was undoubtedly stunting our minds, & we should never be the same again. Then we played with dogs and cats in the garden till Victor came & took us back to Water Eaton, where we spent a lazy morning. I sewed straps onto the kilts, & made 'a gallant silver chest' for the 'Keys'. Hugh & I avoided each other.

In the afternoon we parted forces, & Charley & Hugh & Jack & Kirsteen & Frances went off into Oxford with the harps, while the rest of us went to Aston Bampton & gave a show to the Basque children in their beautiful garden. We had David instead of Hugh & Charley in our car, & tho' less entertaining he was considerably less obstreperous.

The matinée was most successful – to crown our joy 3 real bushes of broom were in flower behind the 'stage' – and the children were a <u>most</u> appreciative audience. They did some dances & songs of their own in the interval which were most spontaneous & charming. We had a meagre tea after the show (we had missed lunch owing to shortness of time) and rushed on to Shipton (where I found my case to my great relief. Joyce's case had been found in the morning at the back door of Water Eaton by one of the horrid precocious Carr Sanders children.)

The others (Charley, Hugh & co) had been there most of the afternoon, but of course the stage wasn't ready. Tom dragged our recalcitrant feet out for a procession, & we awoke the echoes of Shipton & Milton (both under-Wychwood). We trudged a mile or two, & were getting tired & cross when we met Victor plus car, who gave us an exhilarating lift back on the running board at 60 mph.

I got a worried letter from home. Maybe things are worse than I'd thought. Also Hugh produced a 'Worker' which seemed pretty desperate in spite of Pollit's usual optimism. Michael, who has just been called up, writes to make me his 'literary executor', with instructions what to publish should Anything Happen to him. But Michael always did take life melodramatically.[18]

We had a splendid audience to-night to console us. All the Basque kids were there, and <u>so</u> good. And all the five shilling seats

---

[18] MRD Foot (1919-) the future military historian, had been at Winchester with Frank Thompson, and was now reading History at New College (1938-39 and 1945-47).

[19] *The Countryman* was launched in 1927 by J.W. Robertson Scott, journalist and writer on rural affairs. Concerned about the mechanisation of farming, the magazine attracted writers such as G.K. Chesterton, Hugh Walpole, G.B. Shaw and several prime ministers.

were filled up with intelligent ladies, & gentlemen with beards (including Scott Robertson, editor of *The Countryman*[19]). The money simply <u>rolled</u> in, and afterwards the bookstall & collection did excellently well. We were inspired, & gave them a really good show for their money. 'Tam Lin' went better than it's ever done, & my feet scarcely touched the boards. Someone in the front row remarked of my acting 'Aren't her movements perfectly beautiful?'

Frances told me this – & I embraced her for doing so. Frances herself looked superb beside her harp, in a long brown dress & a golden belt. At the interval a slight contretemps occurred when Jack fused the lights. Jack actually was roaring tight, having just returned from the 'Red House' shortly before the performance, but after we had all cursed him heartily he got them to work again. I enjoyed the 'Lay of the Heads' thoro'ly, & for once felt sure the audience did too. I felt, for the first time, a slight response from Hugh when I kissed him.

Joyce & I are staying with the Groves at the Four Winds – we are sleeping in a double bed, as last night, but everything is perfect otherwise. We had a really pukkah dinner when we got in – & did we devour it voraciously! Then I had a long political argument with Mr Groves who is an ex-Fabian-turned-Tory & specialises in the 'you'll grow out of this nonsense' line. He is all wrong about the Soviet-German pact. Curious how many intelligent people are getting the Soviet Union wrong over this business.

I wonder if this is the end of everything at last? Anyhow, if it is, I am having a very grand finale.

Bicester.
August 29th, Tuesday.
Another perfect day. Had a magnificent breakfast and bade

affectionate farewell to the Groves. Packed our goods and set off. Victor very cleverly induced Moira to take some of our cases on her trailer, so that the back of our car was comparatively empty. Also by some lucky dispensation Charley went on Jack's car, so Joan & Hugh & I sat luxuriously in the back, with Kirsteen, Tom & Victor in the front. Tom held forth in fine style most of the way on how ungratefully everyone was grumbling about their parts, & what a cross discontented set of individuals we were anyway, & 'much better had he devised for us all' etc. While we all sat & laughed ourselves sick. Poor old Tom. We lost the other car on the way, & arrived at Tusmore Park,[20] the abode of Lady Bicester, at 2 o/c. Now Tom had been having a long & most familiar correspondence with one Ivie, Lady B's secretary, & was much looking forward to meeting her. When he was greeted on the step by a white-haired spinster who turned out to be Ivie we were much amused. We weren't expected for lunch, but we were ushered in with all the symptoms of great joy, & led to a huge high-ceilinged dining hall where a sumptuous table was spread with shining silver for our delectation. We had thought Buscot Park magnificent – we had gasped at Leygone Manor (where we stayed the night we were at Northleach) but Tusmore Park put them both in the shade. It was a wide tall tawnily-weathered 18th C. building, with mile-long terraces & a most beautiful lake to double it all in reflection. And within it was like a Byzantine mosque or the Greek church at its most splendid. I could have sworn I smelt incense. It was all <u>too</u> opulent. But the lunch we had left <u>nothing</u>

---

[20] Tusmore Park, built 1766-69 and set in 3000 acres, was proverbially beautiful in the elegant Anglo-Palladian Classical style. In 1960 it was demolished by Lady Bicester's son and replaced by a weak modern house one third in size of the original. A postcard sent by IM home, on 30 August 1939, mentions silver plate and that Lady Bicester was 'particularly taken with my acting'.

to be desired. There was lamb, both hot & cold, sauces & vegetables to our hearts desire, salads *ad libitum*[21], & still Ivie rolled up with plates of veal & ham, & apologised for the 'impromptu meal, as we were not expected'. And to follow (*gaudeo referens*[22]) was apple pie & cream and peaches, & then biscuits & cheeses of all sorts. All washed down with barley water or beer or cider to taste. We made the most of our opportunities. Magpie life develops a hand-to-mouth philosophy of existence, & the general principle is, get a good meal or a hot bath wherever you can, for heaven only knows when you'll get the next. So we set to, & quaffed our liquor from silver tankards, & made the roof ring with our mirth. At last, when contented & replete we lay prostrate about the table, a car was heard, & the arrival of the other Magpies announced. They had lunched on the way, & were most jealous. We came in lordly manner down the wide stairs to meet them. The cider must have been particularly potent. I'd had only one glass, but felt unduly elated, & so apparently did Joan, for all we could do in reply to the envious looks of the others was to shriek with laughter.

This we did until Hugh stonily pushed us out into the open air.

We went on down to the Pavilion, a charming little theatre in the grounds, with a fine apron stage. Here Joan set to work on 'Vilikins & his Dinah', while I wandered off into a far field to practise some of Denys's duets on my recorder. Seven brown horses came & stood appreciatively about me. Before long Denys himself arrived & we tried some of the things with moderate success. We then walked down to the lake and admired the beauty of the place & wondered if we were to die young & what it all meant

---

[21] At one's pleasure.

[22] Joyous to report.

anyway. Went back to the Pavilion & had a good tea on Lady B. (Lady B. herself is sweet & Irish, she waited on us herself when we were up at the House.) Then I went down to the lake again to practise alone, but hadn't been playing 10 minutes before Hugh quietly loomed up out of the wood, & we lay on the grass & moralised. Then Tom arrived, in a crazy lazy mood, & we threw grass at each other & talked nonsense.

The evening's show was a great success. A small but most appreciative audience. Tom watched 'Tam Lin' from F.O.H.[23] for first time & was full of praise. I talked to a charming American girl in the interval & she was rapturous about the whole show. And she said to me 'I just <u>loved</u> Tam Lin. And your hands, my dear, I don't mind telling you, were a delight to look upon. I suppose you've done a lot of acting. What dramatic school did you go to?' I registered mild pleasure & shrieked with joy inside. To-night I am sleeping at a Mrs Quatermain's – one of Lady B's aged retainers. A sweet old woman who drinks stout & refers to her husband as 'her sweetheart'.

To-day Tom read us a rather stiff but charming letter from Cecil in his usual style – saying how he envied us being so cut off in our own little world with our own little problems. Indeed this is a very pleasant nutshell to be bounded in, & we count ourselves kings of infinite space,[24] every one of us.

Chipping Campden.
August 30th, Wednesday.

Better & better. Came up to the Pavilion about 9.30 to find the

---

[23] Front of House.

[24] cf. *Hamlet* II ii 'I could be bounded in a nutshell and count myself king of infinite space were it not that I have bad dreams'.

men in the throes of getting up. They had slept on the floor in horse blankets. ('It's so <u>difficult</u>' said Denys, 'if you're not a horse!') Tony disgraced himself completely. First it was discovered that he had <u>slept</u> on Joan's Broomfield Hill dress, mistaking it for waste material (it <u>is</u> a little like a collapsed parachute) & then, in contrition, he started to clean everyone's shoes – and polished them on Joyce's 'Laird o' Cockpen' dress! He must be crazier than I thought him. Joan was <u>furious</u> & Moira came hunting him, cheered on by all the men, with the avowed intent of slapping his face (which she didn't). Tony got pretty riled himself, & tried to defend himself – unwise.

Lady Bicester – who loved 'Tam Lin' best of all, bless her heart – offered all the men hot baths at 11, so that delayed our start. But we reached Chipping Campden eventually about 2 o/c without mishap, save that Moira knocked a boy off his bicycle when he rushed a corner in front of her. We were just behind in Victor's car & Hugh was out of the door like an arrow, several seconds before the rest of us knew what had happened, & picked him up. (Typical of Hugh, that.) Luckily he wasn't at all hurt.

When we got to Campden we found that Pemberton, our agent, was fuming, having expected us at 11. Guy Pemberton is a big man in the theatrical line it seems, & had given us fine publicity. We heard people in the town exclaiming 'O, the Magpie Players' – just (as Moira remarked) as if they were saying 'O, the D'Oyley Carte!'

I slipped away after unpacking & explored the place – god but it's beautiful – almost completely Tudor. The church is late perpendicular & dull inside, but it looks fine up on its green hill with a very old yew-treed churchyard about it, and a fine view of fields & woods. I lay across one of the graves & thought how quiet it would be to be dead.

We had a procession on a coal cart round the village, and were greeted everywhere with smiles & cheers. And the house we had!

The place was <u>packed to the doors</u>, & we had to <u>turn people away</u>. We rushed out at the last moment & brought in carloads of chairs & benches to make more sixpennies, & even then there wasn't room. They loved the show, & we acted magnificently (to give us our due). And the collection came to 4 7s 6d! We must have made a good £9 altogether. (A good £12 I found out later!)

We went and drank port with the Pembertons afterwards, & then Frances & I left for the Noel Arms, where we are staying. Bad news we had to-day – a wire from Bibury cancelling the performance. This may mean disaster financially.

The Territorials were all called up to-day, Jack says. I feel strangely unmoved.

Yarnton Manor & Winchcombe.
August 31st, Thursday.
Had a fine breakfast on Guy Pemberton in the Noel Arms, & then split forces once more, most of us going to Yarnton for the matinée, while Jack & Hugh & Kirsteen & Tony took the scenery to Winchcombe. Yarnton Manor is a beautiful Elizabethan house with miraculous gardens. A minor crisis occurred when we arrived. Our car (Victor, Tom, David, Joyce, Frances & myself) lunched en route, but Moira, Joan & Denys (in M's car) forgot to (after having been so instructed by Tom) & on arrival they pushed off into Yarnton to eat, quite disregarding Tom's protests, who wanted them to come on a procession. Moira was quite savage & nearly ran Tom down when he stood in the way of the car & remonstrated in no uncertain terms. The rest of us, who sided entirely with Tom, garbed ourselves suitably & rode in triumph on the running board of Victor's car, and waked the echoes. Riding on running boards when the car is going a good forty is most exhilarating sport. When the others returned I gave them icily to understand that they hadn't a leg to stand on, and

my sympathies were for once with Tom, which surprised them not a little.

The matinée went well – it was a beautiful setting 'Tam Lin' especially excelled itself. A huge beech tree, conveniently placed, was 'Carterhaugh' & Denys himself appeared dramatically on top of a wall. Also there were fine steps for me to 'hie' up and down. There was an anxious moment in the metamorphosis scene, when Denys had to run quickly thro' the house & out the front door. Apparently the door was locked & D. had to get the caretaker to open it. And there was I, getting nearer & nearer the 'mother naked man', and wondering when D. would appear. Eventually, about 30 seconds after I'd spoken his cue, he came rushing breathlessly out into my wavering embrace. I gurgled 'Thank God', and we clung to each other in silent laughter.

Tom's latest idea re Tam Lin is that I should wear a girdle in the first scene & leave it off in the second scene 'Because', he said, 'the audience may not realise what Tam Lin has been up to!' We mooted this but finally rejected it as far too subtle.

The journey to Winchcombe was enlivened with a puncture & a first class quarrel. Tom was laying down the law to Joyce about the interpretation of the 'Demon Lover' when I, urged on by Denys, butted ....[2pp excised by IM]...

..... to take the law into our own hands & leave all our costumes & scenery behind the theatre. We unpacked, for the last time, the loaded trailers, & stowed away the beloved grey screens & the noble rostra. 'We shall come back' said Tom, as he stowed costumes away in the cupboards. 'After the war, the Magpies will tour again. But,' he added, 'our show will be frightfully pre-war, I'm afraid.' Tony Cotton was even more optimistic. 'I invite you all to a sherry party in my rooms in Lincoln on the second day of term!'

Victor & Tony went first, taking the hired car back to Reading. I resolved, much against the will of the company to return to London. Hugh remonstrated. 'Do you realise there's a pretty good chance of London being bombed to-night? Don't be a little fool!' But I was unmoved. .... [*2 lines excised by IM*]...

I decided it would be safer to go with all the others to Oxford, & then if no trains were running I could stay with Joan.

Hugh & I rode together in the dicky of Jack's car as it roared over the Berkshire Downs. It was intensely exhilarating. Grey blue clouds & streaks of green & pink sky wreathed the horizon. Hugh put his arm round me & we sighed at our luck.

We reached Oxford about 8, & Jack dropped Hugh & me up at the station about 8.30. Discovered a train for London via Didcot was due to leave at 8.32, and rushed onto platform, armed with a return half of Kirsteen's to Gerard's Cross.

At 9.35 we were still on the platform waiting. But it was a very strong & wonderful hour I spent with Hugh then. I had not realised he ..... [*2 lines missing*]...

Everything was dark – no lights in the trains. I got an empty carriage & half-slept. The train stopped for about half-an-hour outside Didcot.I found there were no trains direct to London, but I must change at Reading. Eventually I got a train from Reading, & found myself in a carriage with 2 half-drunk reservists who had just been called up. One of them, a lorry-driver, turned out to be quite nice, & promised to get me a lift home on a lorry if the tubes weren't running.

His little refrain was 'I know for a fact', enunciated in a confidential & impressive tone. He informed me that for the last 18 months ammunition had been being removed from Woolwich Arsenal to secret dumps in the West Country. This I credited, but I decided he must be a bit tight when he said that 'Sir Reginald Domville, who was his personal friend, had told him months ago that war would begin on this particular date.'

A long wait at Reading. God! It was dismal. Blue lights we could scarcely see by, the place deserted & troop trains packed with singing cannon fodder passing every ten minutes. Eventually a train came, & we got to Paddington. I found the Metropolitan line still working, bade adieu to my lorry driver, & just caught the last train. This was after 1 o/c. When I reached Hammersmith I found the tubes were not working. Waited awhile for a trolley bus but vainly. Then I asked a man who was passing if he knew aything about the buses. He didn't, but he was most willing to be helpful. Far too willing I thought at first. We conferred, & as he was bound for... [*end of text; a page torn out*]

L-R: Frank Thompson, his parents and younger brother Edward c1939, courtesy Dorothy Thompson

II

WRITING TO FRANK THOMPSON
1940-44

IRIS MURDOCH AND Frank Thompson met after yet more theatricals. To show the dangers of Fascism in Britain, Frank and some friends wrote and acted in *It Can Happen Here* which imagined Britain as a Fascist police state and was put on for a Labour Club audience at St Michael's Hall, Oxford, on 6 March 1939 (admission price 6d]. Frank had sighted Murdoch the previous November at a crowded talk about Spain in Queens College: squeezing onto a bench while Stephen Spender made a woolly speech, he noticed a girl leaning on her elbow who wasn't pretty and had a figure too thick to be good.

> But there was something about her warm green dress, her long yellow locks like a cavalier's, and her gentle profile, that gave a pleasing impression of harmony. My feeling of loneliness redoubled. 'Why didn't I know anyone like that?'

This wish was granted in the producer's rooms in Ruskin, where, wanting to make a good impression despite being drunk, he started on politics. He had no use for Liberal or Labour leaders. 'What about the Communist Party?' Murdoch asked provocatively.

> I was dumbstruck... So I said, 'Come to tea in a couple of days and convert me'. Then I staggered home and lay on a sofa ... announcing to the world that I had met a stunner of a girl and was joining the Communist party for love of her.

He wrote to a friend[1] – 'I've met my dream-girl – a poetic Irish Communist who's doing Honour Mods. I worship her'. By the time Iris came to tea in his very untidy rooms he was ready to join. The British Left was inclined to pacifism; the Tories to appeasement. Any young person dedicated to stopping Hitler was easy game for The Communist Party. Frank and Iris both fitted the bill. They marched together in the Oxford Mayday parade in 1939 and got pelted with rotten vegetables; and probably attended the same CP summer youth camp near Guildford that summer, in search of political education.

The Oxford CP was good at infiltrating other parties. Nearly all the committee of the Labour Club, with over 1,000 members, and all the committees of the League of Nations Union, Liberal Club and Student Christian Movement, together with two of the five Conservative Club committee, were also in the CP. So, extraordinary as it seems, were two even of the ten British Union of Fascists![2]

CP members experienced, none the less, awkward moments. The first came when the USSR and Germany signed their non-aggression pact (see Part 1), and both promptly invaded Poland. The CP changed over one week to declaring the war 'imperialist' and the Party line pacifist. Murdoch toed this new Party line,

---

[1] Antony Forster.
[2] LTE from Robert Conquest.

FRANK THOMPSON – INTRODUCTION

which lasted until June 1941 when Hitler invaded Russia: Frank did not. Despite bitter protests from his parents, he joined up on 2 September and wrote a poem defending his action to Murdoch, starting 'Sure, lady, I know the Party line is better': he wished to fight.

Then in November 1939 the huge USSR invaded tiny Finland. Roy Jenkins and Tony Crosland, nauseated by the CP lie that the Red Army was fighting to liberate the small, brave Finnish people just as it had, together with the Nazis, 'liberated' the Poles, broke with the OULC and set up a much bigger Democratic Socialist Club. Meanwhile the tiny rump-OULC continued despite this second invasion to support the USSR, Iris remaining 'apparently rigid on the Stalinist line'. Jenkins spent fruitless weeks attempting to sort out the assets and liabilities of the rival groups, writing to 'Dear Miss Murdoch' as OULC co-Treasurer and receiving humourless answers from her addressed to 'Dear Comrade Jenkins.'[3]

When, on 17 February 1943, Murdoch writes to Frank that 'I don't know if it will mean much to you after these years... but the two clubs, who were always at each other's throats, have now amicably amalgamated', it is to the healing of this bitter split that she refers. Meanwhile both Frank Thompson and Iris Murdoch were still, even in 1943, CP members. Murdoch had resigned her 'open' membership while continuing as a clandestine member. She later admitted to friends that she was after 1942 illicitly copying Treasury documents and, for the Party, making dead-letter drops into a tree in Kensington Gardens;[4] while Frank that year was helping heal conflicts within the Iraqi Communist party.

---

[3] Roy Jenkins, LTE June 1998.
[4] See e.g. John Jones, *TLS* 5/10/2001, 'She loved and sung'.

That this correspondence is between fellow-Communists may not always be obvious, but politics was one ground of their friendship. Hence Murdoch addresses Frank as 'Old Campaigner'; and their mutual admiration for the USSR caused each to learn Russian. Iris afterwards spoke of her CP years as having taught her from the inside how a small, ruthless group of individuals can wield destructive power, and compared a dictatorial CP branch with an IRA cell. But that was later.

■■■

An intense idealist, Frank was brilliant, tall, slim, fair-haired, grey-blue eyed, high cheek-boned, a Wykehamist who spoke six languages and later acquired three more. He was one year younger than Iris[5] reading Classics at New College. He came from a liberal, anti-imperialist and well-connected bohemian family that was also 'quick with ideas and poetry and international visitors'[6]; his younger brother E.P. Thompson would make his mark as the best-known left-wing historian of his generation. Boyhood friends had died with the International Brigade in Spain.[7] While a student, Frank is remembered as charming, shambolic and uncoordinated. 'Stop apologising', friends would say to him. War-time photographs show a face of some beauty, intelligence, and grace. He was also a gifted poet in the making who would write a landmark poem for the coming war, subtitled An Epitaph for my Friends:

As one who, gazing at a vista
Of beauty, sees the clouds close in

---

[5] b. Aug 17th 1920, Darjeeling.
[6] Thompson E,.P. *Beyond the Frontier* (1997) , p 47
[7] e.g. Anthony Carritt, 1937 – see FT's letter to IM, 4 Sep 1942.

And turns his back in sorrow, hearing
The thunderclaps begin

So we, whose life was all before us,
Our hearts with sunlight filled,
Left in the hills our books and flowers,
Descended, and were killed

Write on the stone no words of sadness,
- Only the gladness due
That we, who asked the most of living,
Knew how to give it too.

Before he wrote this, Frank was 'pining green' for Iris, who though sympathetic was interested in Michael (MRD) Foot, who was crazy about Leonie Marsh who adored Frank. This prefigured the erotic symmetries of her novels. Frank wrote bad poems to her expressing calf-love and suffered extravagantly. Michael hid Frank's cut-throat razor from him. Leo Pliatzky, more down-to-earth, invited him to dinner. He stopped sleeping, started talking to himself, and spent a week convalescing at home. On his mother's advice, Frank dug up an entire bed of irises as a counter-charm. On this unhappy love quartet, Frank joked in a parody of Marxist-Leninist Newspeak: 'It's not shortage of resources that's the problem, comrades. *It's maldistribution of supplies*'.[8] Iris Murdoch would later write that Frank was the most remarkable person she met as an undergraduate at Oxford.[9]

■■■

In March 1941 Frank, having transferred the previous August

---

[8] Recalled by Philippa Foot.
[9] Slavcho Trunski, *Grateful Bulgaria*, Sofia Press, 1979, p15.

from the Royal Artillery to 'Phantom', a small communications and intelligence unit, was posted to the Middle East. After this date their correspondence takes off, and fifty years after his murder Murdoch told the present editor that she and Frank had planned to marry.[10] This was never true, no matter what might – or might not – have happened had Frank survived the war and returned to England. It is clear, however, from the letter-run, that Murdoch started to fall in love with Frank. MRD Foot, a friend of Frank's since their school-days, and Murdoch's lover in 1943, endorses this: he felt that he was a 'stand-in' for Frank. Frank noted to his parents that Murdoch's letters whenever she had not seen him for a long time, were full of affection.

The war was a great age of letter-writing, providing a virtual chat-room for a generation. A new technology evolved too. Like visits to the mothers of soldier-friends posted overseas,[11] regular mail was regarded as a vital part of sustaining morale, but the sheer bulk of letters being transported to and from the Middle and Far East was a problem, especially after the Italians closed the Suez Canal and the Mediterranean became too dangerous for sea transport. The sea route around the Cape of Good Hope – a detour of 12,000 miles – delayed mail for weeks. The now forgotten 'airgraph', mentioned by both Frank and Iris, was one solution. Single quarto sheets were distributed and collected by Post Offices, sent to a processing station, censored, given a serial number and micro-filmed with 1,700 messages on 100ft of film. When in April 1941 the first airgraph dispatch arrived in London

---

[10] See also Sue Summers (1988) 'The Lost Loves of Iris Murdoch', *Mail on Sunday*, 5 June. She also dreamt that she and Frank married – see *Life*, ch 7.

[11] IM visited Hal Lidderdale's and John Willett's mothers - almost certainly others too, now lost to view.

from Cairo, 50,000 micro-filmed letters were found to weigh just 13 pounds instead of three-quarters of a ton. On arrival each airgraph was developed, magnified and delivered in a manila envelope.

Iris describes her own airgraphs and letters as 'talk', or direct address. She wrote: 'I'm very talkative on paper' and 'I can live in letters.[12]' Except with remarkably few close friends, face-to-face communication could be shy and inhibited. On paper she experienced freedom, and writing to a distant friend was the most liberating of all. The habit started in 1937-38 with a year-long romantic correspondence to a Belfast family friend called Scott whom she had not yet met. It continued all her life.[13] Frank Thompson replaced Scott as distant love-object from 1941-44, David Hicks replaced Frank from 1944 to 1946,[14] Raymond Queneau replaced Hicks from 1946 to 1956. Pen-friendship offered cost-free intimacy, a point of entry into the imaginative worlds of others, and a stage on which to try out her own *personae*. After she became famous she spent up to four hours a day writing letters to pen-pals who were often fans.

In November 1942 Murdoch wrote to Frank of T.E. Lawrence as 'the sort of person I would leave anything to follow'. Frank had met Lawrence as a child on Boars Hill. But it is possible that her praise of this intellectual-turned-man-of-action influenced Frank in his decision, some months later, to join the Special Operations Executive (SOE), set up by Churchill in 1940 to 'set Europe ablaze' by supplying arms and other support to guerrilla

---

[12] To Hicks, Dec 1945; and to Philippa Foot, undated but mid to late 1960s.

[13] James Henderson Scott, see *Life*, ch. 3; see also *IM NewsLetter* 2007.

[14] Her brief 1946 engagement to Hicks after a seven year correspondence shows that this writing had power-in-the-world, and was not mere 'fantasy'.

and sabotage groups.[15] He at first hoped to go to Greece, but in November 1943 changed his destination to Serbia. He had learnt Serbo-Croat and Bulgarian too.

On the night of 25 January 1944 he was dropped with supplies and a W/T operator onto the high Serbian plateau. Code-named 'Claridges', his mission was to remain on the Serb-Bulgarian frontier and act as a base for the four men in 'Mulligatawny'. The plan was ill-conceived, and ill-executed. For two months on snowy mountainous terrain, hunted from camp to camp, the missions evaded capture, with bad weather blamed for the unpredictability of drops of supplies. On 18 March more than ten thousand troops, mainly Bulgarian, encircled the whole South Serbian plateau. Partisans repeatedly escaped from ambush, at terrible cost in terms of casualties. Together with two Mulligatawny survivors Frank and his Partisans moved towards Macedonia where on 21 April, Frank found time to write his last three letters.

To his parents he laconically writes that he 'now hold[s] the record for the twenty yards sprint for three major battle areas'. He misses England 'where they really know how to organise Spring. But I want to see dog's tooth violets and red winged blackbirds before I go over the hill'. To his brother E.P., then engaged in the long assault on Monte Cassino, he promises a post-war walking-tour, with frequent stops at pubs. To Iris he writes a remarkable letter, citing *Agamemnon* 418-9, and making clear that he has, from her letters, put together a picture of what has been happening to her and warning her against falling for 'emotional fascists'.

This 'emotional fascist' was Thomas Balogh. From 1942-44

---

[15] She influenced another admirer Paddy O'Regan in his decision to join SOE – see *Life*, ch 6·

Murdoch worked as an Assistant Principal at the Treasury, a period when she fell in love with Balogh, who cost her many tears. His was to be a recurrent psychological type in her life. Canetti, whose mistress she was between 1952 and 1956, may be the best-known example, but David Hicks (see Part Three) was distantly related, albeit not, unlike Canetti, actively malevolent. This was the last letter she received from him, and it was not until October of that year that Frank's family and friends learnt that he was dead, a story that merits re-telling.

The extraordinary chance by which these last letters survived was discovered only recently. 'Mail around here doesn't exactly seem very regular' he joked from Occupied Serbia. In 2002 Frank's W/T operator revealed that a group of *Time-Life Magazine* journalists and photographers had also been dropped into Serbia by parachute in April 1944, travelling on horse-back and prompting resentment among Frank's Bulgarian Partisans both by looking so sleek and well-fed, and also by announcing that they had to press on to Albania in order to escape that evening by submarine. Frank's Partisans, ill-shaven, under-fed, and battle-scarred, were considerably less pampered than these journalists, who did, however, offer to take mail with them to Bari. So Frank duly sat down that spring afternoon to write what would prove to be his last letters.

Posthumously decorated, he became one of the heroes of Bulgarian history. There are three books about him in Bulgarian: a new one was published in 2008. A railway station is named after him. Frank remains an immensely attractive figure, a full life of whom is currently being written for an English-speaking readership. A Byzantine coin, sewn into his tunic and kept by a collaborator present around the time of his execution, was in 1977 returned to Iris, as the person Frank had indisputably loved.

Unsurprising that Frank became for Murdoch a character out of romance. She is remarkable among liberal novelists in treating the military profession sympathetically. Frank influenced her portrayals of such admirable soldiers in her novels as James Tayper-Pace in *The Bell*, James Arrowby in *The Sea, The Sea*, and Pat Dumay in *The Red and the Green*.

■■■

In September 1941 Iris Murdoch asks Frank whether he has run into David Hicks 'my old flame…a man worth meeting' a question she repeats on 21 January 1942. At the same time she commends Frank to Hicks: 'he's young & maybe too simple and warm-hearted for your taste, I don't know – but I think perhaps you'd like him.'[16] The two, both posted in the Middle East, might well have met, and Frank indeed was, as she implies, hard to dislike. It may not be an over-simplification to say that Iris Murdoch loved Frank because he was nicer than she was and David because he was nastier. At any rate it says something for the quality of her feeling for both that she alerts each to the existence of the other. She was famous, where her many admirers were concerned, for holding her cards close to her chest.

The number of her devotees is at first sight unaccountable. She was not conventionally pretty and her figure, as Frank observed, was 'too thick to be good'. Yet Frank, Noel Martin, Leo Pliatzky, David Hicks, MRD Foot – to go no further - at one time conceived themselves in love with her. That the ratio of men to women at Oxford around 1940 had exceeded 6:1 is significant: attractive girl undergraduates were spoiled by attention disproportionate to their charms. Still, when she and her war-time flat-mate Philippa Bosanquet once decided to tell each other of the men who had

---

[16] On 7 April 1942 and again in January 1944.

asked to marry them, Philippa's 'list' was soon done. As Iris's list went on and on Philippa asked crossly whether it might not save time if Iris listed the men who had *not* yet proposed.

John Willett is a key witness – at school with Frank and also a close friend of David's, and mentioned in both the letter-runs that follow. Although fond of Murdoch, Willett was never in love with her. He suggested that what magnetised others about Murdoch was her spiritual quality. Be that as it may, she was furious when told that Aristotle had argued that one could be in love with only one person at a time: her own experience told her that Aristotle must be wrong. That her approach to love appeared strange to some never bothered her. She accordingly ran close friendships and love-affairs concurrently.

Frank 1940-44

Oxford.

[early summer 1940]

Thank you Lieutenant for the letters, & for sending me a poem, which so few people do now. I liked the poem because it was like you. Simplicity tinged with melodrama. You're a darling!

Yes, I have no time. There is no time. Life is a perpetual crisis. Every day consists of the problem of how to fit 24 hours work into 18 & leave time for meals. We are waging a running fight with the proctors which makes things worse. Don't worry, old Campaigner,[1] we shall not go down without striking a blow for our liberties!

I am making (in the way of academic business) the acquaintance of Professor Price of your college.[2] He is, as I expect you know, a felinist like yourself.[3] His lectures & his books abound

---

[1] IM had talked FT into joining the CP in March 1939; they almost certainly marched together in the 1940 Oxford Mayday parade, when IM, like others, was pelted with rotten tomatoes: see intro to this section

[2] H.H. Price (1899-1984), Wykeham Prof of Logic.

[3] 'Felinist': FT's letters are decorated with drawings of cat's faces. A 1940 poem of Frank's entitled 'Loneliness' ends: 'Learn like the cat,/The stately cat, soft-prowling through the grass,/silent and proud, to stalk and think alone'.

with cats – cats that are observed in one corner of the room, then cross the room unobserved in the other corner, cats that stand behind the sofa with their tails sticking out, cats that are positively known to like milk – & other cats whose partiality to milk is mere induction. Cats in general…

Better still however are Professor Price's bubonic tendencies (I hope that word <u>has</u> something to do with owls). Have you seen his owl collection? I wonder if I kept some 50 owls in my room would I be as wise as Prof Price? – It might be worth trying.

You must pardon me for not writing a proper letter. It is 3 am & I have just finished a monumental essay on Leibniz (God bless these Germans. What would we do without them.)

I am very tired & on & off life is pretty overwhelming.

Write to me again & send more poems. I can hardly wait to hear about Lev Davidovich Bronstein Trotsky….!

My love to you, brother.

London[4]
[late 1940]

Dear Frank,

I am truly, without exception, the most ungrateful individual on the face of this earth, and fully deserve whatever torture the Inferno has in store. (I forget what particular form they take.) I love getting your letters. They always make me realise that the human race in general, and a classical education in particular are good things after all. In fact, the more letters I get from you the more I admire you. Perhaps humans & humanity can conquer anything, after all. So you see I'm extremely sorry I didn't reply at once. I had an incredible amount of work & just cut out writing to anyone.

---

[4] This letter in IM's m/s hand.

I am particularly distressed that you are worried about the world. I was, but am much less so now – remember, your environment is probably less likely to induce clear thought than mine is. Let's meet after Christmas, if heaven & your colonel (or whatever it is holds the strings of your destiny) permit – and have some μακραι λεσχαι.[5]

I expect you know that Léonie is going to marry Tony in January – unless Somerville makes last minute objections to her staying up after marriage, which I don't think they will. I only hope Michael doesn't take this too hard.[6] He was in Oxford towards the end of last term, and was pretty despairing, because Léo more or less told him she had no wish to see him again. He has pledged himself so irrevocably to this forlorn hope. I was terribly sorry for him, but couldn't do anything except look sympathetic and tell him in no very decided tones not to be such a fool. This sort of damn silly fidelity is rare enough in this bloody matter of fact *chacun pour soi*[7] existence.

Michael sent me the remnants of his poems. As poetry they lacked clarity & originality – but revealed a very sensitive appreciation of the beautiful & an intense desire for it. Like most people's juvenilia, I hope so. Does one's capacity for suffering decrease with the years? I hope so, in Michael's case.

You're right, I'm afraid, about the minimum prerequisites of a successful poet – leisure & comfort. I who still possess them have doubtless incurred a great responsibility to posterity. O to hell with posterity! They're the cause of all our troubles. It was my

---

[5] Long discussions. The phrase is used in Euripedes' *Hippolytus* 384 (Liddell and Scott), to which Frank's last letter refers – see footnote 41.

[6] Michael (MRD) Foot was then in love with Léonie Marsh, who had herself recovered from being in love with Frank, marrying Tony Platt in January 1941: see also intro to section 2.

[7] Each man for himself.

confounded consideration for them that first drove me from my cool sequestered vale or my ivory tower or whatever goddamned metaphor you care to use. (Not that I regret it one bit – I could not love thee, Poesy, so much, loved I not Honour more. And now to God the Father…)

Pardon these surrealist heroics. I am really the luckiest of people (& in my saner moments realise it) and my mind (tho' you might not think it) is crystal clear & quite devoid of doubt. Let me know when you are coming to London. I don't know if the enclosed are of use to you, if not, use them to corrupt the Fascists. Courage, heart of gold, & not to worry about things. *Au revoir.* *Love I.*

> 9 Waller Avenue
> Bispham
> Blackpool[8]
> September 16th, 1941

Dear Frank, Much thanks for the bitter plant & the sweet verse. I like your gentle contemplative strain. Not vastly changed, though now it's hyssop & apricots in place of honeysuckle and fritillaries. I'm very glad you are still writing – it is always, at the very least, a good gesture – & some of your poems are more than that. You are a lucky dog – at least, in my mental picture of your environment drawn from your latest letter, you are a luckier dog than most of my friends. You always hit upon the picturesque – in life as well as in words. Or is it just temperament, one of the *a priori* determinants of your experience?

As for myself – existence is superficially serene & happy – but volcanic movements sway the unplumbed depths. I have reached one of those stages in a 'negation' let us hope in some occult

---

[8] This letter in IM's m/s hand.

dialectical progression – in which all one's hard won knowledge and carefully thought-out conclusions suddenly seem to be commonplace. So far one gets – far enough to impress the laymen – but always stopping short of originality. Just as, when writing a poem – the thing is well enough – but some springing, startling shattering metaphor is required – & never comes. This sort of feeling, of course, arises from an overdose of υβρις [hubris] & a habit of taking life far too Absolutely. And I get a certain sad pleasure too from seeing my minor Dogmatisms brought to their knees. The next lesson however is not to be learnt in Oxford, but out in some nebulous place called the world – being the antithesis of the university. Hence my impatience at another year. Greats is fun – but the philosophical part at least seems a bit frivolous at times. I pretend I am being taught to think clearly – but really an enormous intellectual chaos is being created, from which I may find myself retreating in a cowardly manner, instead of girding my loins to disentangle it all – just because it doesn't seem important enough to deserve the attempt – involving such strain to my modest intellectual powers. The only problems that [matter] are the moral ones – & there I speak a different language from Aristotle, Ross & Pritchard.[9]

I feel perpetually upset about the Russian business without being able to put any practical yoke on my wild-horse emotions. I suppose I hanker for the dramatic & heroic – ridiculous. I can almost see myself joining the WRNS just to demonstrate my vicarious suffering for Leningrad – & my contempt for Oxford.

My God, how that woman talks. Thou. I've no idea where you are, but if you are anywhere near the precincts of the foam-born

---

[9] Sir W.D. Ross (1877-1971) and H.A. Pritchard (1871-1947): among the major figures in Oxford moral philosophy during this period.

lady[10] you might run into my old flame David Hicks (in the British Council) who is I believe in that region. A man worth meeting. Is Hal Lidderdale[11] on the same pilgrimage?

I had a letter from Noel who sounds glum & hasn't yet got a commission. Léonie, by the way, is going to have a baby! Which is the very best thing that could happen.

Have been thinking much about Ireland of late – people & books put it in my mind. That's an awful pitiful mess of a country. I guess it's a bit like me – so full of pretences & attitudes – so barren of solid achievement. But Ireland at least has had her baptism of blood & fire – me, I just talk. Snap out of it. [It's] time to negate this negation.

I'm reading Proust – delicious, subtle, beautiful – Life has its exquisite compensations. He too teaches one to forgive – a precept I'm learning from all quarters just now. Characteristic of all great writers? Shakespeare – Tolstoy – James Joyce – for the last of whom I am developing an enormous enthusiasm. Have now read everything that survives of Tacitus – except the *Germania*.[12] I tremble & adore. I suppose old Leo isn't near you any longer?[13] Be

---

[10] Cyprus: Aphrodite, the foam-born goddess was in legend born out of the sea near that island.

[11] Hal Lidderdale read Greats at Magdalen and was remembered [LRB, letters, 31 Oct 2002] as being 'as near to being her boyfriend in 1940 as… anyone else ever got.'

[12] Tacitus, Roman historian, wrote the most detailed early description of the Germans at the end of the first century CE.

[13] Noel Martin, b. 1919, had attended Liverpool Grammar School as Leo Pliatzky was at Manchester Grammar. Both were at Corpus Christi College, where both got 1sts at Mods, neither continuing on to Greats. Noel dropped out from Corpus in 1940; Leo changed after the war to PPE. Leo Pliatzky – 'the old cynic himself', Iris was to call him – was later a Secretary of the Fabian Society and a knighted Treasury civil servant. He was Jewish, Manchester-born and poor, with a St. Petersburg-born father who gambled. He had been rescued by Harold Laski from working at 17/6d a week in the Houndsditch Warehouse company; Laski paid to complete his education, and Oxford was memorable in part for offering, for the first time in his life, three square meals each day.

careful, my gentle one, when the big pushes come. I miss you.
Love I.

> 9 Waller Avenue
> Bispham
> Blackpool[14]
> [December 24th, 1941]

Frank me darlin'. It is Christmas eve & I in Blackpool. There is
the hell of a wind blowing over the house & I feel a bit with-
ered away already. I have just received a box of expensive Turkish cigarettes from Michael. Dear old Michael. A lost soul too.
(The trouble is, I have been reading Virginia Woolf, the darling
dangerous woman, & am in a state of extremely nervous self
consciousness. The most selfish of all states to be in.)

The most important thing of course is that the Russians
are winning at last thank God. May they go on winning. I feel
ashamed of my defeatist mood of a month ago – then it seemed
that nothing could halt the Germans this side of Moscow –
now I feel that nothing can halt the Russians this side of Berlin. An equally false optimism of course. The war begins to affect me emotionally far more than it did – possibly because my
watertight rationalism has broken down. It's all damn complex
& confusing. I don't have a clear line on it any more. I feel myself approaching the state of $\alpha\pi o\rho\iota\alpha$[15] which I imagined only
Liberals & the New Statesman suffered from – it couldn't hap-
pen to me, this pathetic confusion & suspension of judgement.
But it has. Actually in a way I'm quite pleased, because such a
condition contrasts favourably with the suspension of thought

---

[14] This letter in IM's m/s hand.

[15] Aporia: Impasse, uncertainty, doubt.

which preceded it. And of course the foundations are as sound as ever. It's only a lot of the fancy superstructure that's been blown away.

Last term was good. I got face to face with my work for the first time since Mods – & the results weren't too depressing. I was beginning to be afraid that my brain had decomposed in the interim. It's too late I'm afraid as far as schools is concerned – but I've got a lot of satisfaction out of doing philosophy & getting my mind clear on one of two questions. This man MacKinnon[16] is a jewel, it's bucked me up a lot meeting him. He's a moral being as well as a good philosopher. I had almost given up thinking of people & actions in terms of value – meeting him has made it a significant way of thinking again. (Obscure. Sorry.)

Soon my charming American lassy[17] & her kid (now 2 years old) are coming to stay. That will be good. I'm feeling a bit vampirish & want to have my friends around. Her husband is in the M.E. (in artillery. One William Holland, in case you ever meet him.) She's upset about her country too. I'm afraid I can't muster much emotion about the Philippines[18] – except that it's bloody that all these people are killing each other – but that's probably because I'm no strategist.

What is important too is whether you are in on this Libyan business. It's very hard, sitting here & looking out at the cabbages & the semi-detached villas, to imagine you in a war –

---

[16] Donald MacKinnon (1913-1994), later Emeritus Professor Divinity at Cambridge, was an influential theologian and philosopher of religion. Like another of her Oxford tutors Eduard Fraenkel, MacKinnon was in love with IM (see Part Three).

[17] Sally Holland, whom IM had known since 1929.

[18] Three weeks earlier, on the morning of Sunday 7 December, the Japanese had attacked the American fleet at Pearl Harbour, Hawaii, and soon assaulted Singapore, Thailand, Malaya, Hong Kong, Guam and defeated the USAF in the Philippines too.

killing, people maybe – you & Leo & Hal – I can't imagine it at all. Whereas I <u>can</u> imagine you at the Coptic monastery, swimming in the cistern. God. I do feel bloody, sitting here writing self-conscious letters.

I wish June were over & I were (even) in the ATS.[19] I don't care how tough the job is so long as I can use what mind I have. The primrose path is getting me down a bit. It's unsettling looking forward into a blank, though. A sort of queer interregnum has set in. I feel I've outgrown my old personality & not yet acquired a new one. I guess I shan't get a new one till after June. Then I shall learn some things.

I've read Gorki's 'Mother', – yes a darling book. My Czech lassy[20] is more like Sonya than anything I've ever met. As for being simple & warmhearted – fine, grand – but unfortunately we aren't peasants with a straightforward line on life, we're just bemused intellectual misfits – or at least I am. I think. I'll know for certain after June & I'll tell you.

I'm reading Mallarmé who suits my mood again – exotic, restless, obscure. He passes me, *laissant toujours de ses mains mal fermées Neiger de blancs bouquets d'étoiles parfumées.*[21] But Gorki is better. Of course – if only one could & were. I must go to America after the war.

I'm writing a little poetry again. It has its moments. I hope you are safe, dear Frank. Good luck.

Love I.

---

[19] ATS = Auxiliary Territorial Services, into which roughly 200,000 women would be drafted.

[20] Chitra Rudingerova, a half Czech, half-Jewish refugee whose first name comes from Tagore, was taken into Badminton when IM was there: its Headmistress favoured what Nazis termed Mischlings – those of mixed race.

[21] Stephane Mallarmé's poem 'The Apparition': '...from whose ever opened hands /White bunches of scented stars kept snowing in'.

Somerville College
Oxford[22]
January 29th, 1942

Greetings, my brave & beautiful buccaneer! I have just received from you a rich haul of letters, viz item one airgraph dated Dec. 21, & two letters dated Nov. 10 & Nov. 21 respectively. The airgraph was mainly preoccupied with sand – but I loved the tales of your adventures in the letters. (My God, I can imagine you for the 50 postwar years, electrifying some senior common room with doubtful tales of the mule driver you met at Haifa way back…!) Thank you for the cyclamen, & for the story of the gentle Sophia (I'm sorry you wouldn't tell me the other stories), & the story of the renegade Bolsheviks & the story of the policeman's horse & for copying out several pages of Gorky's 'Mother' in German (ignorant alas of the fact that a) I know no German & b) I read the book long ago & loved it.). And thank you very much for the translations of Gusyev – I was fascinated by them – especially 'Glory' – what naivety – what pure faith – And I loved the Prologue too ~ <u>And</u> I was so glad to think of you translating them – a gentle civilised activity. What's more, you have read the latest New Writings,[23] in which respect you are one up on most of us so-called intellectuals here. Oh but I was glad to hear your voice again, *gaudeamus igitur.*[24]

The trouble is though, that I hardly like to talk to you about what I am doing these days, for it must seem so unimportant by comparison with the things that you are probably doing

---

[22] This letter in IM's m/s hand.

[23] 40 vols of *Penguin New Writing* edited by John Lehmann came out, starting January1940; small enough to fit into battledress pockets, these editions were widely read. Together with Cyril Connolly's *Horizon*, *PNW* offered a good chance during the war to get to grips with contemporary writing.

[24] Let us therefore rejoice.

now (may the Gods guard you there. I hope you have had no struggles with lions. And by the way, news please of Leo & Hal & anyone else I know out there! (David Hicks of the British Council, in case you've met him, too.) Letters from England must seem odd & irrelevant & faintly insulting – or so I imagine. However.

Oxford goes on, you know. You didn't dream it. I take schools next term. I begin at last to understand philosophy – but I'm afraid the fact that I did no work all last year spoils what vague hope I <u>might</u> otherwise have had of getting a First. My mind probably isn't good enough anyway. Still I get a lot of satisfaction out of sharpening & polishing what there is of it. It's not a bad little instrument in its way – I only hope to God I'll be able to keep it from rusting after June.[25]

People get married right & left. Anne Cloake has wed Teddy Jackson – Léonie's baby comes this month – the Club is full of an array of bright & new faces – so young – I can't avoid a feeling of matriarchy.) Alastine Bell has wed George Lehmann (if that conveys anything to you.) All sorts of incompetent people are being outrageously successful in Ministries & the Forces (which encourages me) & all sorts of moderately intelligent blokes & girls are getting stuck away in corners doing nothing (which depresses me.)

Me, I carry on. I have this incredibly fine guy, MacKinnon as a tutor, which makes things lively. It's good to meet someone so extravagantly unselfish, so fantastically noble, as well as so extremely intelligent as this cove. He inspires a pure devotion. One feels vaguely one would go through fire for him, & so on. Sorry if this sounds like a superman – There are snags – such as the fact that he's perpetually on the brink of a nervous breakdown (due, according to popular theory, to the fact of being unhappily

---

[25] June: when final exams ('Schools') happen; after which IM joined the Treasury.

married.) (The merest surmise.) He is perpetually making demands of one – there is a moral as well as an intellectual challenge – & there is no room for spiritual lassitude of any kind.

Gentle gloom bloody hell. I get so sick of that myth. I'm not
a Blessed Damozel you know, at least not any more. There isn't
even a trace of Burne Jones –& the faint aroma of incense has
perished in the high wind. Perhaps it's just the last 6 months,
when everything has gone to pieces. I haven't a face any more.
I am prepared to give up the clear contours & the cutting edge
which were formerly my ideal. I feel generally ikonoclastic [*sic*]
– the εικων which I most want to smash is the pretty golden
image inside myself which I've preserved so carefully. Com-
pleteness horrifies me – I have no more pat answers. I want
to hurl myself down into the melée & the mud & I don't care
how filthy it is.

Sure, this is just rhetoric. But a dialectical change of some
sort <u>has</u> come about. I fear for my future – fear a slackening of
effort – It has been like a salmon leaping – one moment it's there
with the sun on its scales, clear and perfect, & then there's only
dark moving water & indistinct glimpses. Frightful spiritual pride,
I suppose. I expect one shouldn't agonise like this – should reject
this profitless subtlety. It's a bloody enough world already without all this unnecessary agony. Better, as you say, to be simple &
warmhearted. Much better.

I envy you your Greek booksellers & [*illeg*] maestros. Yes, I'm
jealous. Men have a freedom we never have (it's a conventional
complaint, I know) – achieve a comradeship, an easy friendship
with the world at large that women miss. To hell with sitting
around & being subtle.

Not that I'm in the least unhappy (except by occasional fits)
oh dear <u>no</u>. Somerville is full of charming people – (our first year
really is the goods – intelligent & lively & all it should be. Every
other lass a potential bureaucrat.) And I get a certain pleasure

from wielding a certain influence. There are pleasant unselfish friendships to be had – & the inevitable μακραι λεσχαι[26] – and the classics sitting soothingly on my shelves – & an essay decently attempted for MacKinnon – and Oh yes Oxford under a foot of snow. Life is very sweet, brother, still.

(I wish this letter sounded like me – it doesn't quite. I can't put myself on paper the way I used to do. Some other medium seems required – an X ray picture of my soul or something.) (It would be lurid, I suspect.)

After June (after June after June a magic phrase) when all my problems are going to be miraculously solved, All is Revealed & so on – I plan the things I am going to do – learn jujitsu – learn German – translate Sophocles into rather intense English verse – learn to draw decently – buy expensive & crazy presents for my friends – really go into the subject of comparative mythology – read many very basic books about politics – learn about America, Psychology, animals my God I could go on forever – (all of this, of course, in the intervals of a [mere?]10 hours a day war job!) and that – because the world appears to be full of a number of things.

Tell you who blew in the other day – John Willett – remember him?[27] A very pleasant & talented guy. He represents to me the Oxford of my first year – utterly Bohemian & fantastic – when everyone was master of their fate & captain of their soul in a way that I have not met since. These people just didn't care a damn – & they lived vividly, individually, wildly, beautifully. Now we are all more earnest, more timid – no more careless rapture. Did you ever see any of John's drawings? They are extraordinarily good,

---

[26] Long discussions: see n 1.

[27] John William Mills Willett, reading PPE at Christ Church 1936-39; later the foremost British expert on and translator of Bertold Brecht.

& concern one subject only. David shewed me some in my first term & they made my hair stand on end – I think I should rather relish them now.[28]

Another thing (said she irrelevantly) which I must do after June is a) read the Bible and b) go into the history of the Roman Catholic Church (which <u>fascinates</u> me, as all enormous institutions fascinate me. I love the Roman empire for the same reason – it's such a monstrous huge conception – ramified by such a variety of myths & devices – far more interesting than the petty quarrels of the Greek city states!) Christianity, you know, when you get away from it a bit & really <u>see</u> it, is a most amazing & almost incredible phenomenon. How does it look from Galilee? What a beautiful queer unexpected world it is. Christ, what a miserable, humiliated, broken & altogether bloody world it is.

I do believe in the future, though – I believe tremendously. My God, we'll make something out of this hole & corner planet of ours.

Frank, old friend, I love hearing your voice crying in the wilderness – cry often, & at great length preferably – & oh for christ's [*sic*] sake don't get hurt in this business.

I did like those translations, very much.

Love. I

STILL NO DEFINITE JOB
ATS SEEMS MORE & MORE PROBABLE
TEACHING OR CIVIL SERVICE
ALSO CONCEIVABLE

[Airgraph]
Somerville College, Oxford
April 24th, 1942

Dearly beloved, an excellent letter has come all about Bachtin,[29]

---

[28] Willett, when asked in 1998 about these drawings, said that they then lived in his French house and were entirely unexceptional…He took IM's surprise to be a symptom of her innocence.

Bully & Biscuit. I imagine it had been overtaken by a later letter as I was puzzled a few weeks back by unexplained references to Biscuit, whom I took to be perhaps your troop commander. After Schools (a period which in optimistic moments I endow with all the properties of the Golden age – & which in pessimistic moments [which now grow more frequent] I envisage as a mixture of the deluge & the destruction of Pompeii) I shall read Bachtin, even if I have to go to Bodley, a grim resolve). Noel Martin was here today. He is on Search Lights, an officer now, bored & disillusioned in the extreme. I was very sorry. However, I expect shortly to be myself among the ranks of disillusioned which may be a more active form of sympathy. A rather depressed letter from Leo which upset me. A contrast to your letters – or is it stiff upper lip stuff on your part?? Give me a line on that. I suppose you never manage to see Leo now? Seeing you would certainly raise his spirits! Continue to write at such admirable length – your letters always give me great joy. Sorry the export trade is poor at present. Will probably not write again till after Schools.

The gods be with you

Love Irushka

WF Thompson Lt
GHQ Liaison
MEF[30]
June 7th [1942]

Irushka, flaxen-haired light of wisdom!
You ask me in an airgraph about Life & whether I am disillusioned. Strange beetles keep bumping into the lamp & falling onto my writing

---

[29] i.e. Mikhail Bakhtin, 1895-1975, Russian philosopher and literary critic.

[30] MEF = Mediterranean Expeditionary Force (though known to some of its soldiers as 'Men England Forgot').

paper. I must censure you for a serious abuse of the English language.

For a materialist there can be no disillusionment. For he or she has no illusions. Surely that's obvious & platitudinous enough. The harder you twist it the truer it remains. Not all your philosophical training can get you away from that.

Apart from that, I'm <u>not</u> keeping a 'stiff upper lip'. I'm far too malleable for that. If I had any cause to be depressed, I should sound gloomy enough in all conscience.

At the moment I feel only shame – shame that while Russians are dying at Kharkhov & my own countrymen facing living hell beneath the Libyan dogstar, I am in another part of the Middle East with nothing to fear but scorpions. Surely fate must have a reckoning for me not so far around the corner.

I have now got a puppy call Timoshenko. He is a white puppy with one brown ear & a brown spot on his back. He already shows eponymous ferocity.

The other day I met Evans-Pritchard – anthropologist, old Wykehamist, a fellow of Exeter College. As a 'political officer' he is rumoured to be a pushover, but he has already accumulated anthropologous data for a complete new book. Rather more important really, if you know anything about our efforts at politics. Together we drank arak, watched a French general dancing with his mistress, talked most about Winchester but a little also about the decline of Western Europe & the coming ascendancy of Asia. I followed that up by staying the next night with an Armenian Doctor, Dr. Altounyan, who has published a long poem on the death of TE Lawrence called 'Ornament of Honour'. I wonder if you've ever seen it. I confess myself quite incapable of taking the measure of it.

Altounyan also let me read an unpublished essay on 'the mechanics of poetry', which was interesting as first-hand testimony. He is a believer in inspiration par excellence, regarding anything born of trial & error or second thoughts as spurious. He may not write for years on end – (this poem – his only published one – was written after the age of 40) & then he will be seized by a fit which may last for several weeks. During this time poetry is continually flowing through him. He carries on with his normal work as a surgeon, but every spare moment is spent on jotting down poetry & putting it away in a drawer, with no need for further revision. On a previous occasion he wrote 13,000 lines off the reel, but they 'somehow just didn't come out right'. Looking at this other poem about Lawrence he said to me with quiet assurance 'that is real poetry. Auden, Elliott, all these people – they just don't begin to write poetry. It's not their fault. The inspiration has never come to them. But that – that has the stuff of real poetry. That will live.'

I wish I could tell you about some of the places that I've seen – the individuality of each dirty & honorable [sic] city. I've seen a great many 'historic' rivers but only Jordan is the equal of the Cherwell & Ichen. The bigger ones have water-meadows – even with yellow flags in them – but they are nothing to the water-meadows that lie round St. Cross. It's not a bad place, England, when all's said & done. After the dust & heat of the near East I can even imagine spending an enjoyable week-end in Ireland! How one's ideas change with the years!

By the time this reaches you, you should know the results of Greats. I hope they are all you expected & more.

Join the WAAF,[31] get a job as a cipher operator, & come out here. I'd love to see you again. I'd love to see anyone who makes sense.
With lots of love   Frank

WF Thompson Lt
GHQ Liaison Sqn
MEF
July 27th [1942]

My green-haired Sibyl,*
*[*Frank's footnote*] I attach importance to this epithet. With this I feel I have trapped your personality. A good green, mind you – none of your ghoulish pre-Raphaelite stuff. Hair that flows naturally in dreamy shamrock tresses. That is your ego materialised in hair.

---

[31] WAAF = Women's Auxiliary Air Force.

This afternoon I have been pondering anomalies. It will surprise you that I found these anomalies within the statutes of our own British army. Did you realise that it will be a financial loss to our gallant cadre of British officers, if we hurl the enemy back beyond Matruk? Anyone serving west of Matruk has his colonial allowance docked by half. Once there, however, they will find a powerful incentive to go further. Beyond the Libyan border the price of whiskey drops by 5/- a bottle. The teetotaller however receives no such stimulus, the price of lime-juice remaining virtually the same. The rank & file, receiving no allowances & unable to afford whiskey, remain unmoved through the titanic flux of battle across continents.

I hope you have read Beatrice Webb's 'My Apprenticeship' – Pelican, 2 vols. Not only is it of great interest to all sub-species of the genus Socialist, but Beatrice Webb is such a charming woman. In a desert whose most depressing feature, – worse than flies, heat or sandstorm, – is the predominant masculinity of its inhabitants, I found it wholly delightful to follow the thoughts, perplexities and sorrows of a highly intelligent woman. I wish there were a few more of them about.

I confess myself a little tired of militant socialists who have no historical perspective & make no allowance for the class background of individuals. I was discussing *My Apprenticeship* with one such & he poured scorn on the naive, slightly condescending way in which Beatrice Webb & her confederates presumed to examine working-class conditions as if they were clinical material. What does he expect? Does he want poor Beatrice to leap in one bound from Mayfair of the 1880s to the Victoria Dock & give stirring harangues to casual labourers on the way in which capitalism is digging its own grave? All said & done, Charles Booth's inquiries into the conditions of London, proving as they did for the first time that 30% of the population were below subsistence level, were an achievement that anyone could be proud of today.

Similarly he was very contemptuous of Pares' Penguin on Russia. With the triumphant severity of a skilled heresy-hunter, he said drily 'Yes, I'm afraid he goes very badly wrong.' Well, damn it all! I wouldn't expect him to agree with some of the things which Pares says, but Pares knows a great deal more about Russia than you or I do. Furthermore he has a great love of Russia & a certain amount of sympathy with the

Soviet régime. What he says, deserves to be examined with some care. Where one disagrees with him, one should not dismiss him abruptly with some catchword like Whiteguard, Trotskyite, or Social Democrat, but try to work out whether what he says is possibly true, how much chance he can have had of testing its veracity, & how much he may have been prejudiced in his observation by his own mental background. A book like 'Assignment in Utopia' needs to be studied with far more care than is normally given it, before it is rejected. Lyons went to Russia as a sympathiser & stayed there a long time. That much was wrong with his mentality is obvious. But people who dismiss him as a 'Trotskyite' are ostriches.

To such serene wisdom as your own, these conclusions must be foregone. I had better confine myself to the small talk which suits me. I'm still waiting to hear your Greats Results & the details of your future employment. Whatever you do for the duration, I hope very much that the post-war world will find you a job which is congenial. Won't there be scholarships again after the war which will let you go & unearth the vast wealth of black-figure vases still lurking in the Negropont?[32] By that time you may have discovered how interesting & pleasant the Civil Service can be itself.

Lest you should think our present life is one high-keyed epic of blood & sand, I will tell you how I passed this morning. I spent it at the head of an armed posse scouring two Bedouin encampments for a couple of latrine-seats which disappeared last night. Our portable latrine-seats, constructed by an ex International Brigadier, are justly the pride of our unit & we were anxious to retrieve them. So we searched every one of the filthy patchwork tents, with their furniture of petrol tins, old boxes, dirty rugs, goats, hens & dark-eyed women in black dresses with painted foreheads, who fled shrieking before our approach. No result. A solitary donkey laughed us off the premises.

How, you ask, can I write you 5 pages of nonsense when Rostov & Stalingrad are in danger? If I were capable of writing 5 pages of lucid

---

[32] Frank had spent some of spring 1938 excavating on Crete with John Pendlebury (1904-41).

sense, how would it help poor Rostov? Oh, where is this Second Front, Irushka? Do people at home realise that, if Russia goes, we shall have to fight back from the Americas? Do they realise how long this would take, if, indeed, it is possible at all?

But I still think Timoshenko has a dagger or two up his sleeve, not to mention a hefty punch in his strong right arm. A drive down from Voronezh might change the whole situation.

I told you about seeing Leo in a letter-card. Hal writes wittily as usual. Give Léonie my love if you see her.

Keep plenty for yourself. I hope I see you again some time.   *Frank.*

PAIFORCE (addressed MEF.)
September 4th, 1942

...I must tell you about the stream I bathed in yesterday – a swift cold stream that could still remember the mountains. For most of its course a shallow stream, but at the place where we bathed the rocks came down and forced it into a pool, shoulder-deep. On one side, the meadow-side, willow bushes and agnus-castus hung like Narcissus with their heads close to the water. On the other, among the rocks, tall feather-grasses were graceful and I wish you could have sketched them. Looking above and beyond we could see the sheer arrogance of mountains in the evening sunlight.

Strange occupation for soldiers, while there is a battle in Libya? But <u>someone</u> must field long-stop to our brother Ivan. A role which will entail I fancy, more watching than action. For Ivan is the best wicket-keeper in the game, and who can bowl the ball that would slip past him?

I thought of you when I saw my first Russian soldier. His cap was tilted back on his head, he was driving a 'Jeep' and he sang all the way down the dusty road in a loud unbroken monotone.

I thought also of my best friend, Brian Carritt, who has just died in England. I don't think you ever met him, though he was at Oxford for the first year of the war. But you must have heard the name. Noel Carritt fought in Spain and Antony Carritt was killed there. Gabriel ('Bill') Carritt was well-known in the Youth Movement and once stood for

Parliament. Brian was the youngest son and the most gifted. He was brave and gay and I shall always be glad at the thought of him.

PAIFORCE
October 7th, 1942

...From 10.30 to 12.30 at night I can pick up Radio Moscow on the wireless. From 11 onwards it sends the news at slow dictation speed, and I find I can understand nearly every word. The reason for this slowness is that this programme is providing front-page copy for local newspapers all over the Union whose editors tune in and take it down word for word. It is amusing to feel oneself at one, crouching over a small wireless at midnight, with the editors, fat and bearded, spectacled and cadaverous, small and electric, of the 'Kuznetsk Kommunist', the 'Bokhara Bolshevik', and 'Tomsk Truth'.

[Airgraph]
5 Seaforth Place
Buckingham Gate SW1
October 12th, 1942

You must be thinking that I don't love you any more. That is most definitely not so. It is just that lately life has been disturbed, inconvenient – I have suffered from a scarcity of blackout curtains, a surfeit of odd jobs at home & at the Treasury.

Your last letter delighted me (especially your remarks apropos of Collins) and soon I will reciprocate with a long letter full of the funny thoughts that are going round & round my head. Life is curious just now & not without its subtle shades of colours.

I am learning Russian but haven't got much beyond the Good morning, here is my long green pencil stage.

I hope things are alright with you – interesting & not unpleasant. Look after yourself, my dear.

Love, I.

WF Thompson

GHQ Liaison Squ.
PAIFORCE
October 17th [1942]

My dear Irushka!

It seems strange to compare your gentle letters with flint but the simile has this much aptness. They strike fire immediately. And when one arrives, as has yours, of the Augustan Ides, I am impelled forthwith to answer it.

First let me tidy up this little polemic that has started. I think you wrong me by taking me out of context. 'Materialists have no illusions' taken alone and without wrappings certainly sounds an exceptionally stupid remark BUT

1.   In the first place it is written in a letter to you, who I know were never one to take nonsense at its face value.

2.   It was written with special intent, inciting you to snap out of it, after receipt of one of your more particularly Chehovian [*sic*] missals.

Dash it all, after more than three years away from a University I am not very clear what a materialist is. Nor could I tell an illusion from any other type of cosmic phenomenon, unless you gave me a set of ready-made rules such as

1.   A Genuine Illusion will always turn litmus-paper red.

2.   A Genuine Illusion can always be recognised by the delicate question-mark etched in brown on the white fur of its forehead. Specimens where this mark is inclined towards the right ear belong to the sub-species of the Optical Illusion.

3.   A Genuine Illusion must have played cricket for Eton two years running and been elected a member of Pop by unanimous vote. etc. etc.

I know very well that I'm full of them myself.

And you still cherish one, my dear, if you think that life out here is lived in 'a varied & lively environment from which one can perpetually learn new things.' But no. I won't say what I think. I should be doing myself and the glamorous east injustice, if I allowed myself to describe it under the influence of jaundice.

Two things I will say.

1.   There is no country more varied and lively than our moth-

erland. (Count Ireland in with the rest. It's all much of a muchness [*FT's drawing of cat's face*].[33] No country breeds more numerous and more delightful lunatics. And no country, for all its varied surprises, is more restful. Out here I find what my father found, that the utter poverty and human degradation is a thing which comes to weigh on the mind incessantly, until one can get joy from nothing. This is not cant. I'm not posing as a sensitive, big-hearted Emotion Boy of the Beverley Nichols variety. The misery of the east is a thing which you cannot imagine. Unless you have a very robust intellect, the misery threatens to edge out all other impressions.

2. It is <u>not</u> possible to <u>live</u> as one is placed at the moment. Life, for me, more than anything else, means working in close comradeship to a clearly-sighted end. I get only a secondary pleasure from sensations and experiences. As you can imagine, I shall never realise this ideal of Life as an officer in the British Army. Of all the people I have met since the war started, there is hardly half a dozen that I want to see once it's over. (Startling disparity when you put it alongside the countless friends and potential friends whom I met in my last term at Oxford!) They have, I suppose, aims in life, but, on the rare occasions when I was able to discover them, they failed to ring an answering chord in me.

I knew it all along. I should never have taken up my pen, with the yellow jaundice on me. Jaundice must be easily the gloomiest disease in existence. Like other maladies, it depresses you beyond measure and reminds you much too clearly of the vanity of the flesh. But unlike others it fails to depress you so far physically that the whole question is one of indifference. One is just wide awake enough to feel thoroughly sorry for oneself.

When you went to the zoo, I hope you payed [*sic*] due respect to the Wombat. I think I had written to you before of the Noble Passion of Dante Gabriel Rosetti for that Lord of Creatures. If only he had written <u>poetry</u> about Wombats instead of Blessed Damozels and all that Poppycock!. But come off that Zebra stuff! Give me a brush and

---

[33] see footnote 3.

a bucket of paint and I'll fix up a horse for you far more artistically in half an hour.

Three years & a bit since I joined the Army. More than that since you & I first exchanged *Weltanschauungs*[34] in a room at Ruskin. Now I am 22 instead of 18, and you 23, almost a matron. Looks like being another three years straight before we meet again. We shall probably find we have both changed out of all knowing and have nothing any longer in common.

Write whenever you can. An airgraph is a pleasant way of saying 'I haven't forgotten you.' But a letter is a golden gift, a winged gift, – worth more than half the world to a mortal in depression.

I'm greatly cheered by the picture of Staid Iris Murdoch reading Homer in the underground. Does the train ever stop suddenly leaving your words to ring out in all their natural clarity? If so, many must be the tired stockbroker whose heart is melted and his vision beautified. Doubt if I could scan or construe a line of Homer now.
Lots of love.   Frank.

[Airgraph]
5 Seaforth Place
Buckingham Gate SW1
October 19th, 1942

Frank, my wild & gentle chevalier,
I have two fine letters from you before me now. Beautiful Frankish letters with the genuine Romantic Thompson stamp, and even a picture of a cat. I'm glad you're where you are, and finding life pretty colourful. I like to think of you in delicious brown camelhair trousers – a pity you can't grow a delicious brown camelhair beard to match. Hail, Thompson pasha.

I am settled into my flat, & more or less settled into my job too – though I still lose more files & overlook more important

---

[34] World-views or pictures.

letters than anyone else in the Treasury. I can see myself liking that job a lot, a little later on. It appeals to one's worst instincts I daresay – a love of unimportant power, a liking for machine-like efficiency, a desire to regiment humanity into cast iron categories. Yet it's not altogether bad – certainly not altogether bad for me. I'm learning a hell of lot of new things about how our curious country is governed – & I'm even beginning to think that Administration is a serious & interesting activity, once one has got past the stage of thinking it inhuman and dry as dust.

But do not please on this account- say 'Irushka is dead, long live Miss Murdoch, an official in the Treasury', I still do a thousand and one other things which you would approve of – I am for instance learning Russian at LCC classes. I am writing a little (prose and poetry – exceedingly bad), painting (ditto quality) reading a great deal (mainly Theology at the moment which you mightn't approve of – but don't worry Jesus won't get me. I have always had a great interest in any coherent system of symbolism – and its relation to the accompanying thought structure – and Christianity is the one nearest to hand).

Noel was in London last weekend and we went on a very pleasant pub crawl together. He is a lieutenant now – still pretty browned off, & trying desperately but unsuccessfully to get sent abroad.

Am I happy? (I expect you've given up asking yourself this question – I still do ask it from time to time) (Silly). I think probably not. The Stalingrad business is bloody. Also I am lone-ly and (I suspect) suffering from incipient pangs of frustrated ambition. On the other hand life has innumerable consolations. Soft job, soft living… Jesus Christ. I agree there is one point

---

[35] i.e. philosophy.

at which the real world focuses – & all else is φιλοσοφια[35] –
Keep safe. Write!

My love to you. Irushka

Please tell your brother to call. I'd like to meet him a lot.

PAIFORCE
November 8th, 1942

...Am taking Russian lessons from an old Armenian political refugee. He speaks not a word of English, which means that everything has to be done in Russian and gives me excellent conversational practice. He has no conception of the rules of grammar, but fortunately I am almost past that stage.

He tells me some excellent stories. He was a native of Rostov, a Menshevik, at the time, in 1918, when the Reds were defending that town against the Germans and White Cossacks. The Mensheviks of Rostov, although neutral, maintained a large private army, in which there was an Armenian legion. Terterian, my tutor, although he had seen service only in the commissariat, claims that he was Chief of Staff to this region and consequently had free access to Sergey Ordzhonikidze, the Bolshevik commander. Then things began to look bad, Ordzhonikidze called Terterian and asked him to hide him, in the event of being unable to escape from the city. 'Although he knew I was a Menshevik, he knew that I was a man of honour.' Terterian agreed to. Shortly afterwards the Reds made a successful withdrawal and Ordzhonikidze had no need to avail himself of Terterian's promise.

The sequel came three years later when Terterian was a Menshevik M.P. in independent Armenia; the Bolsheviks came in, to help drive out the Turks, and soon began their programme of arrests. But the Armenian Bolsheviks could not decide whether to arrest the Menshevik leaders. They referred the matter to Ordzhonikidze – then a member of the 'Baku Troika' – (himself, Kirov and one other) – who were credited with ruling the Caucasus. The answer came back swiftly – 'Arrest them all <u>except</u> Terterian,' and one or two others. This was followed by the postscript – 'If Terterian loses a hair of his head, you will answer for it with your lives.' – 'Ordzhonikidze was a man of honour' – Terterian concluded. 'That was why Stalin poisoned him.'

Seaforth Place
Buckingham Gate SW1
November 24th [1942]

Frank, my brave & beloved, your letter dated Oct. 7th has only just arrived – in which you record your linguistic failure with a Ukrainian truck driver. Yes, a fascinating language – not, so far, as difficult as I had expected – but I daresay fearful pitfalls & craggy arrêtes await me. Nor can I yet quite realise what poetry in such a language must be like. Our ambitious teacher has already made us learn a little poem by Pushkin (called *Utro*[36]) – but I can't pretend I feel breathless on a peak in Darien as a result. That will come, that will come.

As I write this the world has woken up with a vengeance & all sorts of encouraging & interesting things are happening in Russia & in North Africa – may it still be so when you receive this. This ingrained inferiority complex must be shaken off – one had got too much into the habit of thinking that the only people who can beat the Germans are the Russians – & they can't do it all the year round. But now, thank God... In a way of course it seems terrible to rejoice at anything which must total up to such a sum of human anguish when considered in detail – especially when one is snug in Whitehall oneself – Lord, lord. I get so damnably restless from time to time. I would volunteer for <u>anything</u> that

---

[36] IM was learning Russian with a White Russian emigrée living behind Peter Jones: Malvina Steen. Alexander Pushkin (1799-1837) wrote 'Winter Morning' (*Utro*) which starts 'Cold frost and sunshine: day of wonder!'

would be certain to take me abroad. Unfortunately, there is no guarantee given one when one joins the Women's Forces! – & anyway the Treasury would never let me go; for, inefficient as I am, I am filling a very necessary post in a semiskilled sort of way. Sometimes I think it's quite bloody being a woman. So much of one's life has to consist of having an attitude. (I hope you follow this, which is a little condensed.)

I trust you are as far from the firing line as ever? I was amazed to observe that your latest letter contained no references to tamarisk or swiftly flowing brooks – however 'PAI Force' seems to indicate that you have not yet left the company of such delicious flora. Long may you stay. I should, of course, like you to be a hero – but I doubt if I could accept the risk – & I am quite certain you have all the qualities of a stout fella, without the necessity of a vulgar display.

News of our friends at this end I have little. What of Leo & Hal & any others that I know out your way? I miss you all, you know – I miss that unanxious society in which we trusted each other & were gentle as well as gay. I miss your burly self especially. Like all sensible people, I am searching out substitutes. The Treasury yields a number of pleasant men & women who, besides being very intelligent (& some of them very beautiful) are good company over a glass of beer or whiskey but they lack withal a certain redness of the blood – a certain human gentleness and sensitiveness. On the other hand, my Soho Bloomsbury & Chelsea acquaintanceship is widening also. 'The Swiss' in Old Compton Street, 'The Wellington' in Wardour Street, & 'The Lord Nelson' in King's Road are the clubs which I frequent in search of the Ultimate Human Beings – and knowledge & experience & freedom. A strange society – composed of restless incomplete ambitious people who live in a chaotic and random way, never caring about the next five minutes, drunk every night without exception from 6 o'clock onwards, homeless & unfamilied, living in pubs & copulating upon the floors of other people's flats. Poetry is perhaps the only thing taken seriously by them all – & the only name they all respect is that of TS Eliot. Politics they do not understand or care about. Their thought & their poetry is concerned with subtleties of personal relations – with the creation of the unexpected in words – 'dredging the horrible from unseen places behind cloaks & mirrors.'

Perhaps it is a betrayal to make friends with these people while our armies are fighting in North Africa. But I cannot help finding these offscourings of 'Horizon' a goodly company in some ways – they seem, indefinably, to be better human beings than these smiling Treasury people who drink, but never too much, & who never in any sense give themselves away. They are queer & unreliable, many of them – but they meet you in a level human sort of way, without the miles & miles of frigid protective atmosphere in between. They have a sort of freedom too, which I envy. I think it arises from a complete lack of any sense of responsibility – (so of course my envy is not wholehearted. I may be flying blind at present, but I would not cast <u>all</u> the instruments overboard. Why, I don't know. A person with a moral sense but no moral axioms is a ship crowded with canvas which has lost its rudder. Failing another rudder, one should strike sail, I suppose.)

In the intervals of my Soho adventures & my grapplings with Russian verbs & rules for the use of the Genitive, I do a large number of things. Seaforth still needs much attention in the way of scrubbing floors & spreading coats of spotless paint over variegated surfaces. I write a bit. I read a lot – am having an orgy of Edmund Wilson at the moment – (good on literature, superficial on history.) and lately I reread The Seven Pillars.[37] I feel a

---

[37] T.E. Lawrence, *Seven Pillars of Wisdom* (1922).

sort of reverence for that book – for that man – which it is hard to describe. To live such a swift life of action, & yet <u>not</u> simplify everything to the point of inhumanity – to let the agonising complexities of situations twist your heart instead of tying your hands – that is real human greatness – it is that sort of person I would leave anything to follow. Also I've read much poetry – various moderns, Wilfred Owen (a magnificent poet) – and Pindar (who always brings you to my mind!)

It is good to write to you, my brother, & try to disentangle for your benefit the strands of my far from satisfactory life. I feel in a peculiar sort of way that I mustn't let you down – yet don't quite know how to set about it. I don't think I believe any more in clean hands & a pure heart. Ignorance I know – 'innocence' I imagine is just a word. What one <u>must</u> have is a simple plan of action.

So what so what so what.

I am on First Aid Duty tonight at the Treasury – an oasis of peace in a far too full life. I must go down to bed pretty soon. (We had one casualty tonight. Great excitement. A man with a cut finger. Christ.)

I think of you often. May the gods guard you.

Goodnight, my gentle Frank –

Much love to you. Iris

Seaforth Place
Buckingham Gate SW1
January 22nd [1943]

Darling the mice have been eating your letters (not indeed that that is my excuse for not writing for so long, my excuse for that is everything or nothing, whichever way you like to look at it.) I am very angry about this, chiefly because your letters are rather precious documents, but also because I am not on very good terms with the mice, & the fact that I have been careless enough to leave valuables around where they could get at them can be chalked up as a point to them. One day I shall declare serious war on the mice in a combined trap-poison operation. At present I am just sentimental with a fringe of annoyance. I meet them every now & then, on the stairs, or underneath the gas stove, & they have such nice long tails.

Look here, though. I don't seem to have heard from you for some time. How are things? Are you still to be found among incredible shrubs & amazing mountains having unsuccessful conversations with Ukrainian truckdrivers? Your silence I think portends action. I hope it has been, is being, effective – & not I do hope too dangerous – at any rate in its outcome. I don't mind how many dangers you face, so long as I don't know at the time, & you emerge in good condition – & don't suffer miseries en route of course. Of course you will have more tales to tell when you come home – you will have the tales anyway, I guess. You are obviously designed by the universe to be a teller of tales! We must write a novel in collaboration when you return. You can write the action part & I'll do the psychological interludes.

Oh I chafe at this inaction. I'd take on any job now – <u>any</u> job – if it would get me out of England & into some part of the world where things are moving. Yes you'll say. 'Baloney – things are moving in very few places (& there they're going <u>too</u> damn fast) and everywhere else you'd be just as browned off as you are in England.' Maybe – but then at least I'd know two ways of getting browned off, instead of one.

Not that I'm unhappy. All things considered, life is OK. I like my job on the whole. It's not strenuous. I have a pleasant flat near St James Park (the Park is thinking about Spring already – soon <u>you</u> will be thinking about fritillaries, no doubt), which (the flat, not the park) is rapidly becoming so full of volumes of poetry of all eras & languages that I shall have to go & camp on the railway line (or feed 'em all to the mice, after they've finished their present strict diet of Airgraphs.) I read a good deal – but not as much as I'd like. I write a little – but Oh Christ not one bit as much as I'd like. That's part of the trouble at present. I have just so damn many very tiring & quite <u>unavoidable</u> activities that I have just no time to live my own life – at a time when my own life feels of intense value & interest to me. Jesus God how I want to write. I want to write a long long & exceedingly obscure novel objectifying the queer conflicts I find within myself & observe in the characters of others. Like Proust I want to escape from the eternal push & rattle of time into the coolness & poise of a work of art. (Agreeing with Huxley for once, I think it is not what one has experienced, but what one <u>does</u> with what one has experienced that matters. The only possible doctrine of course for one who has experienced remarkably little of the big world!) But all this requires peace & calm and time time time which I haven't got oh blazes, hell I haven't got it.

Just as well perhaps. If I ever write an opus it would be an unspeakable opus – remember 'The Importance of Being Earnest?' Cecily on her diary... 'Oh only the thoughts & impressions of a very young girl _____ & therefore intended for publication.'

Frank, I wish you would come home (a simple wish, often reiterated). You & the others. You offered me – & still may it please the Gods offer me – a friendship I'm finding it harder & harder to attain these days. I'm hellishly lonely in my great & beautiful & exciting London, & in my cushy job – Oh I know tens & hundreds of people some wild some tame & all interesting, & most kindly but so few my friends. I feel more independent actually than ever before – no longer at all anxious to seek the mob's approbation, to be admired or impress my intellect upon the chance gathering. But oh so much in need of intellectual intimacy. The patient mind which is prepared to comprehend my own & toss me back the ball of my thought. (This sounds a bit intellectual snob. Maybe. I'd believe almost anything of myself these days. I'm becoming the Compleat Cynick where I. Murdoch is concerned.)

I should tell you that I have parted company with my virginity. This I regard as in every way a good thing. I feel calmer & freer – relieved from something which was obsessing me, & made free of a new field of experience. There have been two men. I don't think I love either of them – but I like them & I know that no damage has been done. I wonder how you react to this – if at all? Don't be angry with me – deep down in your heart. (I know you are far too Emancipated to be angry on the surface.) I am not just going wild. In spite of a certain amount of wild talk I still live my life with deliberation.

Ersatz? Well, yes, a bit – but then all life is rather ersatz now, since the genuine articles have been separated from us & he is a fool who does not go ahead on the basis of what he has.

News of our friends I have little. Noel Martin I saw the other day when he was in town for a medical exam. (He passed A1) He's volunteering for a special air observer job which sounds rather suicide squaddish to me. He's been driven crazy with boredom in his searchlight racket. He's in love with an ATS subaltern age 30 and may soon propose to her. The gods speed his suit. She sounds rather nice. Léonie I hope before long to have staying with me, complete with infant. (I haven't yet seen the latter.)

People here are getting awfully damn complacent about the war. I wish they wouldn't. We're hardly beginning to see the way out of the wood yet. Beveridge is a good thing though – <u>that's</u> alright, so long as people don't start relaxing with a sigh of relief. (I've just been reading Bev. – a fine piece of work – thorough & equitable – & it'll be a good fight, trying to get it put into operation – doomed to failure I surmise, but instructive.)

Poetry (said she slipping around in a random manner from subject to subject, please forgive this) obsesses me more & more – it is a great sea into which, whenever I can escape from my detestable duties, even for ten minutes, I slip with a sigh of relief. Poets I have discovered lately – Louis Aragon – 'Le Crève-Coeur' – the first real war poems I have read that are poems. Dunkirk at last seen by an artist – a handful of real jewels – a limited edition in France, all confiscated. One or two copies escaped to England & have been reprinted here. Then – a favourite of your father's evidently! – archy the cockroach![38] And (rediscovered) Wilfred Owen. And Ann Ridler. And innumerable moderns.

Do you ever read now? Or write? Oh you should have that civilisation you could take part in so richly – too. For the mountains & the truckdriver are very good also. And I do agree with you about the Russian language!

Write to me you frightful cad & say what you are feeling about our pretty baffling universe.

['you write so many things
About me which are not true
Complained the universe.
There are so many things
About you which you seem to be
Unconscious of yourself said archy]

Out in the kitchen I can hear the mice eating something or other. Better go & see what.

Look after yourself.

Much love Iris

[Airgraph]
February 6th, 1943
Frank m'dear, this is to convey the great news that Noel is engaged.

---

[38] Don Marquis *Archy and Mehitobel* (1927).

This time to a <u>really</u> good thing from all accounts. The first inkling I had was when he was in London a few weeks ago and kept calling me 'Carol'. On demand, he furnished the explanation that he was much in love with an ATS subaltern, stationed with him in Somerset. A lass of 30, formerly a ballet dancer. He was going to propose, he said, but hadn't much hope! I told him to be of good heart. Then a few days later he rang me up from Bristol in wild joy to say he'd made it! They're getting married in a few months. I'll be meeting her in London quite soon. I'm certain she's the goods from what Noel's said *Gaudeamus igitur.*[39] The Bad Luck of that man Martin was getting me down a lot. A blot on the landscape is that he's probably transferring to a rather suicidal air-job. Still, he was perishing in London among the search lights, & even granted Carol, it may be as well for him to break away. I hope all is as well with you, my dear buccaneer.

Love Iris

PAIFORCE
February 7th, 1943

...I have spent all this Sunday afternoon sitting in a cafe with a Pole, meditating on the basic sadness of life. He let me read a letter from Tosia, his fiancée, who is still in German-occupied Poland. The dry ink itself seemed to ache with restrained longing and a courage that was only maintained by the most rigid self-control. Cut out all sententiousness about strength through suffering. Think of the millions of people to whom this war has brought nothing but utter irredeemable loss. Piotr and his Tosia are both close on forty. If the war leaves them both alive and sane, they will still find little peace in an embittered and factious post-war Europe. For us, who are young, and have the faith that we can recast the world, the struggle that

---

[39] Let us therefore rejoice.

comes after will be bearable. But I feel very deeply for the countless peaceable people, who can never because of age, or an upbringing and environment which is as fortuitous as anything else in this world, be wholly with us and will never know peace in the one short life allotted to them...

Polish, so it seems to me, is a crabbed and logical language, a petit-bourgeois among the languages, especially when compared to the class-less wild and melancholy grandeur of Russian. The Poles themselves feel this instinctively, are far keener to recite you Pushkin than Mick-iewicz, and tell most of their better funny stories in Russian. But Pol-ish has some fine poetry, which I am just beginning to explore, and would have more had it not grabbed hold of the scaley end of the romantic revival. As far as I can judge from a month's study, the genius of the language lies partly in its vein of inspired gaminery and unfail-ing relish for the ridiculous. If you ask a Pole whom you know well 'How are you?' his most likely answer is 'Very well thanks. I keep a green herring on a chain at home,' – which is after all as good an answer as any...

Another good friend of mine is a moon-faced and quadragenarian writer of Polish children's books. This one is trying to persuade me to learn Japanese and embarrasses me, when we are walking through populous districts, by dancing a <u>krakowjak</u> for my edification or rushing forward on all fours to show how he stormed a Bolshevik barricade near Lwów.[40] His bosom friend is a Russian monarchist, who is trying to win my adherence to the Grand Duke Vladimir and is anxious to introduce me to a prospective saint (feminine) who lives in the Russian convent at Jerusalem. Apparently the current odds are fifty to one on her canonisation so she ought to be worth knowing...

Nietsche, when he began to go mad, sent telegrams to all his friends. 'The crucified has been overthrown stop I am again arisen and am god stop Dionysus'. Piotr told me this, with whom I share a great affection for Nietsche. <u>Also Sprach Zarathustra</u> is a wonderful poem, if nothing else.

---

[40] Present day Lviv, now in Ukraine

[Airgraph]
Seaforth Place SW1
February 17th, 1943

Greetings thou son of a son of a son of a, as they are supposed to say affectionately out in the East. Noel, who sends delirious love, is on the point of marriage,[41] having decided to carry it through on his next leave, which starts in a day or two. By the time you get this then, Carol will be Mrs Martin. Really I feel joyous about this & long to meet the Lady.

I don't know if it will mean much to you after these years & years (they are years too) but the two clubs, who were always at each other's throats, have now amicably amalgamated, & all is unity & progress.[42] This is a fine thing & a real tonic to me. Leo's heart will leap slightly. Perhaps yours too. But what can that small place Oxford mean now ...?

Yesterday I saw a film (in Glorious Technicolour) called 'Arabian Nights', which told the Haroun al Rashid story with much American glitter, wise cracks, spectacles & Lovely Girls. I thought of you – & what a sore upon the universe's face spots like Baghdad probably are in reality. Heigh ho. But you are a Romantic too. Wish I could book you a Magic Carpet en route for London.   *love I.*

[Airgraph]
Seaforth Place SW1
March 20th, 1943

Frank m'dear,
Thanks for letters (I am conscious of a gap in my own flow of

---

[41] Noel Martin and Carol Nethersole in fact married the day IM wrote this letter: 17 Feb 1943.

[42] See intro to Pt 2 p83.

talk which please forgive) especially a charming one about lilac scented nights & Miluska (who sounds nice – I'm glad there are <u>some</u> women on the scene – stop you from becoming utterly barbarous you know.)

All this talk about not taking judies on the ration strength[43] is bloody silly though. It isn't as if we all had endless lives & could say 'OK, we'll put all that off till a better time.'

Christ, this is the only time we've got, poor wretches, & we must make the best of it – our only lives & a short enough time of youth to enjoy them to the full. I applaud Noel's action. (It'll be so good for <u>him</u> too.)

Life is very dreamlike – I wish someone or something would wake me up. I probably read too much poetry – or something. Lately I've taken to reading an English poet I've neglected for many years – one W. Shakespeare. My God, if one ever took to disbelieving in the spirit of man (which I never did) one could pretty soon renew one's faith by a glance at that chap's works! I recommend 'em. Especially 'Measure for Measure' which I've discovered anew, and 'Antony & Cleopatra.'

Chitra,[44] my wild & woolly Czech, is staying with me this weekend. Rather like cohabiting with a hurricane. A very good kid. Life is good when it expresses itself in such people.

Oh Frank, I wonder & I wonder what the future holds for us all – shall we ever make out of the dreamy idealistic stuff of our lives any hard & real thing? You will perhaps. Your inconsequent romanticism has the requisite streak of realism to it – I think I am just a dreamer. Shout in my ear, please.

Much love, old pirate.

    I

---

[43] Judies = WW2 slang for girls.

[44] Chitra Rudingerova: see n.13.

MEF
April 16th, 1943

...I too am very fond of _Antony and Cleopatra_. There is something uncanny about the way in which these slightly sordid middle-aged lovers, who have talked very little else but drivel for the first three acts, suddenly rise in the last two to the very pinnacles of poetry, and blaze their trail across the mind of humanity for all time. It is in a way a promise to all of us lesser folks, who are too warped or too jaded ever to be Romeos, that we might, in our own time and on our own level, provided we still have the grace to be dissatisfied, know a moment like Antony's, – at any rate that we are not doomed to be Octavians...

WF Thompson
GHQ Liaison Squ.
MEF
April 26th, 1943

Dear Old Girl!
Your splendid letter of January 22nd has just arrived. Now that the Four Horsemen of the Apocalypse have begun to take their toll & crosses that I never thought to see are already weathering at Boars Hill & Sunningwell,[45] now that two years of absence have sorted out the friendships that are less enduring, there are only four people left in that country called England who can speak almost as clearly on paper as with their lips. Three of those are my closest kin and the other one is you. When I get a letter from you I have to sit down right away & answer it. If Shelley had not set such an unpleasant precedent, I'd call you my soul sister. As it is the Russians have a better word for it – _tovaritch_ [= comrade] That's what I'll call you.

First I must clear one misunderstanding. My conversations with

---

[45] Frank's family moved to a house on Boars Hill around 1925; two close childhood friends and a neighbour had died, Rex Campbell-Johnson in an air-crash, Brian Carritt of TB.

Russian truck-drivers were not <u>all</u> doomed to misunderstanding. Once I fell into my stride, I fared rather well. There was one particularly happy one which I'll try to describe to you without making it too much of a set piece. You must imagine Persian November at its most radiant. A sky clear except for a few clean white clouds. A sun manifestly enjoying its task of giving light without too much heat. Mountain-tops clean snow-white... Mountain flanks every shade of amber gray & chocolate, varying as the cloud-shadows shifted. Along the [*sic*] lower slopes a special miracle of beauty of the bare poplars, delicate pale-green. The fruitful valley itself a riot of red & yellow leaves. Everything a spirit which said – 'you go to hell! It's worth while being alive, whatever you say!' At a village in this valley there was a petrol pump & at this petrol-pump a Russian convoy was refuelling. Mammoth dark green lorries were pulled in to the side of the road. Russian drivers in greenish-grey overalls & great floppy grey fatigue-hats were strolling up & down, stretching their legs & checking their vehicles. We had to pull in behind one of them, & the driver, an ugly great thug with a mop of yellow tow for hair stood grinning at us.

'H'are ya doing?' I shouted at him in Russian.

His grin broadened as he heard his own tongue. He came slowly towards me, 'How am I doing? Well. Very well.'

He came & leaned on the door of my truck grinning thoughtfully, feeling none of our western obligation to continue conversation.

'Splendid news from Kavkáz [Caucasus]' – I said. We had just heard of the first victories at Ordzhonikidze.

He grinned again. 'You think it is good?'

'Yes. Very good. Don't you?'

He thought & grinned & looked steadily at me for nearly half a minute. 'Yes. It is very good.' Another half minute devoted to thinking & grinning. 'Yes, it is just as Comrade Stalin said. He said. "There'll be a holiday on our street, too." (*budet i na nashei ulitse prazdnik*) And so there will! So there will! There'll be a holiday on our street too!'

We both laughed at this. 'Yes!' I said. 'So there will! There'll be a holiday on our street too!'

The traffic cleared & we moved on, but for hours after my inner heart laughed & sang as it hadn't done for months – as it hadn't done since I was bowling across Libya on some far colder morning with a column of armoured cars, or since, on a half-holiday from Winchester, I found my first man-orchis on Telegraph Hill. You could love those Russians Irushka, as it is possible to love only the best & freshest of our own people.

Yesterday I went to a service at the Greek Cathedral & I learnt something about my education. For four & a half years I went to chapel every day of the School year – twice a day on Saturdays & Sundays. That is not to mention the invariably pleasant & refreshing evening prayers. As a natural result, a frequent visit to church is really necessary for my mental health. In church, from ingrained habit, I begin to think, I become myself. In church, I can break away from the narcotic routine of being an empty headed petty-minded captain in the British Army & take some stock of the world & myself. Only in church or on a long walk am I really a free man. Those Sundays by the Itchen, with two services as decorous as only the Church of England can make them & a long walk among the water-meadows come back to me now as some of the happiest days in my life.[46] And yet you must search far to find a more bigoted atheist.

Now I must sort out my ideas about your virginity. Of course I'm not angry. Anger could only spring from two sources

1. From jealousy – but it must be nearly four years since I thought of you as a body

2. From righteous indignation, at the transgression of some principle but first I would have to decide what were my principles.

So you see, I could have no cause for anger. Nor can I, since I am not conventional after the modern fashion, be unreservedly glad without due reflection. I find two stumbling blocks

1. First, a minor one. I know what men come to say & think about women with whom they have slept, unless they have really loved them. Malraux is very good on this subject in *La Condition Humaine*. I know, of course, that your men are not ordinary men but perfect gentle knights. But it will take you years of sorrow to realise how violently misogynous [sic] most men are *au fond*. – But anyway. What other

---

[46] Winchester College where Frank was a scholar, 1933-38.

people think or say is obviously irrelevant.

2. My other objection can't be explained in a sentence because it depends on a theory which I'm still engaged in formulating. I you see have messed up my sex-life probably beyond repair by taking physical love far too lightly. I have been reduced to a most terrible dichotomy by which women fall into two categories

– Women it would be rather nice to sleep with provided one didn't have to talk with them for more than five minutes

– Women one really likes *avec lesquelles il ne faut pas s'embêter dans un lit*.[47]

Which is of course an insult to both and an outrage against the sex in general – but an attitude, if I may say a word in self-defence, it is perilously easy to adopt when one rarely spends more than three weeks in one place & hasn't had a chance to fall in love since reaching the age of 20. To medicine me from this would probably take years of psychotherapy combined with the best type of free love. (I have of course high hope of achieving a partial cure by similar means). But having suffered all this, I am coming to the conclusion that it is better to abstain altogether until one falls head over heels in love. Men who had never slept with anyone before their wife, tell me that the first weeks of their honeymoon were an ecstasy they have never known before or since – an ecstasy which those who have already partaken of the fruit will never know. But perhaps different approaches suit different people.

This objection probably doesn't apply to you. As you say, two affairs haven't done you any harm. My point is – I remember – thinking that often that [*sic*] a good love-affair would do you the devil of a lot of good. ------- being afraid that you were so introspective & self-sufficient that would soon ------? into a cold virginity from which it would be yearly more difficult to force yourself. So, on the balance, it is obviously a subject for joy. If I've said anything here that is clumsy or stupid, forgive me. I'm afraid there is no finesse about me, Irushka.

Do I write? I've written only three poems & no prose in the last year. Just before that, I wrote quite a little prose. My father got one short

---

[47] Roughly: 'with whom one should not bother oneself in bed'.

story published for me in the *Manchester Guardian* and a selection of my letters <u>without warning me</u> in the *New Statesman*. But at the moment I'm writing nothing nor do I feel the urge to write. I'm suffering stagnation militaris. A change of air & proximity to the Germans will probably wake me up again. But the truth is I haven't much to write about. I have a conventional mind formed along Wykhamical lines. Also I'm very little of an introvert. Only when writing to you or to my brother do I make an effort at introspection. And unless you are an introvert you have not the vision to look into <u>other</u> people's minds. And without that you cannot write as it is the fashion to write today. Mind you I think the psychological novel has had its day. Soviet authors I believe, are searching round for a new line of advance. Ehrenburg, when he tries straight fiction as opposed to satire, has gone back to a style as simple as Defoe's. Personally, I think Tolstoy & Chehov went as far into the minds of our fellow men as it is profitable or seemly to go. Gorki is, to me, an ideal novelist in this respect. No, if I had the ability to tell a story, I should not allow you to mar it with psychological interludes. But the truth is, Irushka, I have a very shallow mind & I've been skating round these last four years on the crust of it. If/when I return to England I look to you & other comrades to re-educate & rehabilitate me in some measure. What nonsense. This war should be developing my mind. I don't know. I don't know what's happening to me. If I get through this European war I want to go to China, & then on, wherever the next phase takes place. Because this war, in which we are now engaged, may have its uneasy lulls & armistices, peace we shall NOT know until the United States of the World has been achieved. And if I get time, wandering from here to there, I may write some of the more memorable things I have seen. But about the conflicts in my own mind, not. They had far better end with the unseemly clay that bounds them.

Nor do I read poetry at the moment for several reasons.

1) I have virtually no poetry books with me. This is a poor excuse.

2) By the time work ends – I'm usually too tired. When work ends, I have a bathe, change, take dinner about 7.30 & go to bed soon afterwards. I should get nothing from poetry if I read it when I was half asleep as I always am after sundown. What spare time I have I usually

spend learning some language or other, for more or less materialistic motives.

3) I need <u>real</u> leisure to read poetry. If I had a whole fortnight free I reckon I could get back into my stride by the end of my first week. What I <u>can't</u> do is come back from some field of work which has no poetry in it, open a book of poems & fall straight in with the mood. If I had even a room of my own it might be different, – if the tempo of life briskens it may well change. But in rifle inspections & correspondence with the paymaster about Signalman Snook's allowances, in the faces & after-dinner conversation of my brother officers, there is no material for poetry. Nor can I sit back & read it in these surroundings.

When I was on a Course last month I led a big discussion on the Beveridge Plan. It was rather a success except with one or two Indian Army Majors. Now let me teach you a little modern Greek.

βαρύ αρμα – a heavy tank (doesn't that do queer things to you?
Actually τανκ – plural τανξ is more common)
η αιθουσα των αξιωματικων – The officer's mess. (Why an officer's mess should be an axiomatic I don't know)
ταλύ πῦρ – rapid fire
αναταράσσω – I blow up

τι ειναι αυτός;
Αυτός ειναι ενας γατας
Αυτος ο γατας ειναι αγριος:
Οχι, ειναι πολύ ημερος
[What is that? That is a cat. Is that cat wild? No, he's very docile]

From which useful little conversation you will realise that ειναι is

now the third person singular. I approve the logical trend towards neu-
trification eg. τό νησί, τό τραπέζι. [*The island; the table*] How many parts
of the body do you recognise below

τό μάτι

τό πόδι

τό χέρι

τό δόντι

τό κεφάλι

τό νύχι[48]

That will be enough for now.

This letter has grown rather long. It should keep the mice in rations
for at least a week.

Do write me more long letters like your last. I talk a lot of nonsense
when I answer them, but maybe I understand more than I let on.

Lots of love   from Frank

MEF

April 27th, 1943

...I have a weakness for mice too – and even (tell it not in Gath or
North Oxford) for rats. Large villainous rats like sea-brigands. I have a
delusion that all rats wear loudly striped Jerseys – perhaps it's a memory from some picture-book by Beatrix Potter. Sometimes I try to build
a hierarchy of furry folk, in order of the greatness of their souls. At the
top come cats who are obviously God and that's all there is to say about
it. Then there are bears, because they are kindly and peaceable when
they might easily make themselves so unpleasant. Then wombats, which
are very solemn animals, and shortly after them marmots, because
they have long whiskers, and because they sit among rocks and whistle.
Then woodchucks and chipmunks. Then rabbits. Mice and rats come

---

[48] Respectively: the eye, the foot, the hand, the tooth, the head, the finger-nail.

pretty low down the list. But I'll never kill them, unless it was a question of me or them. There's a lot to be said for rats and mice, provided they can be taught their place.

Captain Frank Thompson, Cairo 1943, courtesy Dorothy Thompson

MEF
May 23rd, 1943

...Today I want to talk to you about Greeks because they are staunch antifascists, because they are simply among the best people I have met, because they are very much the same as the Greeks who fought at Scamander and Marathon, drove their chariots by the weeping firs on the Hill of Kronos or packed the slopes of the Acropolis to hear the Agamemnon. In the spare time which I get at the weekends I try to drown my nostalgia for the old Hellas by contact with the new. A Greek sergeant who was wounded at Tobruk, his father, an apothecary who insisted on speaking shocking English and tried to recite me the Odyssey (do you know we couldn't get farther than the first three lines?), a cotton-merchant who talked to me about Thucydides and Venizelos, a girl who teaches Greek at the Berlitz School but who is teaching me to dance, – these are my staple diet. On Sunday afternoons I go to a Greek theatre so jambonic that it is impossible, after one has been there twice or thrice, to regard the actors as anything but very good friends who are putting on a maladroit but pleasingly naive charade. I'm on quite good terms with the management and, when the play requires it, lend my hat or my Sam Browne to dress up the odd policeman. And I have heard Sophia Vembo singing to an audience of Greek sailors. Sophia Vembo,[49] to my mind, is unquestionably the most charming, the liveliest and most spiritedly antifascist entertainer whom this war has produced. After galvanising the Greek nation by her pillorying of Mussolini (she writes most of her words and music herself) she stayed behind through that grim year when all Greece was starving and then, two months ago, escaped to the Middle East by a small boat. When she is not singing she stands with her arms akimbo and laughs at the audience. When she sings you feel she could rout a Panzer-Division on her own. Her latest is a dithyramb of triumph, with the refrain,

τωρα ρωταν νι ιταλοι
γιατι !γιατι ! γιατι !

      Now the Ities are asking
        'Why! Why! Why!'

Clytemnestra has nothing on her when, with black hair falling down

---

[49] Greek singer and actress, 1910-78; when Germans invaded Athens in 1941 she escaped to the Middle East where she continued to play her part for the war effort.

over her face she shouts with husky exultation... And the audience are almost as much of an inspiration. On the shores of the Mediterranean, in Greece, Spain, and Jugo-Slavia men realise very clearly the meaning of fascism and the nature of the only forces that can effectively oppose it...

Too bad they wound up the Comintern.[50] There goes my last chance of getting a job after the war.

Thompson is not popular in the mess at the moment. Last night I broke a chair while telling a Russian joke.

HMT

May 31st [1943]

Frank darling hello, (Having got as far as this I was interrupted. Today is definitely a Bad Day, since I am being moved, desk file & telephone, down from my lofty airy 3rd floor room to a warren on the ground floor with bricked up windows where I shall live perpetually under one of those bluish electric lights which are reputed to produce 'daylight' & do I must confess succeed in spreading the atmosphere & dim sinister glare of a chilly winter afternoon, rather toward dusk, with a rainstorm impending. This is depressing – you may notice from now on a gradual falling in my spirits – dreadful diseases tend to break out among us cave-dwellers – palefaced & hissing slightly we creep about the lower corridors & in & out of our hideous lairs – now & then one goes mad & is transferred to the Ministry of Works or the Stationery Office. However, as I was saying, no sooner had my belongings been dumped in this cell in purgatory than various minor

---

[50] When the Soviet Union itself was invaded on 22 June 1941, during Operation Barbarossa, the Comintern had switched its position to one of active support for the Allies. The Comintern was subsequently officially dissolved in 1943.

devils came in to fix me a second telephone (another grievance incidentally is that my room-mate is a charming but excessively talkative staff officer, in whose company work is virtually impossible.) And I fled to the Treasury Library, half an hour early for a meeting on 'Causes of Delay,' meaning to write you a long letter in H.M. time, but was disturbed after the initial greeting by the chairman of the group who was also bent on a pensive half hour.)

That parenthesis completed I advance to the body of the letter. I have just returned from a weekend with Léonie at her new dwelling at (note please) 28 Wordsworth Road, Harpenden, Herts. Léonie has not, I think, changed much since I last saw her [two or]⁵¹ so years ago. (Her name, note also, is Platt.) She is still the same charming, aggressive, nervy, individualist. Definitely three dimensional. A person. I enjoyed her company greatly. There is also, of course, David Platt, age 15 months, & completely angelic. Golden hair & a raffish glance. It all gave me a queer sensation though of time moving yet staying still – & there were so many goddamn memories. If only one could amputate sections of one's past!

A letter from you, my old friend, has arrived, lamenting lost opportunities for youthful nihilism – wrongly, I feel sure. A healthful nihilism can flourish at any age – but only for the very young do certain aspirations & idealisations attain their perfect roundness & brilliance. We shall never feel complete that way again – but it is good to have felt so – tubers, perhaps, stored against this lean season when we are growing hard fibres & impenetrable bark.

As you rightly observe, three cheers for the Greeks. Oh that

---

⁵¹ blank space: words missing.

this war was over & we could visit these people in their own lands & under a decent Government! Carry on the good work, m'dear, only don't get hurt doing it.

Much love, Irushka

5 Seaforth Place
Buckingham Gate SW1
[spring 1943: letter typed by IM[52]]

Frank old darling

My love my greetings to you! It gets harder and harder somehow to imagine you really living in a flesh and blood sort of way out in those incredible regions–what efforts of the imagination friend-ship requires of one! And lord how one fails–

Yes you are right –this is a new departure ,this ty ping racket. Someone has x rashly lent me her typewriter for th e duration,, and Isuppose I'd better learn to use the bloody thing. One may as well try to be a jack of all trades – seeing one is likely to succeed at none and let quantity be swallowed up by eqality Imean the other way round--

This machine is not conducive of xx fine writing –at least at the rate Imanage to get along–because one has so often forgotten the beginning of a sentence before the end draws in a sight!however there are certain compensations, suchas thepicturesque regions of exclamation andexpletivewhich lie ready tobe explored you know *!!?1/2xxx£@!,---and the lovelxy surprise when it does something wild and irresponsible onyou like missing a letter or starting to write in red!I hav eyet to discover any logical reason

---

[52] Ruth Kingsbury from the Magpies had lent IM her Corona 4 typewriter: this was evidently not the first letter IM tried to type, but the only one that survives. After the typewriter was 'stolen' by the poet Paul Potts, IM gave Kingsbury a handsome

forthe arrangement of the letters.

News small events and my own small and rather self conscious soul--nNoel is wed that at least is not asmall event-I havent
yet managed tomeet the lady.Indeed both the Noelsx a re married—you remember Noel Eldridge whom you were unpercep-
tive enough to regard as a snake,?well he has up and married a
Scottess unknown to me[53] —seems very happy and is incidentally
x out in your part of the world—so be kind to hi m you awful
Wykehamist if you meett him!

Otherwise not much to report mon capitaine.Iwatch with
interest your liason with the Pole—she sounds a nice Pole.I'm
glad there are some real women for you out in those wastes.
As a matter of interest,how have you fared with women in the
East,?Idon't mean from the grand passion point of view, but
just from the sex experience point of view.Do you spend your
offdays lying with lovely Iranians? How do you feel about that
racket now?it's terrible Frank, howlittle we know really in spite
of fairly freqquent letters of how the other party is developing
in th ese fast a and fatal years.Perhaps we shouldn't pry into
eachh others minds at this dis tance of time and space—but one
is so afraid of the sxxxa strangeness wh ich is to some extent in-
evitabl God what a difference half an hours conversationwould
make.

I make a little progre s —my Russian is improving slowly—o
a delicious language. A lifegiving stream in the middle of my
bureaucratic desert. Anew language does refresh the heart .

---

[53] Noel Eldridge, whom IM had met through Oxford student journalism asked her
to marry him, arguing light-heartedly that, as he was almost certain to be killed, she
could at least enjoy a modest war-widow's pension. Noel later married Jane Brown
McNab, and then introduced his wife and mother casually, on the street. Two weeks
later he was sent abroad and he and his wife never met again.

(i have even got as far as wonder ing which to start next!xWhat do you say to Turkish,market-value ratherthan aesthetic value being thecriterion,?I am feeling pretty cynical about my post -war job chances already tho'heaven knows I'm sitting pretty compared with most folks.)Then,I read a lot–write not much-- most o f my time just now is spent– wasted rather, ith people. London swarms with acquaintaintanceswhom individually I like but who collectively are making hay of my life! and for my friends living out of London my flat is a convenient hotel! getting bear- like in my old age? Maybee.I prickle all over like a hedgehog–this vacuum in which Im living requires from me greater efforts of self discipline than any Ive ever had to make before.

The tendency to drift is strong– now that the rather artficial but comforting framework of Oxford is gone. If one could pour oneself into one's job it would be different,but I can't –so I'm left troubling about my own unimportant salvation and integritas in a world in whichI should be endeavouring better things. Still ,given that I'vegot to hang around in this goddamned bed of roses I'd better set about organising the only thing left to or- ganise–my mind! And to do that in this strangeempty space is noteasy.

Christ! it must be this infernal machine that makes me talk like this. Slow motion thought. But I can't help feeling (a) impatient at having an easy sedentary job when 90% of the world is taking it on the chin and (b)realising that I've got to xx use thesex years to build up my strengh in any way Ican so that I'll be some good to somebody one day.

Since writing the above I have heard from Noel M. who says he will be in town with his Lady in a day or two and will call. I'll give him your love. (Unecessary a actually, ashe says he has just heard from you and has replied.)We'll drink to absent friends in some cosy pub in soho.

This machine doesnot encourage a n overflowing heart– my

thoughts refuse to be xxxxmarched along at such a funereal pace
Drat the thing &@£*'/%*!!

I'will therefore,O my friend, close down.iI shall I trust be on
the air again shortly with my usual high speed programme.

Write to me,Wanderer,and tellme more tales of the miraculous East.

All xxx9(damn)wild and woolly salutations. Keep safe.
love and xxxxxxx
Iris.
[*sic*]

MEF[54]
June 2nd, 1943

...That is what the peasants of the Urals shouted to my tame white-
collar-girl when she arrived there, an orphan in an alien land. That is
what they said to Krakovian Miluska when she arrived in their midst
after seeing her country bombed and shattered to its fundaments. To
Miluska, who could not have tortured the people if she'd tried to, but
who undoubtedly came from a land-owning family who must have done
so often. To Miluska, who slaved in an office every weekday, in order
to go dancing on Saturday evening and 'lie in' on Sunday morning, but
yet undoubtedly took three trunks with her to Sverdlovsk and two fur
coats. I tell you this not with any counter-revolutionary intent, but to
illustrate two platitudes.

1. How unkind man is to man, without realising it and without
wishing to be. Those peasants of Sverdlovsk were simply recording their
astonishment and stating with classic simplicity a doctrine that was
generally accepted. I conclude that we must cultivate imagination.

2. How stupid class generalisations sound when applied to
individuals. From this I do <u>not</u> conclude that such generalisations are
foolish, but that, however much we steel ourselves to hate institutions

---

[54] In Frank's mother's hand: 'Shore of Red Sea, Training for Sicilian Landings'.

and even bodies of men that are striving for evil ends, there is no point in trying to hate <u>men</u>. We'd be wasting our time…Worse than that – we'd be losing our own virtue.

You may wonder why I suddenly inflict on you this homily. So do I.

You speak lightly in a recent letter of learning Turkish. This is NOT a task of which one should speak lightly. Turkish is a tongue about which I feel rather strongly. It has some virtues, I grant you, for instance an ordered symmetry of grammar for which, I suspect, we must thank the laws of Ataturk, but it does something which <u>no</u> decent language would ever <u>dare</u> to do. Let us take their 'Izafet' or 'definitive combination'. When a noun has another dependent on it in the genitive – 'the King's English – the dog's dinner' – they put that unoffending noun – viz 'English', 'dinner', in the accusative. I wonder the League of Nations hasn't politely told them that this is one of the things that <u>just isn't done</u>.

July 5th [1943]

Frank me darlin' your letters are like a sort of intermittent song heard in the woods at midsummer. Full of quaint trills and curious chirps & nothing of bitterness in them. The picture which they convey to me of your existence in those mythological lands is somewhat as follows.

1) Wake up. Survey beautiful Libyan (or Persian) dawn illuminating hills. Interval for contemplation

2) Early morning chat with Russian truck drivers. Discussion: What Tolstoy means to Us.

3) Bathe in flashing mountain stream or (alternatively) azure sea.

4) Lunch with Miluska

5) Coffee with Old Wykehamists. Talk about Good Old Times (rather sentimental, this bit.)

6) Interval for contemplation

7) Adventures, when heat of day is over, with Greek book-sellers, Arabian mule drivers, Egyptian bank managers, and (if possible) their daughters

8) Interval for fighting the war. (This supposition is entirely *a priori* & has no factual basis.) (Beautiful Libyan/Persian night is falling)

9) Exquisite supper at Greek monastery. Chat with Byzantine Scholars. Discussion: What Alexandria Means to us

10) Stroll on beach with beautiful Jugoslav and Jewish prostitutes.

11) Commencement of long chianti-drinking party

12) Intervals for breaking furniture

13) Write to me.

Your latest letter, dated June 10th, raises the following subjects. a) China b) Epicurus c) Rimbaud d) Blake. To deal first with b) – yes, on looking up the passage in Texts and Pretexts I find that I had marked it also to signify my approval. E. is positively Wittgensteinian in the simplicity & rectitude of his analysis. My general knowledge of Epicureanism derives from Laurentius & Farrington, & is not very thorough. In answer to your questions I should say 1) that you were <u>not</u> an Epicurean. You are, I thank the Lord, far too much of a Romantic & a Damned Individualist ever to embrace a philosophy essentially so serene. The doctrines are, in certain respects, very sensible it is true. But if one is going in for philosophy at all (a dubious activity) one may as well be thoroughly up to date, and I personally find Kant's line on the gods more interesting than Epicurus! But then I may be just an intellectual snob modernist – who knows? Your second question then I would answer in the negative. It is not a Good Thing to be an Epicurean – so far as I understand that far from simple doctrine. It is better to be a Kantian – & better still to believe in the True Gospel.

I have considered carefully your suggestion of migrating to

China after the war & think on the whole I should prefer not to. I shall visit you, perhaps, where you sit in your bamboo shack, surrounded by the complete works of Lao Tze – or alternatively in your cozy machine gun nest on some picturesque hill – but I am a Western person myself. I cannot bear the suppression of the individual which most Eastern philosophies have at heart. I do not yearn for a Nirvana nor even for a Tao. I am one of the damned.

My love to you, wanderer. Irushka.

July 29th, 1943

Frank my dear it is a long time now since I heard from you. There is no recent letter for me to set my foot upon as a stepping stone toward you. I wonder greatly whether that means you are in Sicily? Whether you are actually there or not the Repercussion Wave will probably have lifted you from where you were & sent you spinning round the Med, & writing may well be difficult. Do write though, as soon as you can, even if it's only a postcard enumerating the Sicilian antiquities which you have preserved from the British hordes.

It's curious, you know, this sitting calmly at home, while my friends are flying about the world like rockets. Very very unsettling. Come on, Italians, do your stuff – & let us get that much nearer to a sane world again.

It is a baking breathless hot July evening & I feel unspeakably demoralised. Tomorrow (August Bank Holiday weekend) I am going to Surrey, to walk and (perhaps) to think. I have so little time to do the latter in these days. Later on in August I hope to spend a week in Oxford where I shall not walk at all but shall think the whole time. What about? My chief thought will probably be 'Whether or not I am a writer' – a thought which has obsessed me all the year, & grows in proportion daily, like an angel for wrestling with. I should not be surprised at the end of it all to find that it was really what smart Greats students call a 'pseudo question', & did not admit of any reply.

I have started learning Turkish. A baffling self-conscious language that announces complacently at the outset that it has only one irregular verb. I haven't made up my mind about its virtues as yet. I daresay one will end up with such a nostalgia for the lost glories of Persian & Arabic that one will have to learn those tongues also. My teacher is the secretary to the Turkish Embassy whom I acquired by the simple method of walking into the Embassy one day & demanding that I be provided with a teacher. He is a charming scholarly individual who speaks most of the time in French, imagining, one has the impression, that he is talking fluent English the while.

My Russian progresses also. I perceive at last, faint & far away, the fact that the number of grammatical peculiarities to be learnt is finite after all!

My old friend, forgive this rambling letter, my sleepy murmur on this intensely hot evening. I know your evenings are hotter – but please reply. And, oh, keep safe. The gods protect you.
Much love I

MEF[55]

[31 July 1943]

...July, which the Poles call <u>Lipiec</u>, the month of the linden-trees, has gone by. I've been having quite an interesting time, but now have leisure again. My life has fallen back into its old groove, a chronic state of reading <u>War and Peace</u>, whatever volume, in whatever language, happens to cross my path. At the moment it is the last volume, <u>Guerra e Pace</u>. I

---

[55] In Frank's mother's hand: After the Sicilian Landings.

find to my shame that I can read Italian more quickly than Russian. But then Italian is not a serious language – simply a compromise, for musical purposes, between French and Latin. My other chief occupation, which has never failed to divert me from here to Hamadan, from Alex to Aleppo, is drifting round cake-shops and getting myself in well with their proprietors. The best cake-shop here is run by some Italian Jews and we find common ground in our distaste for Fascism. 'Abbiamo molt[o] sofferto – molto – moralmente. Per noi, oggi, la vita comincia come prima. Siamo di nuovo uomini'.[56] They make rather good cakes, too...

Have been reading the *Orlando Furioso* and find it a little dull. What bad soldiers those *cavallieri antiqui*[57] were! In the middle of a battle they would drink of some magic fountain, go berserk with passion, and spend the next five years chasing some terrified *donzella*[58] from the Pyrenees to China. And what would I say to one of my men who, while drinking from a river, lost his steel helmet in the water?!! Their adventures have none of the reality which those of Homeric heroes have. You could put Achilles and Patroclus in FSMO,[59] land 'em on the coast of Sicily instead of the Troad, and they would be quite at home, would, say and do almost exactly the same things. But Oliver and Rinaldo, chasing round in tanks after women, would look pretty silly.

MEF
August 14th, 1943

...Michael has sent me <u>Creve-Coeur</u>. I haven't had time to digest it yet, but one can see at a glance that Aragon has scored several bulls, which we can chalk up straight away on the scoreboard of eternity. How strange that the only decent poet in this war should be a communist! I can't understand that, can you?

---

[56] Roughly: "We suffered a lot, morally speaking. For us today life starts afresh – we're new men'.
[57] Knights of old.
[58] damsel.
[59] Full Service Marching Order.

...One of my favourite relaxations is glancing through Marlborough's Turkish grammar, but I should never dream of trying to learn it. Please let me have <u>all</u> your observations on this language. Particularly am I keen to know what resemblance 'Ataturkish' bears to the language of the average Anatolian village, – in other words how deep and effectively Kemal's reforms have permeated. After a brief flirtation with Italian, I'm going hard at Greek. I'm ashamed to say that I'm far more fluent at Greek than I am at Russian. Yet Modern Greek is a fragile language, drawing half its charm from its classical associations...

One of these Jewish girls works in an army hospital. She says she can't find words to describe her admiration for Thomas Atkins. Among his numberless good points she lists a natural and almost unfailing courtesy to women. The other day she was treating a shell-shock patient when he had a sudden fit of convulsions. His first words when he recovered were 'I'm so sorry. I hope I haven't upset you.' As a matter of fact, whomever one talks to – Pole, Greek, Frenchman, German Jew, Italian – this theme, 'the courtesy of the English' (and English means British in European parlance) always recurs – *Bardzo szlachetny narod... sorridenti, scherzosi, cortesi.*[60]

Like the Russians we can rest assured that our private soldiers are our best ambassadors.

August 15th [1943]

Old campaigner, you preserve a stubborn (& no doubt prudent & correct) silence about your martial activities, & it is only from Hal that I have learnt where you have been lately. Yes, I daresay it is all just so much more sweat & hotness & sordid scenery for you – but at least you are in the big river – & we at home can't help envying you. I can imagine your comments on that – but Christ, can you imagine how it feels to fulfil a serene daily

---

[60] 'Very noble people' [Polish] ' Smiling, humorous, polite' [Italian].

routine, having to make greater & greater imaginative efforts to believe that a war is on at all, as the memory of the blitzes fades – & yet knowing intellectually all the time that humanity's future is being fought out, & that one's own friends are out there & may get hurt in the process?

Pardon my tiresomeness – just this old restless feeling, annoyance against the easy stay-at-home life.

I'm glad you see Hal now & then. Hal is a very good guy, & as you say, has a special brand of wisdom. In re your suggestion that a photograph of me be forwarded, I have to inform you that action has been taken. Viz. I have made an appointment with Polyfoto for their next free date, viz the end of August. So you may expect the radiant thing to arrive about Christmas time.

You don't mention old Leo. Hal tells me – & indeed I had a letter recently from the old cynic himself – that he is shortly to be commissioned. Your Army takes a long time to recognise a good proposition.

The leaves are falling portentously all over St. James's Park. I am rereading large sections of the Bible & wondering about Man. I am getting on capitally with my Turkish teacher, except that he will call me 'Mudrock' in spite of frequent reproaches. ('What you must never forget, Bayan Mudrock....' 'Murdoch, efendim!' 'Ah yes – now as I [was] saying Bayan Mudrock...') But - and this, the only conclusion of imp[ortance] I have come to of late is that if (I say if, & cannot give the word too horrid an emphasis) I have any métier it is to be a writer.

Writing is the only activity which makes me feel 'Only I could produce this.' Whether or not 'this' is any use is of course the crucial question to which I know not, & may not ever know, the answer. Meanwhile I am writing fairly regularly, both poetry & prose.

The autumn brings melancholy. Will this war never end – will it always be you battening on chianti & cakeshops, I on Burton &

the ABC – & never a united celebration? Soon I shall break into a lament & compare our inconvenienced youth with the fall of leaves in high summer – as they are falling now. What bosh. And the Red Army advancing too.

Later I will write a more virile letter & prove to you that I am not fundamentally downcast.

do thou, oh my brother, prosper.

Love I.

September 19th, 1943

...As you see, I have a new job.[61] There's no job I would rather have in the Middle East just at present, but it takes up a great deal of time.

October 22nd [1943]

Dearly beloved I am very glad you have another & better job & one to your liking – congratulations & all that. You must be changing a great deal, you know, what with all this Experience, Responsibility etc – & it's hard for me to measure the stuff of the change from your letters – which are in the old vein, though so much more adult & so infinitely enriched! It will be very strange meeting you again in the flesh – *eh bien*, one knows that.

Yes your letters are always rich to the taste. A charming one (dated Sept. 24th) has just arrived this morning, & pulled me out of a morass of gloom in which I was floundering. How can one feel gloomy when one has such good friends? *C'est impossible*. Your comparison of Modern Greek to the twittering of the

---

[61] Frank had on 13 September 1943 joined SOE in Cairo, hoping to be dropped into Greece.

[62] *Nekyia*: probably referring to the shades of the dead summoned up e.g. in *Odyssey* XI where they are 'making noises, like birds fluttering to and fro quite terrified'.

νεκυια[62] is of course absolutely it – it's so exact, I can't think why I didn't make it myself! And while we're on philology, your problem about *sorok*.[63] I tried it on a number of people without spectacular results. My Russian teacher – a middle aged white who is learned without being intelligent, a charming woman though) tells me *sorok* is pure Slav, just a fluke & not an importation. She snorted scornfully at the comparison with Kirk. (damn those I's, I always dot them) The Treasury intellectuals (who are intelligent without being learned) were much interested in the comparison but could produce only conjectures. *Faute de mieux*[64] I am believing my teacher, but will tell you if any details come to light.

Turkish continues to delight me. After working at high pressure in private lessons I have now graduated (somewhat shakily into a sleepy & slowcoach second-year class – my fanatical Turk, who takes the class, being unable to find time anymore for private pupils. The class consists of about 15 people, hailing from every European country except England & seeming in most cases farther behind in their English than in their Turkish. No one understands anyone else, & as the teacher speaks, as I told you, an involuntary mélange of bad English & good French, we are a pretty polyglot gathering.

One of the chief sorrows of my existence at this moment is that there is (I discover) a limit to the number of languages which one can learn at one time.

Your remarks about Henry James interest me. 'A comfortable American' – no one with so deep a sensibility & so full an appreciation of what being a human being is could really be called 'comfortable.' 'Liking England for the wrong reasons' –

---

[63] *Sorok* is Russian for 'forty'; but reference lost.
[64] For want of [anything] better.

is there a list of right ones? 'Subtlety one of his strong suits' – yes, here is a difficulty. Where do all these analytical novelists get one, tiptoeing psychologically around? They all appeal to me enormously (by 'all' I intend a sweeping gesture, embracing fundamentally different writers such as Proust, Joyce, de Montherlant, Woolf) but God knows what the ultimate effect is. All I am certain of now is that I would be quite incapable of writing anything 'straight' ever again. My alarm was increased the other day when I read my first Balzac – Eugénie Grandet – & found it left me quite cold. Are you a Balzac expert, & if so will you please tell me what to read next, having due regard to my state of mind?

Three cheers for the French by the way – I am beginning to find my way a little in fields of French literature & rejoice much at the thought of joy to come. Have just discovered a rather subtle contemporary chap called Louis Ferdinand Céline – monstrous rambling, occasionally very good. What a gorgeous language – how much one is exiled from. How much more they are exiled from. I feel gloom about the future of Europe & about my own capacity to do the smallest thing of use.

Your remarks about a) thuggishness & b) Bob Conquest[65] inspire me to request a photograph. My own (not at all like me, but you asked for it) is laid on. *Much love. I.*

Blackpool
November 12th [1943]

Dearly beloved, thank you for *Priyg and Skok,*[66] who have just

---

[65] Robert Conquest, 1917–, with whom Frank had been at Winchester.

[66] Russian for skip and jump: probably Frank had sent IM *Peter Rabbit* [see end of this paragraph] in Russian.

arrived! Yes, it pleases me too to think that these people of blood & iron have their human moments – perhaps after all we are wrong in thinking of them as somewhat barbarous Asiatics fundamentally differing from ourselves. Viva the confraternity of Peter Rabbits.

I am delighted too to hear that a Mayakovsky may be *en route*. I didn't care for translations, which are all I've seen of him – one just got the full blast of the propaganda with no poetic wrappings. But if the man's a <u>poet</u> I don't care what he says. I look forward with much joy & interest to making his acquaintance. When I get back to London I shall send you some of the stuff that is being written now by the Younger School – our contemporaries, God help us – the New Apocalyptics, the 'poetry (London)' gang, the sensibility boys who think with their stomach. You probably won't approve – you may nevertheless enjoy. Just occasionally some of these folks produce an exquisite lyric – & a good lyric is a good lyric, & infinitely to be preferred to the barren political jargonising that even real poets spent so much time on in the playtime of the '30s when we were all conscience-ridden spectators. You mentioned Aragon, by the way, a letter or two ago. Yes, that is the genuine stuff alright. What a delicious language French [*sic*] is when one does the right thing by it..

Which reminds me that I am making a bold attempt at Italian – the occasion being a celestial attack of jaundice, involving a fortnight at home. (You had this curious complaint a little while ago, if I remember.) I feel quite recovered now, & full of mental energy. I enjoy Italian – & of course getting an elementary knowledge is as you say incredibly easy – dreamlike too – the familiar Latin & French constructions, words, verb forms turning up, a little altered, but recognisable. Too sweet a music, perhaps – lacking the solid majesty of Latin & the tang & precision of French? I don't know yet, but a nice taste, & most

gratifyingly simple. Have also put in some work on Russian &
Turkïsh.

I am reading another Henry James called 'The Ambassadors'
– the man is uncanny the way he unravels a psychological situation. He writes in about five dimensions – & in that gorgeous
convoluted style which, if you give it your closest attention, is
nevertheless not obscure. He is the only novelist I know who
really says <u>everything</u> – & gets away with it. To write like that is
self evidently one of the greatest activities of the human mind. I
hope the New World Order will agree!

A tired somewhat sandy letter from 2nd Lt. Leo. I hope you
see him sometimes & cheer him up. Hal seems to have gone
back to his starting point & to be living as peaceful an existence
as ever. I hope your new job pleases you – I'd love to know
what you're up to – (tho' of course I know you can't tell me).
Still, if the Russians, God bless 'em, continue to hare along like
this maybe you'll all be home before too long. Au revoir then.

Con amore, devotissima I

Force 133. MEF
December 1st, 1943

...One lives really far too little. I go about this ancient town in a
perpetual Anglo-Saxon hustle, and miss everything. Then suddenly
something catches my eye; a bearded man passes by, a young man
with spectacles on a bicycle, in <u>galabiya</u>[67] and white turban, obviously a
student from El Ahvaz; he is eating sugar-cane and nonchalantly
tosses a bit to a family of beggars that is dragging its way along the
pavement; or I catch sight from a rooftop of a Franciscan friar striding along a side-street, between poinsettias and bougainvillea...At

---

[67] Frank, like T.E. Lawrence, owned a galabiya (kaftan) himself.

these times, for a flickering moment, I realise that I am a man in a town full of varied men, and that this, on the whole, is rather a good thing...

When I live, chiefly, is when I meet friends. I've acquired a most admirable friend, a schoolmaster and not really a fervent conservative; with whom I hold almost daily commination services. I have been stripped of my few remaining illusions in the last year – (I speak solely of political illusions) – and harbour now a great deal of malice towards some. I have lost altogether the pseudo-heroic mood I had three months ago, when I first volunteered for parachute duties. I still press for more active work because it seems to suit my temperament better than sitting in an office, but I don't worry overmuch. If they choose to keep me at a base now my training's over, they may. I feel it won't be a tragedy if I survive the war. I can see so many evil men and so many myriads of petty men surviving well entrenched, and I don't think that I, for all my manifest vices, am either of these. I believe that every man of goodwill is going to be badly needed in the years that lie ahead. But for all that, I would rather be now on the Sangro River – I know that for certain and don't say it to reassure you nor even myself...

Force 133. MEF

December 26th, 1943

...With the passing of the year I seem to have come to a watershed in my life. In the past few days I have had some profoundly moving experiences. I have had the honour to meet and talk to some of the best people in the world...people whom, when the truth is known, Europe will recognise as among the finest and toughest she has ever borne. Meeting them has made me utterly disgusted with some aspects of my present life, reminding me forcibly that all my waking hours should be dedicated to one purpose only. This sounds very much like all New Year resolutions, but in this case I think I shall soon have a change in my way of living which will give me a real chance. Nothing else matters. We must crush the Nazis and build our whole life anew. 'If we should meet again, why then we'll smile'[68] If not, why then those that follow us will be able to smile far more happily and honestly in the world that we all helped to make. And believe me, no men are more disarming in their gaiety than these men, our allies, who have known more suffering than we can easily imagine.

Captain[69] WF Thompson

April 21st [1943]

Irushka!

Sorry I haven't written for so long. Old Brotoloig seems to have been monopolising my attention. I know forgiveness is one of your chief virtues.

Three airmail letter-cards from you, bringing me up to the end of JAN. A great deal of talk about weariness of soul, even among your good friends. You know quite well there's no danger of your succumbing to it. You have springs within you that will never fail. I want to hear no more of this [*illeg*] nonsense.

I can't say precisely what your role in life will be, but I should say it will definitely be a literary-humanistic one. You should continue fooling about. [*illeg*] shall be able to compare notes. I shall write a preface to your translation of Levski's poems & you will bestow the same honor on my life of Vuk Karadzic.[70] We might organise quite a neat little racket. I think we should let Lidderdale in on it with a special brief to deal with Slovenian folk poetry & Pliatzky will be allowed to write Steinbeckian stories about Greek harbour-towns which we shall approve from our Olympian heights as 'bearing the authentic smell of the Levant'. Foot shall be our chief authority on Turkey.

---

[68] Shakespeare: *Julius Caesar*, Act V sc 1, Brutus: "If we do meet again, why, we shall smile; /
If not, why then, this parting was well made'. In his last letter to IM, Frank quotes a later scene from the same play.

[69] He had been gazetted Major but almost certainly never knew.

[70] These names are intended to help Murdoch, against censorship, identify where he is. Vuk Karadzic (1787-1864) Serbian linguist; and Vasil Levski (1837-1873) great

Does this restore your faith in yourself & your 'mission'? It certainly should.

I can't think why you are so interested in MORALS. Chiefly a question of the liver & digestive organs I assure you. On one occasion when I had to go without sugar for a month, I felt by the end of it as though I could have won a continence contest against Hippolytus.

αμματων δ'εν αχηνιασ
ερρει παο 'Αφροδιτα[71]

My own list of priorities is as follows:

1. People and everything to do with people, their habits, their loves and hates, their arts, their languages. Everything of importance revolves around people.

2. Animals and flowers. These bring me a constant undercurrent of joy. Just now I'm revelling in plum blossom and young lambs and the first leaves on the briar roses. One doesn't need any more than these. I couldn't wish for better company.

These are enough for a hundred lifetimes. And yet I must confess to being very fond of food and drink also.

I envy you and Michael in one way. All this time you are doing important things like falling in and out of love – things which broaden and deepen and strengthen the character more surely than anything else. I can honestly say I've never been in love. When I pined for you I was too young to know what I was doing – no offence meant. Since then I haven't lost an hour's sleep over any of Eve's daughters. This means I'm growing up lop-sided, an overgrown boy. Ah well, – I shall find time, Cassius, I shall find time.[72]

---

[71] Euripides' play *Hippolytus* concerns a man who has his chastity tested by his own step-mother Phaedra at the behest of a goddess and dies as a result. Murdoch made her own translation of this play in 1946.

[72] *Julius Caesar* Act V sc 3, Brutus: 'Friends, I owe more tears/To this dead man than you shall see me pay.— / I shall find time, Cassius, I shall find time.'

All the same, I don't think you should fall for 'emotional fascists' – Try to avoid that...[73]

---

[73] Final page missing: how Frank signed off his last letter we will probably never

David Hicks, c 1940, courtesy Tom Hicks

III

WRITING TO DAVID HICKS
1938-46

MURDOCH'S AND THOMPSON'S friendship had the shape of classical tragedy: it ended with Murdoch's discovery of her feeling for Frank only months before his early death pre-empted expression of this. In their letters she and Frank discussed Shakespeare's *Antony and Cleopatra* and referred more than once to his *Julius Caesar*. Aeschylus' Agamemnon is another common topic. That these tragedies figured in their correspondence has an unconscious aptness.

The shape of Murdoch and David Hicks's friendship, by contrast, recalls a Shakespeare play that, though painful, is none the less essentially comic: *Much Ado about Nothing*. Beatrice and Benedick are played unwittingly by Iris and David, a couple duelling verbally and secretly attracted after a love-passage that leaves both feeling sore and affronted. Probably left-wing politics brought them together in autumn 1938. They flirted briefly, almost at once fell out, and were then separated by seven years of war. David, serving with the British Council, was posted to

Egypt, then Persia, and finally, at war's end to Czechoslovakia. Murdoch, first languishing in Oxford and then from 1942, the Treasury, captured his interest at long distance.

David's time in Egypt in 1942 was, his son Tom believes, the high point of his life. Here he edited *Citadel*, the magazine for the literary expatriates who found themselves stranded in wartime Cairo[1] and became friends with the writers Lawrence Durrell, Olivia Manning, and Edwin Muir. He would long claim to have been the model for the character of Dubedat in Olivia Manning's *Balkan Trilogy*. It is an odd boast, for the character is scarcely attractive.[2] Dubedat, a scholarship boy from a provincial grammar-school, has been hitch-hiking in Europe equipped with inadequate clothing and an unpleasant voice. He is an eccentric elementary school-teacher with a sentimental view of the poor, reflecting David's then firm CP membership. He is described as 'unusually peevish'.

Manning puts Dubedat to interesting uses. A performance of Shakespeare's *Troilus and Cressida*, that disturbingly bitter play about love and war, features importantly in the *Balkan Trilogy*. Manning, accounted by Hicks a friend, casts Dubedat as the spiteful and cynical Thersites, a choice widely applauded by the other novel-characters as successful type-casting. Thersites has a biting wit and rails impotently against the corruptions of the age. This black play ends with Thersites cursing the 'wars and lechery' that typify the times. In portraying Thersites so successfully Dubedat exploits his own 'natural unpleasantness' and love of hectoring. He is twice described as resembling an angry rat, and there are further disobliging epithets. After the play is over

---

[1] See Artemis Cooper, *Cairo in the War* (1989) p156.

[2] That Hicks gets no mention in Neville Braybrooke's posthumously published biography of Olivia Manning (2004) does not disprove his claim.

Dubedat, with help from a friend, rewards a patron for his kindness by first traducing and then betraying him.

It says something for David's humility if he recognised any element of truth in this hostile representation, which is remote from both the athletic Lothario so many women found attractive, as from the decent husband, father and teacher that David Hicks was to become.

David was himself an aspiring writer: in later life Murdoch gave him generous advice about a projected eight-volume auto-biographical novel.[3] He kept not merely almost every letter and card sent him by Murdoch (only one letter is obviously incomplete) but also copies from 1946 of drafts of some of his own replies.[4] These last make clear that he regarded himself as in some sense a reprobate and that this interested her. If she allots herself a role in the drama, it is that of the good and sacred virgin wrestling with the monster in order to save him from himself. At the same time a psychological sub-plot concerns her own need to find a man strong enough to subdue her free spirit, a man whose cruelty secretly excites her. These twin roles she played repeatedly: in 1943-44 with the economist Thomas Balogh, the affair with whom she describes to David, and then most notably with Elias Canetti in 1953-56. Both these female personae – saviour and victim – haunt her fiction.

One of the interests of their seven-year long epistolary courtship is how much Iris Murdoch, like the heroines of Shakespeare's comedies, makes the running. It is she who pursues and engages his interest, appealing ingeniously to his intelligence and

---

[3] Three pages of notes from Murdoch on Hicks's novel-plan survive among the papers in Bodley, and a letter asking David whether he would mind if Murdoch showed his novel to 'an off-shoot of Secker', the Alison Press.

[4] Not only from Murdoch: e.g. Hicks kept every note and letter from his lifelong friend John Willett (later a noted Brecht scholar), in his miniscule hand, too.

narcissism, and slowly awakening in him a passion to match her own. This was a pre-emancipated age, against which backdrop Murdoch's ungovernable independence of spirit is striking. References to the challenge then entailed in being a woman abound in her letters.

> Men have a freedom we never have (it's a conventional complaint, I know) – achieve a comradeship, an easy friendship with the world at large that women miss.
>
> Sometimes I think it's quite bloody being a woman. So much of one's life has to consist of having an attitude. (I hope you follow this, which is a little condensed.)
>
> One of the many disadvantages of femininity, of course, is that it's more difficult to cope with that sort of society & appear neither a whore nor a bluestocking.[5]

She soon found a worthy role model for the freedoms of which she fantasised in Simone de Beauvoir, whom she praised to David both as 'Jean-Paul Sartre's mistress & full of his philosophy' but also as 'more or less everything that the modern novelist should be, and a woman, bless her!' Two months later she dreams that she meets de Beauvoir, whose first play is now running 'magnificently' in Paris. 'What a woman!'[6] And she would write in 1946 to the writer and Gallimard editor Raymond Queneau, whose work also influenced her profoundly, to discover whether de Beauvoir might be '*trouvable*' i.e. 'at home' for a visit.

De Beauvoir was Murdoch's heroine for different reasons. She was what Murdoch then aspired to be, a successful writer. And Murdoch admired her novels – *She Came to Stay* (1943) concerning a ménage-a-trois, and *The Blood of Others* (1945) concerning

---

[5] Respectively to Frank 29/1/42 and 24/11/42 and to David 4/10/45.
[6] 4 October 1945 and 4 December 1945.

star-crossed lovers during the Resistance. Then de Beauvoir was also a feminist heroine whose writings championed new freedoms for women. Her *The Second Sex*, published in 1949 and the most important feminist treatise of its time, was the foundation upon which much later feminist theorising is based. Its thesis was that womanhood was not a biological destiny but a posture wished upon women by the men who victimised them. Although Murdoch would come to believe that victims are partly responsible for colluding with their fate, this book was lastingly important to her, and she encouraged friends and students alike to read it. Lastly Simone de Beauvoir practised in her private life the freedoms she preached in her writing, and Murdoch, who in 1946 started to visit the Latin Quarter of Paris cafes frequented by de Beauvoir, would certainly have learnt of this.[7] Life in the pubs and clubs of wartime Fitzrovia, sampled by both Murdoch and Hicks, prefigured this post-Liberation Paris bohemianism, and was seen as part of the same act of rebellion against bourgeois conformity as membership of the CP. The bohemianism of both cities permeates her first published novel *Under the Net* (1954).

■■■

After nearly seven years apart, David's home-leave was delayed in 1945 by one crucial week during which the United Nations Rehabilitation and Relief Association (UNRRA) sent Murdoch overseas to Brussels. Missing one another so narrowly he and Iris accounted themselves star-crossed. Before long she contrived to return to London for ten tempestuous days together that November. They probably introduced one another to their parents, and certainly to some of their friends, and decided to marry.

---

[7] See *Life*, ch 9.

Murdoch also completed the task of going through Frank Thompson's letters for publication in a family memorial volume. But soon she found herself back in Brussels, and then posted to a series of refugee camps in Austria for another half a year, while the British Council sent Hicks to Czechoslovakia.

In an interview concerning the two years Iris Murdoch spent with UNRRA,[8] she mentions that on arrival in Brussels in 1945 she went to listen to Jean-Paul Sartre lecture and telephoned Chico Marx, the piano-playing Marx brother who affected an Italian accent on film. She wished to meet Sartre, on whose philosophy she was soon the first and foremost English expert, and about whom she would write a famous and still cogent study. The reason she telephoned 'stand-offish' Chico, was because Hicks was crazy about the Marx brothers.[9] meeting Chico would have given David pleasure.

After this lightning romance David rapidly had second thoughts. His letter jilting her arrived, after weeks' delay, at the Austrian refugee camp where she was by now an officer in February 1946. Her reply releasing him is remarkable. 'I don't seem to have a real gift for making you happy, & others have it, that's that… You are a splendid creature David & lots of splendid women will want to marry you'. This was heroically generous. She subsequently wrote a 'querulous' letter that does not survive, to which David answered 'I like you enormously, better than anyone I can think of. But was worried at the thought of being married to you. Probably the same with anyone else, but it seemed more terrifying in your case. Brain, will and womb, you are formidable...' Murdoch's first letter after the break was prescient too: of his new engagement to 'the Dornford Yates heroine' she writes

---

[8] Bodleian Library: MSS.Eng.c.4718, fols.132-62; c.4733, item 16, p13.

[9] According to his son Tom Hicks.

'Remember that you've just nearly made one mistake – don't go & make another. Take it coolly & gently'. David's first marriage indeed ended after only a few years.

David's son Tom believes that he may have felt a lingering regret that he did not marry Iris Murdoch.[10] Certainly his parents were disappointed that his engagement to her ended when it did, and David was very fond of Iris and proud of his association with her. Slowly she and David achieved the feat of turning their erstwhile passion into friendship. She probably helped financially when he had no money. She took David and his second wife Katherine Messenger out to dinner at the Randolph Hotel when they were too poor for a honeymoon on 1 June 1953, came up to Shropshire for his 70th birthday in March 1986 and they met and wrote to each other over the years in between. 'Something of me is stored up with you in a way that I can never regret' and '... everything to do with you still has so many echoes & resonances in all parts of me', she wrote early in the 1950s. She wrote twice to condole with him when his son Barney, after a long depressive illness, committed suicide in 1978, aged 22; David feared his sons suffered from his undisguised contempt for traditional religion.[11] Katherine considered that David and Iris would have made a disastrous marriage – both living, perhaps too much, through the imagination.

David is remembered at work as difficult by the novelist Fran-

---

[10] Two letters dated 1972 endorse this suggestion: 'By God that was the happiest meeting with you I have had for years, and I wept with pleasure on the tube going back to my office' and 'I don't want to meet...you will have noticed I always make a gauche idiot of myself'.

[11] She wrote that she had known quite well three young people who became seriously 'depressed' ['that mysterious soul-ailment so many seem to have now', IM remarked] and killed themselves – one was Caspar, son of Ian Fleming, handsome, rich, clever etc etc 'but *just did not want to live*. The determination to go was in all the three cases, very very deep.'

cis King, a colleague in the British Council where King believes Hicks had few friends. King wondered whether David was not embittered by, among other things, lack of literary success, and that this came out once untowardly. Both King and Hicks had hopes of a job in Japan that King eventually won. When King's novel *The Custom House* appeared, Hicks's was the only hostile review (in the *TLS*). King wrote him to say that he thought that his conduct had been 'mean-spirited'. He replied that the *TLS* – whose reviews were then unsigned – had had no right to divulge his identity, that he had not liked the book and had merely expressed his opinion, as he was fully entitled to do.

Hicks's second marriage was happy. His son recalls his sometimes erudite sense of humour that could intimidate less well-educated visitors. He, who in earlier life had been a formidable climber in the Alps, the Tatra and Persian mountains now enjoyed chess, the *Times* crossword, logic, history, philosophy, music and art. Listening to Bach, Haydn, Beethoven, Monteverdi and Vivaldi brought pleasure as did the paintings of Claude, Monet, Sisley, Corot and illustrators such as Charles Robinson, Arthur Rackham. He was an early admirer of Tolkein and read *The Lord of the Rings* to his children. He did a fair imitation of Paul Robeson in his own excellent bass voice: he also loved Kurt Weill, Lotte Lenya, Mark Twain (naming his youngest child after Tom Sawyer), Ava Gardner (his pin-up), Bertrand Russell... If his own literary ambitions remained unrealised, he took vicarious pleasure in Murdoch's success. She copied into her journal

---

[12] In January 1972 she copied this from David Hicks's letter: 'As the years pass I find I have less and less to say to you, but you have always more to say to me. You do this through your novels, which are obviously addressed to a general public, yet read in many places as if you were telling me something – always an illumination of some obscure corner of my own experience... You are writing some of the most truthful fiction of our age, and the best...'

a generous and moving letter he wrote in praise of her fiction in the 1970s.[12] After a heart attack he took to sniffing snuff, which clogged up his typewriter and every inch of his study.

As for Iris Murdoch, she did not gain David as a life-partner. What she did gain was ideas for future novels. To the good writer even the uses of adversity are famously sweet: and everything is grist to the creative mill. This took time. It is striking meanwhile how many of Murdoch's wartime friends, Frank and David included, saw themselves as apprentice writers.[13] They share their excitement at the work of Louis Aragon, as at the periodicals *Poetry London* and *Horizon*. Murdoch tried (unsuccessfully) to contribute as well as subscribe. She submitted her first novel to Faber and Faber in autumn 1944, gaining from TS Eliot himself a cold letter of refusal. Nonetheless she was training herself as a writer and, like many such, found in Rilke's *Letters to a Young Poet*, which she reads in German, precious advice about the noble, necessary loneliness of the writer's vocation.

In 1944 she wrote to Hicks that 'I suppose I have a myth-making mind'. Two years later she told Hicks she was engaged in writing of a young man 'who makes a dream picture of a woman he has known, writes her into a novel, & then meets her again after a long interval... I can use [this] even if you can't'. That novel does not survive. Two others do. One is *The Sacred and Profane Love Machine* (1974) where the character of Monty Small who 'cuts' relationships abruptly, and has a Nietzschean cult of the will, may recall David. Four years later she won the Booker prize with *The Sea, The Sea*. It concerns a theatre director who loses track of his childhood sweetheart and then re-meets and kidnaps her over forty years later. It is arguably her greatest novel.

---

[13] I was very struck in communicating around 1998 with surviving friends how many had nursed literary ambitions as by how many of these Murdoch had later tried to

If the Hicks saga (among others) informed that fiction, then the time-lag between the original events and their fictionalisation was some further thirty odd years. She could write so well about obsessional love in *The Sea, The Sea* because she had inhabited this from inside. She could write confidently about theatre-folk in that novel, because the Magpie Players helped start her acquaintanceship with that world. And she could bring the 'saint' of *The Sea, The Sea*, General James Arrowby, to life because she had known Major Frank Thompson, whom she elegised to David as 'a brilliant & full blooded creature, one of the best I ever knew'. Through Frank she came to perceive soldiers as possible heroic figures, romantically committed, not just to violence, but to noble self-sacrifice too.

David 1938-46

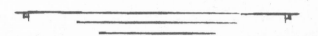

Dear David,

Suzzanah[1] is in a raging fury – Gaetulian lions[2] are as sucking doves beside her – so I think on the whole it would be a good thing to return her typewriter *quam celerrime.*[3]

I have just returned from having a rather embarrassed tea with the Principal[4] – it consisted of a series of nerve-wracking

---

[1] Suzanne or Zuzanne Przeworska aka Popski was, remembers IM's friend Mary Midgley, 'a funny little full-time CP member', a year senior to them, described without being named in Midgley's memoir *The Owl of Minerva* orating to friends in Somerville front hall about the 'extraordinary stupidity of some voters in Jericho whom she had been trying to convert when canvassing in the [Munich] bye-election'. She married 'Akky' = Akiba Schonfield mentioned in these letters, son of a Rabbi.

[2] The lion of the Gaetuli, a warlike Libyan tribe, appears in Virgil's *Aeneid*, Book V, Line 352. This proverbial lion – of fierce reputation – recurs in Horace's *Odes* and Pliny's *Natural History.*

[3] As fast as possible.

[4] Helen Darbishire (1881-1961), literary scholar and College head. Mary Midgley writes: '... she looked rather like an amiable old sheep... probably quite a good principal, but – as is so common – she didn't really know how to talk to undergraduates, so we hadn't a high opinion of her.'

pauses strung together by desperate attempts at conversation, the chief topic being Siamese cats! – what a waste, to go to tea with a really intelligent woman and talk about Siamese cats. I have now come back to the more congenial company of Aeschylus,[5] whom you no doubt consider to be on an equal level of futility – and I admit his plays have no great bearing on surplus value[6] and bills of exchanges.

I hope you have sustained no fresh damage since last we met in fights with fascists or pseudo-fascists – I feel like having a fight with somebody right now – Siamese cats! What a charming world we live in.

Well, goodbye, give my love to the deadheads, and don't forget Suzzanah's typewriter____

Iris

P.S. Don't go starving yourself. We shall all be dead soon enough anyway without accelerating the process.

Somerville tea begins at 3.45.

[postcard]
4 Eastbourne Road W4
December 23rd, 1938

Thank you David,
I find myself quite tolerably disengaged on Boxing Day and shall certainly come if I can thread the mazes of North London. At the moment I have a perfectly hellish sore throat and have to converse in husky whispers (her voice was ever soft, gentle, and

---

[5] Aeschylus (525-456BC) Greek dramatist and father of tragedy: at Corpus college IM attended Fraenkel's seminar on Aeschylus' *Agamemnon*, a play featuring in her and FT's correspondence. See *Life* ch 5 et seq.

[6] Surplus value: a concept developed by Karl Marx in his critique of political economy.

low, an excellent thing in women [*sic*][7]) but I hope that'll be gone by Monday. Isn't the snow glorious? But I <u>wish</u> people wouldn't walk on it.

See you Monday night at 7.   *Iris*

4 Eastbourne Road
Chiswick
London W4
December 29th, 1938

Dear David,

Thank you very much indeed for your charming letter. The weather didn't hurt me in the least and as for feeling 'fooled' – well I didn't come all that way to see any refugees, Czech or otherwise, or any numbers of other Davids. I came to see you and your family. May I say how very much I liked your family – and how much pleasure it gives me to see <u>you</u> in your natural habitat.

I didn't realise you wouldn't be coming back to Oxford and I certainly didn't know you were going to start teaching so soon – you should have told me. I won't pretend I'm not sorry about it. A very short while now I have 'delighted in your company',[8] but long enough to know that you have something I want, and that I've not hitherto found, and I think I have something you want. I am, to use your words, 'a seeker after my own species'.

I shall write when there is time from Oxford and tell you of

---

[7] *King Lear*, following the murder of his daughter Cordelia, Act V sc iii.

[8] Hard not to read this phrase from the song 'Greensleeves' prophetically: 'Alas, my love, you do me wrong, To cast me off discourteously. For I have loved you well and long, Delighting in your company.' The singer later announces 'But my heart remains in captivity.'

Suzzanah's latest affaire and what sort of ties Peter Shinnie[9] is wearing and why I think my philosophy of life is better than yours – and in return I should appreciate an occasional dissertation on the Universe in general and young Hampstead in particular. Next vac – well, the animals at the Zoo will still invite us with their interesting curves, and I should like extremely to improve my acquaintance with your family.

And now I wish you all the luck and happiness in the world. Believe in yourself. You're <u>not</u> so 'bloody mediocre.'

love from   Iris

P.S. And pray cease considering me as a child. I am in many ways considerably more mature than you are.

Somerville College

[Un-dated]

My dear David,

Thank you for the perfectly delightful communication. What a strange amusing creature you are, to be sure! What was it, I wonder, in my letter that made you blossom forth into such an effusion of wounded dignity and inferiority complex. Yes, I suppose it <u>was</u> tactless of me to remember against you one of those too-rare moments in which you doubt that you are the paragon of animals. And it was also foolish of me to allow myself to be so tender towards you last time I wrote – you certainly saw your

---

[9] Shinnie, b. London 1915, after studying Egyptology at Christ Church College, stayed on at Oxford on £3 a week as CP organiser, and temporary assistant at the Ashmolean Museum until called up for RAF war service. Raymond Carr was inducted into the CP by Shinnie at Queen's College in what resembled a religious ceremony, 'with candles and oaths' *Life*, p 614 n 8; and Shinnie believed he might also have recruited IM and FT see KU [= Kingston Shinnie's first wife was Margaret Cloake, sister of Anne (See *Life*)].

advantage and took it pretty quickly.

But seriously, what was your motive in writing that letter? I am most interested from a psychological point of view. Perhaps, realising that I liked you more than a little, and afraid of breaking my heart, your chivalry prompted you to intimate (what I knew already) that you weren't <u>really</u> interested in me – thus effecting, by a little well-timed brutality, a beneficial operation on my feelings. Very noble and touching. But I'm not at all sure that it's necessary. You see, David, I have no intention of being dragged at your chariot wheels. *Mon dieu*! Your vanity is so outrageous that it is positively sublime and almost charming. Do you really imagine that I shall be content to hang round and be a sweet flower to refresh you when the earthy side of your nature has sated itself with less spiritual females? Think again, comrade. I have other things to do. Maybe there's ripe fruit for me to gather too – to use your rather unsavoury and hardly original metaphor – and maybe the prolific orchard in which I dwell at present is rather more sheltered than you believe from the winds of passion. You know you are not the only frustrated artist who has noticed my unfortunate resemblance to a fairy tale princess etc etc. (It must be the way I do my hair – I shall have to change it.) Though I must say 'the good old Freudian idealised female imago' was quite a new line – and most refreshing too, I liked it much better than 'O bright-eyed daughter of the Gods, Born to adore and be adored', which reached me by post yesterday from a love-sick Irishman.[10] But you should have done it in verse – nearly all my other admirers do. 'Straight out of Freud my lady comes' or 'How Jung my love is, ah how very Jung',

---

[10] Probably Paddy O'Regan (see *Life*) but conceivably Cyril Cusack recalled by Margaret Stanier as spending one term acting in Oxford, during which IM and he saw much of each other; IM disconcerted when he left.

or something of that sort.

And now, David, I really don't want to fight with you. You see I still like you very much – though heaven only knows why – I <u>must</u> be resilient. So I tender you my hand and take my leave and shall look forward to seeing you in the vac. Write and tell me how you get on at Beedale's [*sic*],[11] I shall be most interested to hear. And meanwhile I hope you find plenty of nice ripe berries to console you for the absence of Ali.[12] But I have no doubt that your simple wants will be quite easily provided for.

Goodbye.   Iris

Somerville College
Oxford
April 29th, 1940

Dear David,

My greetings. How is it with you? I think of you decorating the skyline on a camel and taking your well-earned siesta in the shade of a pyramid. Or is Egypt not romantic? Yes, I know. I had an aunt once who used to teach the young Egyptians to love God.[13] What do you teach them? I hope it's something with an equally good moral. And altogether, how wags the world in your region of it?

You and your pyramids seem almost as fabulous and mythical to me as Oxford and I must seem to you now. I expect an act of faith is necessary to persuade yourself you ever were here. (But

---

[11] Bedales, progressive and co-educational school in Hampshire, founded in 1893.

[12] Ali = Alastine Bell b 1919 with whom DH was obsessively in love (*Life* p 204]), was daughter of Kenneth Bell, historian and fellow of Balliol College. She studied at Lady Margaret Hall 1938-41.

[13] Isabella Jane Shaw, a.k.a aunt Ella (1894-1990), a one-time missionary

you were, I remember you quite distinctly.)

Everything here seems curiously the same – and yet I don't know why it should, for every month batches of men fade away into khaki, and Balliol is full of glossy civil servants from Whitehall. Worcester is still largely academic – I go there twice a week to hear a highly immoral old man called Pickard-Cambridge[14] talking about moral philosophy. Lectures and all the clubs proceed as before, and the only difference it all makes to me is that I have ten times as much organisational work to do as I would normally, owing to the increasing man shortage.

I have just done Mods, and got the distinguished second which you once so kindly predicted for me. (Damn you. I held that against you for a long time. I suppose it would be unreasonable to bear the grudge any longer.) And now I am doing Greats. The philosophy is not as philosophical as one would wish, but the Ancient History is very ancient (especially in the matter of the dons appertaining thereto) and I find them both pretty good mental exercise.

The personelle [sic] of the university has changed tremendously. Freeling and Lucy[15] are vanished as though they had never been. Carol[16] I hear of spasmodically achieving great things

---

[14] Sir Arthur Wallace Pickard-Cambridge (1879-1957), authority on ancient Greek theatre.

[15] Lucy Klatschko, later Sister Marian and a nun at Stambrook Abbey, came up to Somerville in 1936 to read Modern Languages, and was pursued by DH 'relentlessly' (*Life* p202 et seq and KUAS6/3/97).

[16] Carol Stewart, later Graham-Harrison, also came up to Somerville in 1936 and was also pursued by DH. In 1962 she translated Canetti's *Crowds and Power* into English. She recalled IM in 1998 as possessing something 'aboriginal: simplicity, naiveté, power, and space' and noted both how unusually watchful and observant IM was, even at the age of nineteen, and also, in her own words, how she 'ate people up'.

in the Ministry of Economic Warfare. A few old ties like Jack Dawes and Denis Healey[17] are still here and active. Peter Shinnie is in the airforce and getting incredibly tough – others of them are in the artillery and fleet air arm. None of the women whom you knew, I'm glad to say, has joined the ATS.[18]

Myself, I am incredibly busy this term with committees (E. & B.) and with acting. You see I have achieved one of my ambitions, to play the chorus leader in 'Murder in the Cathedral'. Christ Church dramatic society is doing it, and our stage is the cloister quad at Christ Church with the Cathedral as a backcloth. Also I am bringing out a revised version – an *editio maior*[19] rather – of your song sheet. (Remember?)

The world – yes. It's a pretty interesting and fast moving little world these days. There's a lot to be depressed about certainly, but I can't say I feel very fundamentally downhearted. In fact I've never felt so full of hope and new life as I do now. We're not doing so badly.

Meanwhile this place is raving wild with spring. I met a calf this morning that looked like Michaelangelo's [*sic*] Moses – and the calf's mother was like Epstein's Madonna. I won't tell you about the cherry trees or how green the Cherwell banks are, or you'll be homesick. How homesick are you? Don't be too. Though indeed there's nothing much wrong with the flora and fauna. As I think Browning observed.

I hope very much life isn't boring or unhappy or lonely or any

[17] Like IM, Denis Healey, later Labour politician and Lord, was then an open member of the CP. He was at Balliol reading Greats from 1936-40, and lent IM Samuel Beckett's *Murphy*, which features in her first published novel.

[18] Women could join all three services – army, air force and navy. In the army, women joined the Auxiliary Territorial Service (ATS) where, like men soldiers, their uniform was khaki.

[19] Major edition.

of the things it shouldn't be but so often is. How many English people are there with you? Are they interesting? How hard do you work? What is the work like? Do you still paint? Have you written anything? I tell you one thing you might write, that's a letter to me, if you feel like it, and if you have anything of note to say about a) Egypt, b) David.

The best of luck to you.

Love Iris

P.S. John Willett,[20] from whom I got your address sends his love and says he misses you a lot – but as he said all this some time ago I expect he has conveyed it himself by now.

     I.

> 9 Waller Avenue
> Bispham
> Blackpool[21]
> March 21st, 1941

Dear David,

You will hardly believe, after this long interval of silence, how many times I have been on the point of writing to you. However between the what's its name & the thingummybob falls the shadow as TS Eliot says, & to that shadow I have invariably succumbed – not in this matter only. I liked your letter (your letter alas my conscience of May 22nd 1940) very much. Your gift of words has not deserted you, whatever other noble qualities are being blown away in the sandstorm. It seems an arid noonday world you're living in – but you still very much alive in the middle

---

[20] See Pt 2 n 15.

[21] IM's father worked at the Ministry of Health, which was evacuated to Blackpool – see later in this letter.

of it with the dew not quite dry on your hair – twisted satyr of Palmer's Green. Seriously though, you seem to be pretty good at making the best of what I can well imagine is a hellish bad job. How go the prospects of becoming a great man? Does Hicks pasha hold the Middle Eastern fortunes in the palm of his hand?

Young Alcibiades, according to Grote,[22] had all the qualities of greatness except character. By which he means some sort of moral code. I'm not quite sure what the relevance of that is. I'm not sure whether or not you have a moral code. You sometimes remind me of Alcibiades. You will be successful I have no doubt – good luck to you.

Myself, I continue my work in a faded, disintegrating, war-minded, uneasy, evacuee-haunted Oxford that likes me not. Everyone is younger & far more hysterical. Youthful dons & adult male undergraduates are as rare as butterflies in March. The halt the lame & the blind are left to us. However, I'm enjoying Greats very much – my strengthening mind takes fearlessly to its wings now & learns to scorn the dull earth. (Too much German philosophy, that's what it is.) Ancient history too – not so ancient either if one approaches it rightly – Athenian imperialism in the ascendant – long long talks in the *Agora*[23] – strange new philosophies in Ionia – insolent Athenian penteconters ranging the Aegean,[24] where now the Royal Hellenic Navy (underfeared since the battle of Salamis) chases the miscreant Italians (*non sunt quales errant*[25]) off the sea.

---

[22] Alcibiades (c.450-404BC) Athenian statesman, orator, general, and pupil of Socrates; George Grote (1794-1871) author of *History of Greece.*

[23] The open 'place of assembly' and/or marketplace in ancient Greek city-states.

[24] Event described in Thucydides's *History of the Peloponnesian War.*

[25] The Latin, which has a mistake: – 'errant' should be 'erant' – means 'they are not as they were' and is a pluralising of the first half of Horace's '*non sum qualis eram bonae sub regno Cynarae*', *Odes* 4.1.3, used as a title by Ernest Dowson.

But indeed I don't spend all my time battening on this manna – (though, fainthearted, I sometime wish I could.) You may be amused to hear that I am chairman of the OULC. *Fuit Ilium.*[26] How has our glory departed when such as I have greatness thrust upon them.

England now (you wish you were home?) though by no means in all respects a pleasant land, is certainly a very interesting one. I wouldn't like to have missed this last year in England – It's certainly possible, as you may imagine, to feel very melancholy at the things that are happening. I've seen a lot – in London, Liverpool, Bristol – that has made me very bitter & unhappy at the time & afterwards. I've also seen a lot that surprised & encouraged me. The people of England (who according to Chesterton have not spoken yet[27]) are not such a bad crew. It's platitudinous now to say they're brave – but they have other qualities too. They could build something very fine if they set their minds to it.

I get moods when I want to rush out of Oxford, much as I love the place, & never look back. Oxford is a gentle civilised city full of elderly German Jews with faun-eyes & Central European scholars with long hair & longer sentences. But I am homesick for a world more bitter & beautiful & human than Oxford could ever be. Well, I shall hardly avoid the bitterness, whatever happens. Most times though I'm glad enough to take my fair hour – I may be filling shells soon enough anyway – & I may find later on that fighting for a good cause is a full time job. Heigh ho. Heydiddle-diddle the cat & the fiddle.

I met Alastine the other day. She told me you were in Cyprus. Aphrodite's Island. I'm sure it abounds in ripe berries – but do

---

[26] Virgil: *Aeneid*, 2.325: There once was a Troy; Troy was, but is no more.
[27] G.K.Chesterton's poem 'The Secret People'.

the flowers grow there as fair as they do in England? I feel faintly nostalgic now & then about my first year in Oxford. The people are mostly vanished that could remind me of it – but seeing Aly reminded me very vividly. (And apropos of Aly, are you actually married to her or not? If so, my congratulations. Don't take offence at the question.) I remembered all the people I knew then – Lucy, Freeling, Carol, (who has just got engaged, by the way) John Willett, you (how I loved you & hated you) Tony & Lionel & Graham.[28] Now, alas, everything seems infinitely less exciting, less beautiful – less painful & alarming also. There are fewer interesting personalities, fewer good conversations, fewer significant friendships. Or is it just that I'm not such a bloody romantic fool as I used to be?

I oughtn't really to be complaining though, for I have been & am very lucky in my friends – both men & women, they have paid me with a loyalty & tenderness which I never earned. Individually the human race is pretty good.

As you will see from the top of this letter, I am in exile by the waters of Babylon. My father was moved here at the beginning of the war & now I am trying to get used to calling this godforsaken place 'home'. It is a dumb treeless town with no music in it. In the season of course it's gay & coloured & positively abandoned & I do like it really. Also, on clear days we can see the Pennines out of one window & the mountains of the Lake District out of another – not bad for Londoners who are used to having their horizon a hundred yards away above a block of flats. On a sunny March morning it's as good being alive here as the next place – winds blow the seagulls inland – the wasteground is covered with yellow coltsfoot – my father is planting potatoes in the garden.

---

[28] Possibly Lionel Munby and Graham Hill from the OULC; Tony unidentified.

('Hurray for the Murdochs. They are digging for victory.') I never write anything these days – I paint a lot instead, & am evolving a style which I hope does not owe too much to Paul Nash[29] – grey stony inorganic. How are your two books progressing? What do you write – what do you read – on your desert island of the spirit? What parts of an Oxford education are any use to you in the sandy lands of the south? What does it all mean now, our earnest striving for intellectual integrity, our attempts at emotional sincerity?

I suspect that you suffer moments of hell which all your cynicism cannot save you from – and I'm sorry. I am wary though of offering sympathy, remembering the rap across the knuckles I got last time I did so. (Let me disarm you by admitting I was a fool in those days.) Anyway it could be very ill-informed sympathy at best, as I have only the tenor of your last letter to go on.

I wonder if this letter will reach you. Curious to think that many months from now a dirty looking envelope will arrive on your breakfast table bearing the faint reflection of what I was thinking one sunny March afternoon, sitting by the window & watching the starlings eating up our onion seeds.

I have not forgotten that things have been happening in Egypt since last I wrote. Were you in them? What did you do & suffer in the Famous Victory?[30] I'm afraid I imagine you more in the company of phoenixes & ibises than machine guns & light tanks.

---

[29] Paul Nash (1889-1946), then employed as a war artist.

[30] Operation Compass: the Italian Tenth Army was no more. British and Commonwealth forces advanced 800 km in ten weeks, capturing 130,000 Libyan and Italian POW's including 22 Generals, 400 tanks and 1,290 artillery pieces. See *Life Magazine* 10 Feb. 1941: 'Mussolini Takes a Bad Licking in Africa.'

Write to me again, when you have the time & the inclination. Goodbye, phoenix. I wish you most sincerely happiness & serenity of mind.

Love.   *Iris.*

9 Waller Avenue

Bispham

Blackpool

April 7th, 1942

Well David, how is it with you? Are you still spending your time teaching our beautiful language & less beautiful habits to the Damned of Cairo? – and struggling under enormous weights of cinema apparatus – and exploiting your personality for the benefit of incipient bureaucrats? Have the books been written? – or has the *Khamsin*[31] wind made your spirit too dry & dusty by now? It's very difficult to continue to believe in the existence of someone one hasn't seen for years – straining one's imagination on the strength of a few odd & notoriously fallible memories, with a letter written in 1940 bridging the gap. However, with an effort I can still believe there is such a person as David – though even when decorated with palm trees & pyramids the background is rather unconvincing. It's harder still to think of you as an independent three dimensional entity developing parallel to myself in time – and changed far more radically than I have in my 4 beautiful circumscribed & surprisingly happy years at Oxford.

What's Cairo like now? I suppose it's full of Magdalen & Balliol men. Ornaments to the landscape & consolations to your exiles no doubt. I heard from Hal Lidderdale[32] the other day that

---

[31] Dry, hot, dusty wind blowing in North Africa and Near East.

[32] Lidderdale, see Pt 2 n 11.

he had caught a glimpse of you. How do the happenings in Libya affect you – a sort of dusty ....or nearer than that? They haven't put you in uniform, I hope? I met John[33] in Oxford the other day; he'd had no news of you for a long time & we wondered how things were.

Next term is my last in the dreaming city – for which I'm both glad & sorry. I've loved doing Greats – it was worth it – and I feel some regret at having to leave philosophy just when I'm beginning to see what it's about. It has of course struck me from time to time that to worry seriously about conceptual frameworks & concrete universals while the Red Army is fighting for its life shews a certain lack of any sense of proportion. But at other times I dismiss this attitude as sentimental & emotional. One does the job that is set in front of one & if it's interesting *per se* so much the better. Also I have come to believe in the Oxford education myth – at least I have noticed the mists & fogs & Celtic twilights gradually clearing from my mind during these last years – I feel as if I were sharpening & polishing some intricate instrument. (for what?) Or maybe it's just that in my case there was far more rubbish to remove so that an approach to the norm constitutes a noticeable advance! (I think I believed in Absolute Beauty *inter alia* when you first met me? Ye Gods) Schools?[34] I'll get a second of some sort with luck (my philosophy tutor expects me to get a first but he suffers from delusions anyway) And thereafter? God knows. Powers at Somerville want me to try for a classical lectureship at some London college – but I doubt my ability & inclination for such a job. More likely possibilities are ATS, nursing, civil service… Whatever happens it's an invigorating thought that in 6 months from now someone will be employing me to do

---

[33] John Willett, see pt 2 n 15.

[34] Referring to her final examination, in which she won a First.

something – & even paying me for it – I only hope I put up a decent show for them, whoever they are. I do feel a certain invincibility at present – intensely alive, physically & intellectually – ready to learn anything, do anything. (Sorry, if that sounds like an ATS advertisement.) Probably all illusory anyway – simply the result of youth & spring winds & 4 years of the humanities. A few months at some tedious & exhausting job may knock all such notions out of me. At least it will be interesting to see what happens. And meanwhile where are <u>your</u> native wits taking you?

Oxford these days? More & more barren of interesting people & more & more infested by the very young doing dismal one year courses. About the only person left I really enjoy talking to is my philosophy tutor, Donald MacKinnon, whom you probably wouldn't remember – a religious cove – but a very fine philosopher & a most exceptional person in every way. (This sounds bloody superior I know. I wonder is there a point after which one gives up trying to imagine one doesn't like being labelled a Deracinate Intellectual, & ceases to pretend that one hankers after having an Ordinary Citizen, and is not ashamed of the satisfaction one gets from surrendering oneself to damnation with the rest of one's class? Complicated. But that's how it is.) I imagine that from where you are it's pretty obvious what's silly & what isn't in our scheme of things here. What sort of philosophy of life does one evolve on the fringe of the desert – pretty negative? Maybe it's a superfluous luxury anywhere. I wish I knew.

Lately various problems have become clear to me – I don't mean the answers – that's too much to expect at 22 (probably at 40 one realises there aren't any answers) – but just the problems themselves. This illumination has occurred subsequent on a change in my outlook in the course of which I jettisoned many minor dogmatisms. My view of life is much less Absolute than it was. I hold onto the main sheet anchor of course – there's nothing else – but I feel entirely different about the whole thing

– (Having reached a state to which I trust you had attached long before I first met you!) For better or worse – more detached, more cynical, less fanatical – & I think more able to understand & more eager to forgive. A pity maybe. It's dogmatists who make the world go round (But do they ever write good novels?) On the other hand, my lot is cast in the midst of obscurantist & idealistic liberals – & it's as well to be able to appreciate what goes on inside their heads – which I can do now & certainly couldn't before. The trouble of course is that if one lacks a one hundred percent creed one is left at the mercy of the random promptings of 'conscience' – or whatever name one gives to that aura of sensitive self-accusing muddleheadedness which still lingers round us – hence these problems. I suppose worrying about one's 'integrity' etc etc especially at a time like this is just so much self pity – & persuading oneself that one is successfully walking a knife edge between blind dogmatism and cynical detachment is the worst form of spiritual pride. *Eh bien* – at the moment of action OK – we are all dogmatists – & meanwhile I have time to sit & think, lucky me, while chaps like you are working like hell. And trite sentiments occur to me, such as that the most important thing in this interim is to learn to understand human beings – to endeavour to get inside every sort of mind, to give free rein to natural impulses of love & sympathy – for one day I shall be an exile too in some sandy place where there is no earth. I suffer from an intense desire to write a novel & objectify certain of the things I have been realising lately about people & the puzzles that beset them – but after schools I daresay even if I have any spare time, which I doubt, the impulse will have departed.

About Alastine. I'm very sorry David. I hope very much you aren't feeling too upset & fed up with life. Don't. I know it must be entirely bloody to depend on people & things in England when you're so hopelessly shut off from them. Buy maybe by now you've built up a satisfactory existence out there. I hope so – and I'm sorry.

Other friends I have little news of. John [Willett] is a Lieutenant in the Intelligence, as I expect you know, & is moderately bored with life (Address HQ 56 Div. Home Forces in case you think of writing) Carol has married this Harrison cove – a civil servant – I've got no line on him but suspect nobody is half good enough for Carol. Lucy has vanished – & most of our other old friends seem to have done likewise – tho' I see some of them infrequently for wistful & embarrassed half hours when they pass through Oxford. Sometimes I feel lonely, like something left on the shore by the receding tide. But I soon snap out of that – for really I'm considerably less isolated than most of you. Oxford is still habitable, & though letters & hasty meetings are no substitute for an easy, unanxious & uninterrupted comradeship, yet I have managed to keep in touch with many of my friends.

I suppose I ought to comment on the political situation. But nothing rises spontaneously, I confess & since I have ceased to be a bureaucrat (I was chairman of our club last Trinity term[35] Ha Ha) I no longer feel it a duty to fill my letters with political wisecracks. Anyway, by the time this reaches you Christ how different the set up will be.

Incidentally the comic address you see above denotes our place of exile for the duration. Maybe I told you in some previous letter written many years ago – I forget if it was before or after you last wrote to me. This is a vile redbrick wilderness – but there are exuberant people to be seen in the summer, & there's nothing wrong with the sea & the sky!

Also incidentally, a pleasant chap in case you ever run into

---

[35] Our club = Oxford University Labour Club (OULC); Trinity = Summer term.

him in Cairo is one Frank Thompson, Lieutenant, GHP Liaison squad (Edward Thompson's son) he's young & maybe too 'simple and warmhearted' for your taste, I don't know – but I think perhaps you'd like him.

I hope very much that all's well with you – that you're happy, if that word still has a meaning, that life doesn't seem too dry & devoid of purpose – that there are human beings about you. If you're feeling low, then take this letter as a vote of confidence, however inadequate. If you're not, then that's fine. It may be foolish – & it's certainly difficult – to try to keep alive at this distance of space & time a friendship which was difficult & unequal at the best of times. But I can't help remembering you & wishing you well.

Don't feel any obligation to reply unless & until you want to. A Kantian would hold that letters written from Respect for the Law have greater moral worth than those written merely from love of one's friends. But being no Kantian I'm only interested in letters written from the latter motive. And anyway, you never had any respect for the law.

Good luck to you, David.

love Iris.

5 Seaforth Place
Buckingham Gate
London SW1
January 20th, 1943

Dear David,
About Ali – she's married to this Lehmann[36] alright (as you have

---

[36] Alastine Bell married George Lehmann on 31 January 1942. Lehmann b.1922, read Modern Languages at Queens College, by 1943 in the Army; much later at the University of Buckingham.

no doubt by now discovered from Hal Lidderdale or some other chap who's penetrated your backwoods.) What's Lehmann like? Well, the chief thing about him is that he hasn't grown up yet (age about 21, I think.) He's rather beautiful – slim & redhaired & so on – and when he loses the boyish look he'll be pretty devastating. Highly intelligent. Has the right views on most things. (Read Modern Languages. Is now in Army.) My chief objection to him is his immaturity & a certain insensitive conceit which accompanies it. He tends to bounce – (He was incidentally chairman of our club when I was secretary, so I know him pretty well) – but all this will doubtless mend in time. Feel homicidal? I'm sorry. Yes, really I'm sorry – it's hard to know what to say on this subject. I hope you're not still feeling like suicide. <u>Please</u> don't. I daresay though that you give yourself plenty of good advice on this point, – about forgetting & and so on – & don't take it, so any admonitions must look pretty silly. Oh hell. This is just a sympathetic murmur.

I was amused by your letter too. It had that tinge of lively churlishness which I always associate with you. Some people don't get their personality across at all in letters – but your letters all have a strongly Davidish aroma – which is very nice for them as cares for it. Yes, I suppose your view of things in Cairo is just as distorted & partial as ours in London – though your rumours are probably more interesting & better authenticated. Cairo must be a pretty rum joint by now; there must be almost as many Oxford men as Egyptians. God help Egypt.

Talking of Oxford men, I don't think I have any news of people for you. Most of our friends seem to be out your way rather than mine. I lost touch with John Willett some time ago – I have a vague feeling he's in India, but that may be quite wrong. Henry Collins is rumoured to be in West Africa. Suzannah is (I think) still in Oxford, & not yet married to Akky.[37] Stuart Schultz & Maureen are also in Oxford. (Stuart's working in an Abingdon factory.) In fact, no sensations of any kind.

You ask about general affairs here. Little to tell again. Mass meetings in Trafalgar Square periodically demand a Second Front in Europe – less frequently though since the North African offensive opened. Just now there is a dangerous tendency to think that the end is in sight. There is much armchair admiration of the Russians. There is also the Beveridge plan.[38] I have just been reading that great document & am much impressed by it as a large scale constructive suggestion – putting it into practice is of course another matter. But the fight to prevent its being filtered away to nothing by a long series of reactionary hairsplitting sub-committees will be an instructive fight which it will be well worth putting up. If the British people can be made to understand this not impossibly complicated scheme & have the spirit to do something about it, they may get somewhere someday. If not, then it'll be just too bad. How does Beveridge look (if at all,) & how is he being presented, out your way? Organised collective hallucination? Maybe. But it looks the right way. The first thing of course is to win the bloody awful war. (I have just turned on the news & heard that the Russians have recaptured Millerovo.[39] Gaudeamus & 3 loud cheers for the Russians.)

I took Schools in June & started work in July in H.M. Treasury, as an 'Assistant Principal' – ie a very junior administrative officer. All day long now I administrate. That is, I sit at a desk 8 feet square amid heaps of blue files tied up with tape, with a loquacious telephone at my side, & I devise new Regulations

---

[37] See footnote 1.

[38] William Beveridge's November 1942 'Social Insurance and Allied Services' report was to form the basis of the post-war Welfare State.

[39] 'Millerovo's capture was one of the major tests of whether Russia's southern offensive could break through to Rostov, linchpin of the whole German southern front': *Time Magazine* 25 Jan 1943.

(many of them involving forms with names like 1437/63538 90m (14) etc) and amend old Regulations and think out lines of policy & answer tedious & silly letters & adjudicate on tiresome Borderline Cases & all the rest of it. It's a rather comic job. It's in the Establishment Division of the Treasury – ie that section which supervises the rest of the Civil Service & sets down what civil servants may or may not do in all the conceivable situations of life (eg what happens when a Temporary Clerk grade III in the Exchequer & Audit dept. has an illegitimate child??) Much of it is tedious & requires no intelligence – only a capacity for Dealing with Papers. (I haven't got that) – but some of it is very interesting & instructive. I never before conceived of Administration as a real activity in which a definable class of people are engaged. Now I appreciate that administrators exist & that there are good & bad ones. I am a bad one at present – but I can recognise a good one when I meet him & am filled with feelings of honourable emulation. (The principal for whom I work is first rate, which duly inspires me.) I am not so bad at Framing Policy, & I can even make a shot at Devising Regulations – but I am quite hopeless at the Day to Day Working of the Machine. I have a natural tendency to concentrate for days on X to the complete exclusion of Y & Z which are probably twice as vital. Urgent letters sojourn neglected at the bottom of my tray, & the notes of important telephone calls which I write on the back of OHMS envelopes get lost somehow. I get a kick out of it all though – it's a damned interesting side-light on how our great country is run – & the people are decent & endowed with senses of humour.

I am living by myself in a somewhat crazy flat, whose address you see above, being a long & erratic studio on top of an empty warehouse down a rather dark alleyway. It's near enough to Whitehall for me to hear Big Ben. Life on the whole is rich – & I suppose I'm fairly happy, in so far as one can be happy in a rather bloody world. There are too many things and people – a good fault maybe if one can stand the pace. I am learning Russian (a strange & beautiful tongue) & polishing up my German. I am reading a good deal – poetry, politics, theology – & writing just a little (& to little purpose.) I am getting to know new varieties of human animals. I have, for instance, made the acquaintance of part of what is left of London's Bohemia, & feel pretty much at home with the odd creatures. They attract me because, in one sense of the misused word, they are a Free People – though they pay a greater price for their freedom in terms of personal irresponsibility than I could ever pay. They are incorrigible time wasters & live thoroughly unorganised existences – but they are warm & spontaneous. (I need that) and though there is a distinctly dangerous aspect to their friendship, there is also a liberating aspect.

This is beginning to sound like what you would call the 'phonus-bolonus' (a phrase I dislike). O.K. I'm sorry by the way you take unkindly to the 'attitude stuff'. You are of course quite right in a way. My approach is unduly theoretical & I have a curious moralising tendency (of the *video* & *probo* rather than the *sequor* variety,[40] of course.) But I can't help that in the main. My mind is made that way & my life hitherto has not been a particularly hard & practical one. You say 'start in on things.' Unfortunately, brother, it's not so easy. I am not a simple minded person like yourself who thinks that a girl's troubles are over once she's left her maidenhood behind. My troubles are only just getting going. I have, I should add incidentally, abandoned what you call my 'quaint virginity cult' some time ago, & haven't regretted it for one second. There are however remarkably few men who have ever stirred me to any sort of passion. You, for reasons which I can't conceive of, were one of the few – and could be again

---

[40] Latin: video, probo...sequor = 'I see and approve rather than I follow'.

perhaps given the correct context. A wind that bloweth where it listeth etc.[41] (not but what, if you got over your tendency to sneer at people & hurt them unnecessarily, you wouldn't be quite a nice bloke.)

This long-distance acquaintanceship is very tiresome; it means in effect that subtle changes & adjustments in a friendship which would occur in 2 or 3 days of normal conversation take about 2 or 3 years to happen, & may be misleading & unnatural at that. (Don't be so self conscious about it, my girl! OK OK)

It's damned hard, David, to write you a spontaneous letter really containing <u>me</u> (Oh what a treat) when I know it's going to take x months to reach you & so on & so on. One feels that some sort of summing up is required – & human lives are essentially not to be summed up, but to be known, as they are lived, in many curious partial & inarticulate ways.

Look after yourself, *mon vieux* – & please don't break your heart about Alastine.

Love
Iris

5 Seaforth Place
Buckingham Gate
London SW1
January 17th, 1944

Dear David – hello.

I'm sorry to hear you are marooned in Teheran with the black tragic Persian women; I can't imagine Teheran anymore than I can Cairo, so it's not much different from my end. I hope though that you're not getting to despise life too heartily. At any rate

---

[41] *John* 3:8, referring to a wind that blows where it wishes.

there were people in Cairo – more people, I sometimes think, than there are left here. London is a bit like Plataea after the young men had all gone to help the Athenians[42] – only the adolescents & the middle-aged remain!

I am very glad to hear you may be coming on leave! It will be good, though of course alarming, to meet you again! As you say, our friendship (if that is the word) is a queer business. Disasters I've met with lately make me mistrust relationships which go on from writing to meeting; but, after all, you always were a casual cynical chap, & I'm getting that way, so we shan't expect anything particular or get any shocks (I hope). Your memory is accurate. We met remarkably little. I suppose I have a myth-making mind – I certainly created a character for you; which was probably all wrong then, so God knows about it now. I should be happy to start again from scratch!

One thing I liked about you was your straight male humanness underneath your horridness (pardon this obscurity.) That I've missed among these Plataeans. Or maybe it's just that, being older, I now see through people more quickly. Oxford began well, but toward the end, what with the war & my 4 years, I found I was so much stronger than most of the men & women about me that it took the pleasant sense of effort & newness out of life. And since then too much of my time has been spent succouring the weak & not enough in battling with the strong! I've had a number of affaires which have I suppose been good for me in some negative way, without any of them being particularly remarkable either for delight or pain. That is except the latest one. I am rather badly in love at present with someone who is quite the wrong person – ie I can't quite bring myself to marry him, & there are various reasons against a

---

[42] The battle of Plateia happened in 479BC.

long affaire.[43] Ergo, a painful break. It's bitter that when at last I find I want something I have at once to cast it away. I tell myself this too is probably 'good for me'. Toughens the sinews, & so on. Jesus!

All this while the Russians etc. My contact with the war seems limited to buying the evening paper, noting how many miles the Red Army has advanced, & offering up prayers of gratitude. I dislike this solipsistic isolation & the self pity it breeds. I observe the same distress in many civilians over here – that (ie a healthy guilt complex) or else, amazingly & more commonly, sheer apathy. We are at an extraordinary moment in time – any number of interesting & alarming things may happen in Europe in the next few years – but the folks here are so sheerly incurious; they will hardly speculate, let alone study the thing. Uneasy University chaps (like me) are hellish interested, but more than a little bewildered – so we read Aragon[44] & try to dream some wholesome dream about Europe! Or else curse the government for being nasty to Beveridge – or oneself for being unable to rise to History's great occasions. Still, History (that blessed abstract) may give us some chances yet. The people of Europe will probably forgive us for not having suffered – if we can forgive ourselves sufficiently to get down to the job. But this 'we' is a wretched little group. One has yet to see what the real British – the 8th Army I suppose it comes to – will be up to. I wonder how it all looks from your side? I suppose one goes on thinking in

---

[43] IM probably refers to her 'affaire' with economist Thomas (Tommy) Balogh – see letter dated 11 November 1945 and *Life* ch.7.

[44] Louis Aragon's *Creve-Coeur* ['Heart-break'] was an iconic text enjoying cult-success, banned in the UK probably because it addressed Dunkirk, but smuggled in from France, acclaimed by Connolly and Charles Morgan for its poetry and patriotism alike. FT to IM 14 Aug 43 'Michael [Foot] has sent me Creve-Coeur... Aragon has scored several bulls'. See D. Johnson on J. Bennett's *Aragon, Londres et la France libre* in TLS 10/12/99.

terms of Europe wherever one is.

My private post war plans are in a state of flux. I feel I am not at all built to be a civil servant. I am inefficient, & administration depresses me. I shall not really be sorry to part company with H.M. Treasury. I'd much like in a way to escape from this half-baked intellectualism into UNRRA's Europe[45] & do some thoroughly menial & absorbing job, tying labels round necks of refugees & so on (chancing being knifed in the back by some intelligent patriot). Then come back to England at the age of 29 or so – to what? To drift – to play the experienced woman round what's left of Bloomsbury – to visit my old friends & bring teddy bears to their children – to become a literary camp follower, a rather less than demi-intellectual. This business of not being a specialist begins to worry me. It's all very well if one has (as you for instance obviously have) a gift for affaires, a grasp of practical life. I haven't that. My only guiding star is a commonplace literary ambition – & that hasn't delivered any goods as yet. I suppose I'm feeling my age (24 by God!) and panicking! Also looking the matrimonial hippogriff[46] in the face recently has shaken me up. Sometimes I'm much tempted to make a bolt for the academic *feste Burg*[47] but it mightn't be too easy to get back in. All this is pure funk, & an object lesson in how not to deal with the 20th century. You're probably dealing with it much better. One needs the casual approach, dash & so on; not this protective deliberation.

---

[45] IM worked for the United Nations Rehabilitation & Relief Association [UNRRA] in London and abroad, for the two years from June 1944 until the end of June 1946. In 1947 UNRRA ceased its existence, to be succeeded by the Office of the present UN High Commissioner for Refugees.

[46] Hippogriff: legendary animal, part horse, part griffin: hence any 'impossible thing'.

[47] Alluding to the hymn made out of Psalm 46 ascribed to Martin Luther: '*a Mighty Fortress* is our God', familiar from Bach's musical setting.

I hope you aren't still feeling sad about Alastine. What's got into one that sort of way takes some eradicating. I can understand Ali's gloom too – an absentee husband, probably in for a war with the Japs, isn't a perfect asset. Everyone's lives are being mucked up – any sort of venturing seems to end in that.

I was interested in your words about our friends in Cairo. Hal Lidderdale I hear from quite frequently; he manages to retain his charming & somewhat dilettante soul under conditions of the most frightful boredom & sandiness. Of Henry Fowler I have no news (indeed the only thing I ever knew about him is that you wept when he went away to the West Indies! Accurately remembered I hope.) If you run into a man called Frank Thompson (probably in your part of the world on & off) I hope you'll like him. One goes on believing in friendship.

This is a somewhat depressed & selfish letter. But one always survives – & though there may be bombs I give up expecting angels through the roof. I feel, even at the lowest moments, such endless vitality inside me.

Best wishes to you, David. Don't utterly hate & lose faith in the human race. I much look forward to seeing you. When are you coming?

love from   *Iris*

> 5 Seaforth Place
> Buckingham Gate
> London SW1
> May 20th, 1944

David, I was very sad to hear that you were not coming home. I suppose I wanted to see you rather a lot. Maybe it's just as well though. We might have detested each other or we might have become entangled in some unhappy way or we might have been just bored & anyhow things might have been difficult – whereas now, without friendship in the icebox, we can go on in an Old

Man Riverish way for years, until we are both become silver-haired & tolerant & the heyday in the blood is tame.[48] Nevertheless I am very sorry you aren't coming back & I hope your chiefs may relent & let you come after all.

It's hard in letters quite to hit the mean between being earnest & sounding damn silly & being smart & sounding rather slick. I notice that I tend to the former, you the latter extreme. Not that it matters actually, since I suppose one persists in considering the other person as something quite separate from his letters. One is in such a desert in these personal matters – & a glimmer of human feeling from someone whose personality attracts or excites in some way becomes so important. It's being lonely – oh God, how quite terribly & intolerably lonely in spite of the thousand & one jolly acquaintances – that makes for this eagle eyed searching for a different sort of relationship & having something of warmth & sincerity as well as something of life or originality. And this blind holding onto it when it seems to have turned up among all the bloody blanks one has drawn. Heigh ho. Or Selah, as Dornford Yates[49] would say.

I am afraid I am not yet really eligible for inclusion among the harlots of history. I still take my love very seriously & let it tear my guts out every time – & although at the moment I am actually running two affaires concurrently that doesn't signify as only one is *pour plaisir*, the other being completely from a sense of duty only.[50] Also I am very inept and keep involving myself in

---

[48] *Hamlet* III iv: the 'bedroom scene' in which Hamlet commends chastity in middle-life to his mother Gertrude.

[49] 'Selah': Hebrew for 'amen': Yates (1885-1960), remembered today for his Chandos novels from 1927, thrillers set in Central Europe.

[50] Her lovers at this time probably included the French diplomat Olivier Wormser [see KUAS6/2/42 et seq] and John Fulton at the Coal Board and later UNRRA [KUAS6/3/46].

excruciatingly embarrassing situations. But I do take it all heavily & seriously & feel that there is no depth of pain & humiliation to which I cannot descend where such matters are concerned. The emotional tangle which I have just lately got into with somebody makes it all the more essential to get out of England after the war.[51] This plan however will prove difficult of execution – for even if I could wangle a job in UNRRA, for instance there would be no guarantee of escape, since the European H.Q. will almost certainly stay in London. The thought of spending the post war years here appals me to the point of suicidal mania.

I liked your remarks about Carol. But one needs to be happily married really before one can let one's liberal education spread wide about one, as it should, until one is, in a Henry Jamesish way, just 'so wonderfully' living. Fine. My bloody education is just a piece of grit that won't either disappear or produce a pearl. Go back to the academic world? No – not in this period of unrest & not without having wandered first. Any way, the only subject I'd wish to have truck with at a university is philosophy, & the number of jobs in that line is pretty limited. I'd like to see Carol again & see how she looks as a wife & a mother, but I feel a sort of paralysis about it. I did try, over a year ago, to meet her, but there was some organisational hitch & we didn't manage it. Somehow I can't bring myself to try again; the awful doubt I suppose about whether other people are really interested. Not that Carol is likely to think anything in particular either way; we knew each other so little. I have a very dashing & pleasant mental picture of C. & I shall leave it at that.

I do notice a difference incidentally between her generation & mine (university generations I mean.) The women who are now nearer 30 than 20 strike me as having much more of the

---

[51] Most probably Balogh – see n 43 – and Foot; see letter dated 11 November 1944.

jungle animal than my own contemporaries & successors. (*Bien entendu*[52] that I speak only of the 'intellectuals') Maybe it's just the war, & having a sense of responsibility (of a sort) forced on one at an early age & not having enough decent men around to develop the fighting instincts. Or is it that one becomes more of a cat in the course of time? I think I am growing long sharp claws in self defence which I never had before.

I'm glad you still write. That is about the only sort of 'truth', I imagine, that 'makes free' chaps like you & me. (Apart from this personal truth between people that it's so hard to hit on.) The sense of occasionally creating something puts away for the moment the feeling that one's wings are quite hopelessly caught in the net. Maybe you don't have it though. I expect you can put so much of your multiple personality into your job that you don't feel perpetually frustrated to danger point. Is everything as various as ever? And how <u>do</u> you take your relations with men & women now. Do they seem to you significant or is it all a tinkling cymbal?[53] It's unfortunate how one does (or I do anyhow) depend so much on meeting the right people. It does seriously interfere with the business of being captain of one's soul. As for writing, I have written one novel which is extremely bad & ought to be torn up & am writing another which is less bad but much harder to write since none of the characters is altogether me whereas in the other they all were. Poetry I write all the time & very indifferently in the latest smart & incomprehensible idiom.

Talking of poetry it's sad about our old friend Sidney Keyes.[54]

---

[52] 'Take it as understood that'.

[53] 1 *Corinthians* 13.1 'Though I speak with the tongues of men and of angels, and have not charity, I am become as sounding brass, or a tinkling cymbal'.

[54] The poet Sidney Keyes, b.1922, at Queens College Oxford from 1940-42 when he published his first book of poems, was killed in Tunisia on 19 April 1943.

There is a bad tendency here though to refer to him as 'the Rupert Brooke of this war' which is undesirable & inaccurate (unless is meant more precisely what is said than, I'm sure, is intended). I don't like Keyes' stuff very much, or Alun Lewis's either. But let us indeed praise the soldier poet. He is probably much better for being a soldier than many Bloomsbury poets I know are for spending all their evenings in bars. Did you ever meet Terence Tiller[55] when you were in Cairo? I like his rich & heavily imaged stuff.

Here in the political world things are a bit more lively since the political truce has (virtually) come unstuck. Everyone is very muddled, but there is a certain amount of enthusiasm going round & an ill-informed faith in the Power of the People over Parliament. The air is better to breath [*sic*] now & everyone is getting interested in home issues again. But oh alas the muddle thereof – & the usual lack of unity & intelligent leadership on the Left. Lone wolves (black sheep like Shinwell & Bevan[56] do much of the talking – but they are a bit disreputable – so what? The usual impasse.

June 7th

I didn't finish the above, for some reason. I think I was feeling very depressed. I have been suffering many extremities for love & finding life too involved & wearisome & much. Since then various things have happened, but notably the happenings of yesterday.[57] The excitement here over the invasion is quiet but pretty

---

[55] 1916-87, poet and Fitzrovian, later in the BBC.

[56] Mannie Shinwell (1884-1986), was chairman of the Labour Party from 1942. Aneurin (Nye) Bevan (1881-1951) one of the main leaders of the left in the Commons, opposed the wartime Coalition government.

[57] 130,000 Allied troops landed in Normandy on June 6, D-day, with many more following later.

intense. The hysterical voices of the BBC 'men on the spot' obviously 'come over' in a way nothing else quite has in this war so far. People are really moved. It would be odd if they weren't of course – but it's not just 'come on, our side!', or I don't think so – it's something of 'we're setting them free' too. (Accurate I hope.) I feel tremendously moved myself by it all. A sensation of wanting to cry & cheer at the same time that I can't remember having before except at certain moments in the Spanish War. Mass hysteria? A bit of that. But by Christ! It's good to see the bloody English people getting really thrilled about something. (The thrill will wear off pretty quick I daresay & one will become conscious that chaps are being massacred. That hasn't quite penetrated yet.) Not that they're so bloody at that. There was a cheer for Tito[58] the other day in a cinema that thoroughly heartened me!

Another thing which has happened is that I have got a job in UNRRA. I start there next Monday. I'm very glad to leave the arid though intellectual portals of the Treasury, & of all the shows open to me at present UNRRA is the one I most wanted to get into. I don't expect great things though I'm on the wrong R__. Rehabilitation, which will I'm sure turn out a dead end – who's going to listen to UNRRA on rehabilitation? – & which will mean my staying in London. I wanted to be on relief, which will be a lives issue & might mean going abroad. As to the question of escape though, I do not give up hope. The number of people I know in influential positions who are devoted to my cause has increased in the last year & I shall see what disgraceful string pulling can do. All that much later though. Today the struggle.[59]

---

[58] Marshall Josip Tito 1892-1980, leader of the Yugoslav Partisans (anti-fascist resistance movement); later, and until his death, of the Socialist Federal Republic of Yugoslavia.

[59] The phrase 'Today the struggle' recurs in W.H. Auden's 1937 poem 'Spain'(later excluded from the canon).

Oh Christ I wish this bloody business were over. One feels such guilt all the time being safe out of it. How has it all affected you? Any moves in your regions? Any prospects of return to Europe or even to England?

I find I haven't many 2 ½ stamps left in my book. The post offices are shut, & if I keep this letter till tomorrow heaven knows what will happen to it. In my present frame of mind I shall probably send it away to the Admiralty at Bath or the Ministry of Agriculture & Fisheries at Lytham St Annes. I will write again in a few weeks & send some more stamps.

Let me have instant news of you. I am truly sorry you are not coming back. I was relying on your help to solve some of my problems! Well, I shall have to solve them myself, which will be much better for my character.

My love to you

Iris

I hope this route of yours via the FO will work now. I'll try it anyway.

5 Seaforth Place
Buckingham Gate
London SW1
(Sunday) September 4th, 1944

David my dear, your letter, thanks. But oh Lord what a picture of deserts & bad Persians & awful Englishmen. It hurts that one can't <u>really</u> imagine the cockroaches or the heat or the fever. I can a little imagine the hatred. I was moved – but it remains all too vague this picture of you & of Teheran. Or else a little too mythological, with Black Girls & Leopards & so on. And your voice, still sounding familiar, in the background. I hope you haven't been ill again. And have your chiefs turned decent & is life reasonably calm & sane? The main thing obviously is that you must come home pretty soon – but you've thought of that your-self. God! How one gets to loathe these distances & irrevocable partings & keepings apart & all this business of not being one's own master. Not that it'll be all that much better in peacetime – but as it is, it does give one the feeling that one's life is being lived unnaturally – eg away from the people one would most like to talk to & the places one would most like to see etc (All of which is a bit phoney, as I can't imagine what would correspond to the concept of 'natural' here. Being appallingly rich & immoral, I suppose.)

You ask about UNRRA. UNRRA, to be brief, is a pretty unstable show at the moment It's rather too full of inept Brit-ish civil servants (whom their departments could well spare; me for instance), uncoordinated foreigners with Special Ideas & an imperfect command of English and go-getting Americans & Canadians. The result is pretty fair chaos. There are a few able people here & there & very many noble-hearted good intentioned people – but they drown in the general flood of medi-ocrity & muddle. Yet maybe I paint too black a picture. The ma-chinery for repatriating 'displaced persons' (the one job UNRRA certainly will have to do) is being planned with a fair amount of sense & energy – & if we do the right thing by these 8,000,000 we shan't have lived altogether in vain. My own part in this great show is small. A sort of jungle life prevails at my level (survival of the fittest etc) & I have to spend much of my energy preventing myself being (quite genuinely mistaken for a clerk or girl mes-senger by new comers from Washington. The nervous strain is pretty considerable; I'm certainly not enough of a go-getter for that sort of existence. Prospects of going abroad are nil at the moment. (I nearly got a job the other day on a 'flying squad' in connection with repatriation, but was rejected because I can't ride a motor bicycle! What a useless character I am.) Altogether gloom & obscurity prevails about the future. I might try to get some academic job – but that mightn't be too easy & anyway would I make the grade? Heigh ho. I suppose the trouble is I have a little too good an opinion of my intellect – thus I easily get fed up with mediocre jobs, & imagine I'm being victimised while all the time (maybe) I'm just not rising to occasions. A problem. Well, I shall learn. I still cherish the illusion that I can write, though that too is getting a little battered by the waves of time. *Eh bien.*[60] Meanwhile, most of the people at UNRRA are perfectly charming (especially the Czechs – I like next best the French, Dutch, Belgians, Poles, British, Americans & Canadians in that order!) and so one is not perpetually in a state of (righteous/unrighteous) indignation. (It's revolting to observe the extent to which a little social success relieves & rehabilitates one's vanity.)

On other fronts change goes forward at its usually breakneck speed. Shortly after I wrote to you last I tore myself away, with agonies which I could not even have conceived of a year ago, from the utterly adorable but wicked Hungarian with whom I'd been living. Now that I'm no longer bleeding at every artery I see this was a very good move. At present I'm having a rather decorous affaire with a French diplomat, which is at any rate good for my French.[61] Nothing very world- or soul-shaking. I must say, though, I am rather in love with France. *La lointaine princesse*[62] maybe. (London shewed considerable restrained enthusiasm about the liberation of Paris, & one sees a suitable number of tricolours about.) My own passion grows & grows. A large percentage of sheer romanticism of course. Yet too the feeling that if France lives Europe will live – meaning that

---

[60] Ah well.

[61] See note 50.

[62] The distant 'princess' or, as in romance, object of desire.

there will be something left not Russianised or Americanised. Meaning too that France is likely to be a decent progressive force & will be useful to have around. And oh, all the rest – French people, French films, French songs, Baudelaire and Mauriac & the dangerous intellects of the Church & Giraudoux & Aragon & Jeanne d'Arc[63] and what have you. (I got very vividly your picture of the French women who wished they hadn't married Persians.)

Incidentally, I have just sent off to you (by ordinary book post, since I feared printed matter mightn't go via the FO. Give me you views on that) a copy of Aragon's poems (Le Creve Coeur and Les Yeux d'Elsa.)[64] Maybe you already have them though? (I'm still hazy about degrees of civilisation.) I don't know why I chose that out of the infinite books I might have sent – it was the only one which seemed definitely right. It's pretty rotten of me, now I come to consider the matter, not to have sent you some books before. Is there anything particular you'd like me to send? Please say – or else give a general preference (eg poetry preferable to philosophy) (This sounds business like) and I'll try to overcome my normal inability to send off parcels.

I hope the Cyprus novel has gone well. I agree, one can't really talk in units of less than 10,000 words. (And can one even talk then?) Carry on. I hope you haven't had any more breakdowns, nervous or otherwise. How nice it would be to be Catholic & to be able to light candles for people & feel it was some use. (Today Sunday & the angelus from Westminster Cathedral, which is 200 yards from here, has just ceased ringing.) Anyhow, keep well, my

---

[63] Charles Baudelaire (nineteenth-century poet), Francois Mauriac (prize-winning Catholic author), Jean Giraudoux (playwright), Joan of Arc (fifteenth-century French nationalist heroine).

[64] For Aragon, see n 44.

dear, & get that home leave. Let me know about books. I hope I'll remember to put some stamps in.

Much love to you, David   Iris

5 Seaforth Place
Buckingham Gate
London SW1
October 4th, 1944

My ill-informed attempt to send you books, *mon cher*, has been defeated by guardians of the regulations who have sent the Aragon back to me with instructions in officialese to the effect that I must have a PERMIT. This I will start seeking after when I get home (I am on leave in Blackpool at this very moment actually) – I believe it can be got without undue difficulty via booksellers. So continue to let me know about what you want. Something of a *creve coeur* though it was to get the damn thing straight back after having with such *éclat* sent it off![65]

Yes, I am on leave – a miserable week – I mean miserably short. Gales & rain keep one in the house, & there I read & write & reflect & feel not altogether hopeless – which is a lot to say considering how much time I now have for thinking. By the way, any tendency to involution which you may be noticing in my style (a greater degree of it than usual that is) is mainly due to excessive reading of Henry James. Tell me, are you an addict of that incomparable man? I have just finished *The Wings of the Dove*,[66] which just broke my heart, as most of his novels do.

---

[65] Implying how 'heart-breaking' to have the book returned after the 'flush of success' entailed in posting it.

[66] James's 1902 novel concerns a plot by two penniless outsiders to arrange a marriage to a rich but ailing American 'princess' and then enjoy her wealth after her death.paragraph] in Russian

I suppose I take them too seriously & always manage to identify myself in the first volume with the rather splendid but definitely unsound character whom the author slowly & ruthlessly
crushes in the second volume. Such a style though, such splen-
dour – such <u>style</u>! Words fail me. And more than almost anyone
he makes me want to write.

Sorry about this outbreak. A momentary intoxication. Let
me make a request now I've kept forgetting about. Will you send
me an up to date photograph of yourself? I find I've entirely
forgotten what you look like. And I hate not to know what my
friends look like. I hope you won't need to wrestle with permits.
Better still, of course, come home – but if that's not to be in the
immediate future, send the photo instead.

The war looks good for another six months worse luck (though
who knows?) Still no one will send me to Paris. I'm lighting candles for your health & happiness.

Love to you, old dear,   *I.*

5 Seaforth Place
Buckingham Gate
London SW1
December 12th, 1944

Dear David, a long time ago, as I may or may not have mentioned,
I sent you off some Eliot & some Aragon, by ordinary book post.
Anyhow that was a long time ago. If those chaps are to be seen
on every bookstall in Teheran, my apologies. I cannot stop imagining your city as consisting of three mud huts & a bazaar.

Since then, I have a feeling, all sorts of things have happened. I
heard the news of the death of my old friend Frank Thompson,[67]
– you may have met him in Cairo, I forget. He used to be at New

---

[67] FT was shot around June 7th. This news only reached home in October.

College. He was a brilliant & full blooded creature, one of the best I ever knew. I suppose only now I'm beginning to realise the war isn't just a short interval after which one resumes – something. There's nothing to resume. Oh it was all very golden & beautiful & pure hearted, all that time – but now one is quite different & wants different things. A very obvious conclusion, but I hadn't up to now felt it so violently, that severance from the golden lads & lasses period. What the present period should be called, I really don't know. What does it consist of? Oh whirls of charming people, & much hard work directed to no very clear end (& which anyway will probably all have to be scrapped when we finally clear up our relations with the military!), and loads of Henry James & Kierkegaard, and lots of French things – French books and French conversations & Frenchmen. At last there's a reasonable flow of news from Paris, & one begins to feel that that's a city, after all, in the same universe as one's own, & which one might even conceivably visit. One's friends go off there for a week & come back. A few books come across. All that's very refreshing & exciting.

The main thing in one's mind, I suppose though, is Greece, & all the thoughts & feelings it inspires, & which I leave to your imagination. At least it wakes one up – & a few other people here & there are waking up.[68] One sniffs the post-war political atmosphere. If only one could feel any confidence in the Labour party!

This isn't a letter, it's just a note, & I refuse to commit myself to another page. Considering the quantities of stamps I've sent

---

[68] Greece was liberated in October 1944. On 3 December during a demonstration in Athens fighting broke out, with more than 28 killed and 148 injured. Thus began a 37-day period of full-scale fighting in Athens between pro-Communist ELAS and the forces of the British Army and the Government – start of the bitter, second Greek Civil War, which continued until 1946.

you, I think I'm getting a pretty poor return. Write, you cad. Any news of that leave of yours?

I met Henry Collins the other day, by the way (found myself sitting next to him in the theatre at a performance of Somerset Maugham's 'Circle' which is a surprisingly Oscar Wildish little piece) & many curious memories were stirred up. Henry was as stout & as gorgeously Jewish as ever; I was glad to see him. He's still non-commissioned in the RASC[69] or some dismal corps. He was with one Edie of Ruskin; I forbore to ask news of Joan. My chief feeling, I regret to say, was one of relief (or something like it) to find how far I'd come since the days when I was tongue-tied & unsure of myself & frightened of everyone especially Henry. (And here I am, well onto the next page, which just shews you.)

I heard recently too that Noel Eldridge[70] had been killed in Italy. I felt very sad about that. Noel was one of those 'hopeless' characters that contrive to be terribly lovable. Oh well, what's the use of funeral speeches – one wants to praise people when there's no longer any point in it. A sort of conscience money perhaps.

This letter might be to anybody, & not specially to you, which is a pity but it's largely your fault. *N'importe.*[71] Send me a photograph of yourself. And write, old dear, about the wicked Persians & your black girl & the loathsomeness of officialdom & what you yourself are thinking & doing in the midst. I hope you are well & not miserably prostrated with real or imagined illnesses. Somehow or other, I thirst for news.

My love to you.
Iris.

---

[69] Royal Army Service Corps.

[70] See Pt 3 n 33. Eldridge was killed by a sniper somewhere along the Bologna-Rimini road, with the Queen's Royal Regiment in September 1944.

[71] Doesn't matter.

5 Seaforth Place
Buckingham Gate
London SW1
February 10th, 1945

Dear David,

May I complain, mildly, about your silence. I hope you're not ill, or plunged in melancholy. I daresay you aren't. Anyway, suppose you write & tell me so. Spring's coming again, thank God, to this bloody island. I've never wanted it so much. We had a real winter, with snow & cold, & that absolute failure of the imagination to conceive of ever being warm & human again. However, we had a soft time on the whole. We had fires. My colleagues in Paris reported much greater misery. SHAEF[72] was warm, but no one else had any fuel. Anyhow, thank God for the sun again & blue skies & air one can breathe with pleasure instead of inhaling in agony.

At the office I make plans & unmake them again with great efficiency. Nothing practical is ever decided. If I could think of anywhere to go to I'd resign. The military want us as their stooges & we obligingly sign contracts blindfold. We're a washout in the Balkans & most of our job on displaced persons will probably be done toughly & quickly by SHAEF rather than sissily & slowly by us. I feel sick & degraded & incompetent. Possibilities of going to Germany or France still very vaguely exist. I'd welcome any move for base reasons of variety – but doubt much if I've really any job to do anywhere. No University posts seem to be going at the moment, at least none that I can lay my hands on. So I sit & swear at the universe.

The war looks like ending after all. It will be good to stop

---

[72] SHAEF, pronounced 'shafe' was the Supreme Headquarters Allied Expeditionary Force, HQ of the Commander of Allied forces in north west Europe, from late 1943 until the end of World War II with General Dwight D. Eisenhower in command.

thinking that one's friends are in danger. Noel Eldridge, as you may have heard, was killed in Italy lately. I forget if I told you too that Frank Thompson (<u>did</u> you meet him in Cairo?) had been killed in Bulgaria. A partisan show. He was one of the best men I ever knew.

Meanwhile I continue to learn Russian (at leisure) & German (intensively) & to read much philosophy, and kid myself I'm a philosopher, & much poetry, & kid myself I'm a writer. I finished my second novel in July, & tried it on Fabers in the late autumn, who wouldn't have it. I so hate the sight of it, I haven't the heart to try any other publisher. I'm in the middle of another novel by now, but it's bad. It's all 'automatic writing' – I'm not really forcing & tearing the stuff out of myself, just skimming oddments on the surface. Lord, how one's life is tied up in silly vanities & paltry ambitions. I spend so much time cutting a figure to myself & so little time being myself.

I had a dream about you & Carol the other night, in which I felt very childish & frightened. It's odd how one's mind behaves. You must have met me at an 'impressionable age'. Last week I met Lucy Klatschko in Charing Cross Road. She seemed dejected, is working in some government department. I shall see her again soon. Thus, and thus, one grows old.

Write to me, David. I don't know why, but I find your voice soothing, even when you're cursing the universe too.

Au revoir. Love Iris

> 5 Seaforth Place
> Buckingham Gate
> London SW1
> March 8th, 1945

Hello to you.
Your admirably variegated letter arrived last week & illuminated

one of the darker patches of the 'flu that I have had all this winter without much interruption. Am back at the office now, & well immersed in the familiar atmosphere (which is enough to make anyone ill) of inactivity & gossip & intrigue for better jobs. While you seem to attract tasks & responsibilities from every side, work just flies from me as from the plague – never yet have I managed to land myself a real <u>job</u>. My own incompetence & dreamy unpracticalness may have something to do with it. I begin more & more to be nauseated at the business of 'making a career'; not highmindedness I daresay – just inability to cope.

I was amused by your picture of me – it's not a bad likeness. My hair is rather longer now, though, & worn in a bun, or knot (*simplex munditiis* etc[73]), which creates, or so I hope, an effect slightly less arty & juvenile. I remember your looks quite vividly in an impressionistic sort of way. And talking of looks, a tall fairhaired Miss Stewart who attends some of our committees haunted me with a likeness, until I realised that, obviously, she was Carol's elder sister. She's handsome, liker Michael actually, than Carol but lacks Carol's pleasant voice. She tells me C. is having (or has had, I forget) another child, that Michael, after being drummed out of Lisbon for some diplomatic *faux pas* of a minor technical kind, is happily installed in Rome, & that David has been invalided out of the Army (fevers & stomach troubles, I gather, not wounds) & is at home in a rather nervous state. That was sad – I liked much what I saw of David[74] in the old days.

Your stuff about penetrating with mules through snow-beleaguered passes & coming down through jungles to the Caspian Sea is very picturesque & impressive. I looked at the map & learned some basic geography. I've been wondering, do you meet many

---

[73] Simple or plain of appearance.
[74] Neither 'Michael' nor 'David' identified.

Russians in your day to day business? It's so long since the papers have mentioned the matter, I've quite forgotten the political subtleties of that area. Be careful though – I'm thinking of rock faces, hard as iron, without any holds this time, not of Russians. Don't fall, or if you must, see you break your neck quickly & cleanly. No, I don't think taking risks is one of the things that make life worth living! – not that kind of risk anyhow. I admit, I always feel compelled to dive off the highest board in a swimming pool, although I hate high diving – but I regard that as a sort of neurotic urge which has nothing to do with joyfulness & youth. Creating things, on the other hand, obviously <u>is</u> one of the things etc. That, and having real friends. Of the latter, I find I have increasingly fewer – or perhaps the criteria change. There are lots of people I like & like being with – but mighty few, for whom I feel a real *tendresse*, whose company makes me feel more alive & more myself. (So many of one's dear friends are folk with whom one can just wear a more than usually pleasing mask & get-up.) You've always had a fairly electrical effect. God! how one dies to life [*sic*], when there's so much to live for & to be amazed at! Anyhow, enjoy your mountain – & if your compulsion neurosis drives you to the top, don't let it push you over the edge.

Dostoevski is very hard to get, even in 'civilisation', & I'm afraid 'the Brothers Karamazov' is out of print at present. However I'm sending you my copy & will get another copy for myself when it comes into print again. 'Sons & Lovers' (a book I particularly disliked, I forget why) is also out of print, & I haven't one of my own – if I see a copy around I'll get it for you, but doubt if I'll be lucky. Must reread the Brothers K. soon. I reread 'The Possessed' a few months ago & decided it really was the greatest novel in the world. I'd put it above any other Dostoevski (as I now remember them), above 'War & Peace', – & the rest are nowhere of course. It positively batters its way through one's spirit & creates copernican revolution in one's thought. The first time I read it I was distracted by involuntary feelings that Stavrogin 'ought' to have married Lisaveta, and that it was 'a pity' he married the mad woman, etc etc – but now I find I can more nearly accept the puzzling dreadful enormity of the thing. One has to go down into the pit with the man – it's no use standing on the brink & peering. If ever I taught ethics to students I'd make them read that sort of thing – not Sir David bloody Ross on 'What constitutes a promise?'[75] When one starts comparing novels though one gets soon in a tangle because types differ so – & how could one say that anything was 'better' than 'Ulysses', the 'Recherche', 'The Golden Bowl'?[76]

Have also been reading your old pal Rilke lately, in honour of my slightly refurbished German (I do German, by the way, in UNRRA's time at UNRRA's classes – this eases the organisation problem) – the Elegies & the Sonnets – with helpful translations on the opposite page – & feel suitably excited & bewildered & 'melted'. (I can't think of a good word for that liquefaction of the inner organs which fine poetry produces –) And Valery,[77] whose later stuff (I can make little of 'La Jeune Parque') is so crystalline & perfect. Someone told me the other day that, outside of France, Valery is most understood & appreciated at Persian universities! I can think of no plausible explanation for this probably incorrect statement! (Not that England would compete. His poems have never once, so far as I know, been published over here.) I hope the 'Creve Coeur' arrived & that you like it.

One day soon I must give up reading books – I read too many. And do what? Write them instead? God forfend. Go on the

---

[75] David Ross (1877-1971) philosopher, see p 99 n 9.

[76] By, respectively, James Joyce, Marcel Proust, Henry James.

[77] Rainer Maria Rilke (1875-1926) among the greatest of German-language poets; Paul Valery (1871-1945) the influence of whose poem 'La Cimetiere Marin' is clear in a number of IM's novels.

booze. Or lie under a tree & watch clouds or be someone's efficient private secretary. Or peel potatoes at a British Restaurant in a Garden Suburb or something. Life is feverish with too much ill-controlled thought & feeling.

I am leading a comparatively sober & celibate existence at present. I don't seem able to take affaires gently & light-heartedly & haven't the nerve just now to take them otherwise. The most loved of my Frenchmen have gone back to France. The men I know best here seem mainly to be middle-aged clever Jewish ones, usually married, whose company I enjoy. (I find my proSemitism becoming more & more fanatical with the years.) I spend many evenings at home, & long lonely weekends too when I walk up & down my long & spacious attic & brew tea at hourly intervals & write & read poetry & stand at the window watching the trains go by, & then go & walk round St James's Park & come home for more tea. All this is good, & I feel more life in me after every hour of being alone. Sometimes though I feel desperate again for human intimacy & a man & the insanities of being in love. Especially when I've just been to a French film! (I come more & more to the conclusion that the French are the real Master Race.)

Am looking again at your description of your day's work, written after 2 beers 2 vodkas ¼ bottle wine. Not quite what I imagined – but I forget what I did imagine – something more commercial & less cultural I daresay. I take exception to the allowance of 2 hours to billiards, that seems excessive. Otherwise it all looks charming. Some other time I will describe to you the slightly irritated dream in which I spend my days at present. (Was interrupted at this point by an argument with an anti-Yalta Pole[78]– very

---

[78] Despite the fact that in September 1939 the UK and France went to war 'to defend Poland', the conference between Stalin, Roosevelt and Churchill in Yalta in Feb 1945 awarded Poland to the sphere of influence of the USSR. As it turned out, for the next 43 years. No doubt IM's sympathy for the USSR overrode other considerations.

disturbing – I feel sorry for these people but still can't help losing my temper. He obviously thinks it impertinent of me to have any views on the subject at all.)

One last item of news (I may have told you), our old pal Denis Healey is Labour Candidate for Otley & Pudsey (some division near Bradford). I've had no news of John Willett. *Au revoir, mon cher*. Be careful on those bloody mountains. The sour & caustic element you provide is rather necessary to me.

Love to you, David.

I.

> 5 Seaforth Place
> Buckingham Gate
> London SW1
> May 13th, 1945

Hello.

It is extremely hot & I am sobering down after the uneasy excesses of VE.[79] We did all the right things in London, such as dancing in Piccadilly at 2 am. Now I suppose one will cool down, think about poor old Europe, & wonder if our rulers have learnt a great deal from all this. Yet to hell with such gloomy reasonings! Thank God part of the damned war is over. I did thank God very earnestly in the RC Cathedral on Tuesday where the emotion was as thick as incense & the Cardinal (or is he a Cardinal) made a dreadful speech which was happily soon drowned in the Hallelujah Chorus. After that I went & got drunk, which was good too.

I hope you reached the Caspian alright with your mule & got back again safely & met many charming Russians on the road.

---

[79] VE = Victory in Europe Day, Tuesday 8 May 1945.

When are you coming home on leave? Do these extraordinary events make any immediate difference to your life?

Sometime or other you will receive the Brothers Karamazov which I at last managed to get sent off. When I next remember & am in Charing Cross Road I will send you some French books. I am getting some fascinating stuff over from France at the moment. As a result of late repercussions from Kierkegaard & Kafka[80] the French novelist seems to be in a dilemma, wondering whether to write a philosophical essay or a novel. Some, like Albert Camus, write first the one & then the other. Maybe the French have been that way for some time (Gide... Mauriac...) but the malady is certainly intensified now. Poets too are getting philosophical about the nature of language. The Silence of Rimbaud is becoming a great subject for metaphysical speculation. Out of this hurly burly a lot of exciting & maybe good literature seems to be getting written. I'm quite intoxicated by all this. The intellectual fumes are strangely mixed, very strong, overpowering.

I saw Hal Lidderdale, home on leave, a few weeks ago. I like Hal a lot. (He looks much less like Chatterton[81] than when last I saw him) I like his warmth & humaness, his lazy pleasure in life's good things, & his lack of petty vanities & meannesses [*sic*]. A good chap. He's now in Germany. He's had a fairly peaceful time throughout the war, & didn't in the last phase, discover any Germans who wanted to fight.

Now I am going out into St James's Park to look at the tufted ducks.

Au revoir.

Love, I.

---

[80] Soren Kierkegaard (1813-55) Danish proto-existentialist theologian; Franz Kafka (1883-1924) great German-speaking writer of Czech-Jewish descent.

[81] Thomas Chatterton (1752-70) – brilliant poet, and forger, who failed to make a living, starved himself to send expensive presents to his family, and died by his own hand at seventeen. Famously painted by Henry Wallis.

5 Seaforth Place
Buckingham Gate
London SW1
June 1st, 1945

David dear, your fine epic <u>did</u> arrive, a few days after I sent off my last letter. Maybe it was too heavy, & that delayed it. Heavy or not, I consumed it with joy. I envy you these flirtations with a Nature wilder than anything I've ever seen. I've never met with this Monk Lewis sort of Nature.[82] Sorry about the snow – however you were both so thoroughly British & determined about it.

Czechoslovakia? Good god. What shuttling to & fro you chaps seem to do. I can't think at the moment whether I'm glad or not. Of course I'm <u>very</u> glad you're getting out of the backwoods – you were due for that anyway. But I wish you were coming a bit nearer home than Czecho. I feel an occasional dash to Prague will probably be beyond my income. I hope you'll be coming to England en route? Well, yes, I think I <u>am</u> glad. I like to think of you in Prague. There seems an obscure suitability about it. Maybe that's because of a dim prewar memory of your telling me how you stood with some Czech on some balcony looking down on the fair city with him saying sadly 'für Hitler's Bomben' – or did I dream that? It must have got shelled, I suppose, at the end – perhaps it's not too bad. Baroque, baroque – what else? Not much else I can connect with the picture of Prague. Nevermind. Maybe you'll be in Bratislava after all. Know any Czech?

Yes, I liked your epic: pondering now over the preludi-

---

[82] 'Monk' Lewis was the nickname of Matthew Lewis (1775-1818) because of the success of his Gothic novel *The Monk* (1796).

um. I was amused by your stuff about our Master Raceness. I
suppose you get stuck right up against this problem. For me, I just
don't see it at all. I suppose simply because of staying put here in
England & not ever having to think about putting anything
across. I feel <u>now</u> that I'm not of any particular country. There's
Ireland, there's England – but if I have a fatherland, it would be
something like the literature of England perhaps – & so, one es-
capes from Chauvinism. Or does one? Yes, I know I will change
some of this after I have lived outside England for a while. Even
a few months in UNRRA have shewn me that universal brother-
hood is not a condition that comes naturally to people. (Canadians. Grrr!) I wonder will you hate Prague too? I can't believe
that. But oh Teheran – I shudder in sympathy. Come out of it,
David, soon.

Peace, & all that. They have brought back about 50 pictures to the National Gallery.[83] Oh heavenly bliss! Sir Kenneth
Clark's favourites, I suppose. Well, they're alright. The Van
Eyck man & pregnant wife. Bellini & Mantegna Agonies. Tit-
ian Noli me Tangere. Ruben's Bacchus & Ariadne. El Greco
Agony, Rembrandt portraits of self & of an old lady. His small
Woman Bathing (lovely!) A delicious Claude fading into blue
blue blue – blue lake, mountains, sky. Incredible distances to
breathe. Two Vermeers, so blue & lemon, honey stuff, girls at
the Virginals. And then oh more Bellini & Rubens, & then the
Ruisdaels [sic] the Hobbemas, & chaps like Cuyp that one had
forgotten about. I still feel delirious with the first shock. It felt
<u>really</u> like peace. And all the people wandering round looked
dazed.

The UNRRA wheels are really turning at last & I have far,

---

[83] These paintings arrived back from the disused slate mine in North Wales where they
had been moved for safe-keeping during the bombing of London.

far too much to do. I'm liking it though. Just now & then one can, for a moment, grasp the whole tiresome chain of causes & effects & realise that what one does in one's office has some remote connection with someone or other over there being fed, clothed, calmed, who wouldn't otherwise be. Outside office hours, this damned election is taking my time. I spent last weekend sitting on an interviewing board to look at chaps who had the effrontery to offer themselves as possible Labour candidates in Westminster. They were uniformly frightful (ignorant, opinionated, careerist, insensitive....) – well, I suppose we shall have to choose one of them. Alas for England. (Never mind, he won't get in.) Heigh ho, Russian exam on July 2nd General Election on July 5th, & UN-RRA Council opens in London on July 12. In June, however, I'm going to Scotland & will stay at the gayest hotel in Edinburgh. In August maybe, Ireland... island of spells, provincial pigsty. ('Little brittle magic nation dim of mind.' Joyce, of course.)

The other day I came up the steps on one side at St James's Park station, & up the other side, meeting at the top, came Denis Healey. He was with Edna Edmonds. Remember those characters? D. is Labour Candidate for Pudsey, his home region. He looked bronzed & sleek & tough & handsome & very pleased with himself. I was glad to see him.

Am just reading Koestler's 'The Yogi & the Commissar' (shall I send you this, or can you get it out there?) Why am I convinced K. is Satan? He's so well aware of so much that no one else notices or can comment on. He sees what are the real moral problems of now. He's a better moralist than Sir David bloody Ross[84] & all the Oxford & Cambridge chaps rolled together. Well, just for those reasons. He makes the Left self conscious

---

[84] See n 74.

– good – but he administers no corrective, no antidote... It's the same old dreary cynical undertone. There's No Solution – let's just be conscious of the problems – fine subtle intellectual chaps seeing the problems & understanding our neuroses. He quotes Pascal 'Man is neither an angel nor a brute – but in trying to be an angel he becomes a brute.' We'll never find Koestler trying to be an angel. Oh what tangles, what circles... Seductive whirlpools. The best moralists are the most satanic.[85]

Evening. I must do other things. How fantastic, that business of the avalanche. How fantastic to think of you back in Europe. Give me news of that soon. If I think of it when I'm shutting up the envelope I'll put some stamps in. Whistle if you want that Koestler. It will annoy you. There's a lot of potboiling stuff in it too – written for Yankee magazines. God! And any other books you want. I'll raid Charing Cross Road for you soon.

Au revoir cheri. I.

5 Seaforth Place
Buckingham Gate
London SW1
June 20th, 1945

My dear, you are perfectly maddening. You mention on page, let me see, 3 of your letter, apropos of sending books, that they are not likely to arrive before 'your departure'. Departing when, where to? Not Cairo, I assume, since you are wanting to move things there – & hardly Prague, since they wouldn't be likely to send you there direct. It looks therefore as if you are coming to England. A matter not without interest. Can I have some more

---

[85] Koestler had importuned her roughly at a party – see *Life* p169.

details immediately? Thank you.

I'm glad you heard from John W. I was wondering how he had been getting along & whether he was alright. What is he going to do in Wien? Yes, you're both right about the international intellectual contact stuff. God, how one thirsts, after getting it for so many years just strained through the columns of 'Horizon'.[86] Or not even that. After this, I want silence, time to wonder, to think & to feel, to look at different cities & speak different tongues, & become wonderfully anonymous & lonely. Yet to meet people too – new people, free people – above all French people! How far, I wonder, will one be able to – with no money, & with a nagging useless irresolute sort of conscience?

Your question about our bothering to contest Westminster shews how little you realise how things have changed in England. A labour candidate might just stand a chance against the Tory here if the Left was united. (We are hoping that the Communist will withdraw. He certainly would not get in.) After all – Covent Garden, Millbank, Soho – it's not a hopeless constituency; – & even Marsham Court is not as solid Tory as it used to be. Yes, sniffing the air, & taking the informed opinions, I begin to feel it conceivable that Labour might win this Election. The Tories are being foolish enough to let loose Beaverbrook & his filthy Press to go as far as they want to & pour out the ancient ancient stuff.

Your Persian paradise sounds beautiful & makes me all the more eager to part company, for a while anyway, with Tottenham Court Road & Victoria Street. On Saturday, actually, I am going to Scotland. That will be good – the hills & then Edinburgh.

I must stop now – no time even to dispute your attribute to [Henry] James of 'dry colourless sentences' – how unjust! Write,

---

86 *Horizon*, influential review of Literature and Art founded by Cyril Connolly in 1940.

old dear, & tell me what your movements will be.

Love to you. I

5 Seaforth Place
Buckingham Gate
London SW1
July 6th, 1945

OFFICE 'PHONE

MUSEUM 6898

David darling, this in great haste. Some good/bad news. In about 10 days I am going to Brussels. At least, that is the plan at the moment, though it may be changed. It seems, and oh how bitter & unlucky, that I shall just miss you. How long I shall be away, I don't know – several months anyhow. I am to work on a 'welfare' supply programme for displaced persons, & I may make occasional dashes into Germany, & may be back to London as well, in which case I might glimpse you. If you should happen to get onto the continent, I could be located at the UN-RRA office in Brussels, or through the Palace Hotel, Place Rogier. However, I will give you details of all such in due course. Meanwhile, please let me know your moves. My departure may be delayed for quite a long time. I don't want to miss you.

Love to you. I

5 Seaforth Place
Buckingham Gate
London SW1
July 21st, 1945

My dear, as you see I am still *in situ* – & likely to remain so for quite a time, as things look at present. I may even still be here on September 1st. But God Knows. Hell blast this damned Administration, nothing ever remains the same for two days together. There is now a plot that I should go to Frankfurt. In

■ 231 ■

any case, my departure to anywhere looks like being indefinitely delayed. The nervous strain is frightful. I always guessed that international organisations needed employees with iron nerves. At least at Geneva one could go swimming or drown oneself in the lake or go & contemplate the Dents du Midi & feel that it would all be the same in a thousand years. Not that this is an international organisation actually. Your picture of mouselets on office stools is quite wrong. You have no <u>idea</u> how we live. We are not run by quiet bowler hats from Ealing & Dagenham, who at least behave approximately like gentlemen, but by the citizens of Milwaukee & Cincinnati & New Haven, Conn., let loose in their myriads to deal a death blow to tottering Europe. They do not sit on office stools but lounge, with cellulose belts & nylon braces, behind enormous desks, & chew gum & call their fellow citizens by their christian names. Oh God. However, I must admit (& this spoils my race theory) that I have got quite fond of a number of these *Herrenvolk*[87] – these are mainly disgruntled intellectuals from Cornell, Ithaca, who have found in UNRRA the means of having a long holiday from the Ithacans: Odyssey in reverse.

Oh David I feel so tired & angry these days. I wish you were coming home earlier than September blast you. As for seeing you I feel quite confident that I shall manage that, once you're in Europe, even if it means hitchhiking 500 miles in jeeps or unofficially chartering a Lancaster. I have some leave left which I could take in England <u>if</u> by any chance I am gone before you arrive.

We shall all freeze next winter in our respective capital cities. But I shall see you before then. I will write again soon when I am

---

[87] Members of the master-race.

feeling a little less enraged. My rude beloved David with nine leaves in your hair, *my love to you.*   I.

5 Seaforth Place
Buckingham Gate
London SW1
July 27th, 1945

Oh wonderful people of Britain! After all the ballyhoo & the eyewash, they've had the guts to vote against Winston! I feel really proud of them, & ashamed at not having believed in them. I thought they would be fooled. But they have sense, they can think! I feel proud to be British. This <u>is</u> the beginning of the new world.

My own affairs are damnably delayed & god knows when I shall get away. It looks as if I shall be going, for a while at any rate, to Frankfurt. Dismal but educative.

Oh David, what a time this is! I know they will make endless mistakes & it will be bloody hard. All the same I can't help feeling that to be young is very heaven!

Much love   I.

5 Seaforth Place
Buckingham Gate
London SW1
August 3rd, 1945

OFFICE 'PHONE
MUSEUM 6898

David old dear, still no definite news of my movements. It seems possible now that I may still be here on September 1st – I hope so. However, if you get a chance of getting away a little earlier please take it. It would be maddening to miss you by a week or two.

Note my office phone number above. Seaforth has no phone.

My local tube station is St James's Park. Seaforth Place is a narrow alleyway running off Buckingham Gate at the confluence of B. Gate and Caxton Street. Mon dieu, perhaps I am really going to see you again. It seems quite incredible. Dear David, <u>hurry</u> back – come as <u>soon</u> as you can.

   I will write again if any more news turns up.
      Love to you. I.

                                             5 Seaforth Place
                                             Buckingham Gate
OFFICE 'PHONE   London SW1
MUSEUM 6898   August 11th, 1945
Dear David, Thank God the Jap war is over, or looks like being. London is going mad about it anyway, & the great game is to shower torn paper out of windows, in imitation of New York. Meanwhile, the Red Army, I notice, is getting on with the job – which will probably be helpful to the Reds in China.

   But now my own affairs, in the midst of this general relief: I am told now I must get to Brussels as quickly as possible. It will take me a week, or a little more, to get uniform, & then I may have to wait a few days for transport. It certainly looks as if I will be gone before September 1st. There <u>may</u> be other unforseen [*sic*] delays, since this is UNRRA, but I can't count on them any more. So darling if you can possibly get home even a few days earlier, <u>please do</u>. Oh what desperately bad luck this is, after six years!

   I might be able to take some home leave during September or October, or official business might bring me home – but there's no certainty. My blithe remarks about jeeps & planes are probably pretty wide of the mark. God knows when Prague will be accessible. I suppose your chances of being able to come to Brussels en route are equally slender. Our stars are being just as contrary as they could be.

I want to see you very much – so hurry, David, if you can. Write anyway, whatever the news is.

If you do arrive in August, or indeed whenever you arrive, phone or call at once.

Much love. I

PS And give me your address in London.

5 Seaforth Place

Buckingham Gate

London SW1

August 17th, 1945

OFFICE 'PHONE

MUSEUM 6898

Well, the hanging around process seems to be proceeding satisfactorily so far. Even when I have £50 & 162 clothing coupons I find it very hard to buy the things I need in this city. Prospects of delay are fairly good. However, September 7th is still a long way off & my presence is being urgently requested in Brussels, so, please, the directive stands that you are to get away earlier if you possibly can.

Could you let me know your London address & 'phone number? Ring Museum 6898 on the off chance when you arrive, tho' I doubt if I shall be at the office. Call as soon as you can at Seaforth Place, & leave a note if I'm not in.

All for now. Write me any changes of timetable. I'll send another bulletin if there's anything to report. *Love to you, old darling.*

I.

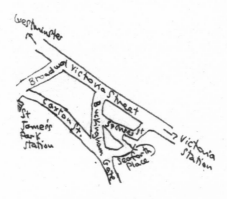

5 Seaforth Place
Buckingham Gate
London SW1
August 25th, 1945

David,

I am booked to go on September 1st. Transport complications and weather may delay me a day or two, but not more. It seems I shall miss you. This is just heartbreaking. I have lingered as long as possible – but an interview I had yesterday with my new chief, together with the precariousness of the whole situation, makes it necessary for me to get over as soon as possible if I'm to seize the job at all. I can't delay any longer. It's damnable. I'm sorry. Maybe I'll be able to get back sometime during September or October, though there's no knowing.

Maybe in a way it's better not to have a hurried meeting, crushed between your arrival & my departure. We'll meet again under better circumstances. I hope England doesn't disappoint you. Write me what you think about it, & about things generally. I can be reached at: UNRRA, c/o British Mission to Belgium, FPO, BAOR.

David, it's just hell missing you like this. All my blessings on you. *And much love.*

I.

UNRRA
c/o British Military
Mission to Belgium
FPO BAOR
Tuesday, September 4th, 1945

David, how bloody to miss you! I hope all's well & that you like being home. <u>Write</u> to me, please.

I can't judge yet what my chances are of getting back before you go again. Not much, I fear. Everything here at the office is topsy turvy. Brussels itself is quite crazy & utterly charming. I arrived just in time for the *Fête de la Liberation*! My only objection is, too many people speak English. More news of all this later.

Write to me, dear David. I wish I could fête your return in London.

Much love I.

UNRRA
c/o British Military
Mission to Belgium
FPO BAOR
September 16th, 1945

Today for the first time since I arrived here I have felt a sort of loosening of the knots, a sense of being myself again, & an interior eloquence which I always have when I'm really well! Wandering the city a few days ago I came on a highbrow bookshop, the very Zwemmers of Brussels, where to my delight the assistant adored all my favourite authors & was clearly expert on the genre of *roman existentialist*,[88] using the term with a casualness which shewed it must be already an accepted usage! We gossiped, & in his enthusiasm he lent me, since I couldn't afford to buy it, a recent effusion of this school, *Un Beau Tenebreux* by Julien Gracq – a remarkably thoughtful & well written book about a young man who, not content with a superb mastery of life, decides death must similarly be mastered & brought within the simple category of 'act,' & with long deliberate preliminaries, which have interesting repercussions on the people he happens to be with, commits

---

[88] Existentialist novel. The bookseller was almost certainly Ernest Collet (see *Life* ch 8)

suicide. It's interesting to see how we have come round again – on a 'higher' plane? certainly a <u>different</u> one – to that godlike approach to life, that fascination with death, that one connects with the early nineteenth century. Julien Sorel[89] etc. etc. This modern French school have a similar, though different, desire philosophically to <u>denude</u> life in their novels. One great difference perhaps is that the whole process is now much more self conscious. Most of these writers are very interested in language – they could easily become obsessed with the 'temptations' which hedge in the process of expressing thought, especially in such a perilous medium as the novel. They are acutely 'moral' in their attitude. The question of power over oneself, of selling one's soul, the endless traps whatever it is that the Church calls pride lays for the fine spirit which is not susceptible to grosser snares – all that excites them. In fact the Church is very much with them still – & in this they are, for me, so far more exciting than the English novelists. They have left Mauriac behind, or so they say – but it is still the same eternal Good & Evil which is in question.

You must excuse this impertinent reverie about authors which you probably haven't been lucky enough to get hold of yet. Much generalising from a little evidence, I fear. It's just that at the moment I'm absolutely feverish with the desire to talk to someone intelligent. Apart from 20 minutes chat with that bookshop man, I haven't had a real conversation since I came over – & just now I feel quite deliriously full of thoughts! That intellectual exaltation – how one feels sometimes that it will never come back again. Remember that poem of [Paul] Valery's – how he waits, calmly, for *cette pluie où on se jette à génoux.*[90] Conscious of being Valery, he

---

[89] Hero of Stendhal's novel *The Red and the Black* (1830).

[90] 'This rain in which one throws oneself to one's knees' i.e. in genuflexion.

could well be calm. And thou, o my phoenix. Time passes, & people fall behind or diverge far away. But I've always felt that you, to say the least of it, kept pace, & not too far distant. A rash thing to say perhaps. The sources of confusion & misunderstanding between people are so infinite. There are times though when in despair & loneliness & self hatred, finding oneself unable to achieve the things one constantly dreams of, one can only become real & stable again by thinking of those few others who are not too far from one's own path.

All this, in my old lofty vein, that you used to mock at! Quite rightly, of course. Mockery doesn't touch me now though, as it used to, – because I suppose one is so much more detached & alone now & has no more any 'social' worries about how one appears, & because anyway one has come to mock oneself much more savagely than any outsider could.

Well, now you are in London, enjoying the pains & pleasures of the returned exile. I wonder how it seems to you. Does your 'youth' come back, with a rush of emotion? Do you feel you must revisit people & places? Will you go & see Ali? Or can you play cool cynical & disillusioned? Maybe just being in England again is very good in a simple sort of way. I feel so bitter that I was not there when you came back.

I will do my best to get home again in October, but it may very well not be possible. I am not quite senior enough to be able to charter a 'plane & no questions asked! – & I am getting already horribly involved in the network of intrigues & manipulations which is European UNRRA. I'll try hard though. Tell me exactly when you expect to go to Prague & whether there's any prospect of your coming through Brussels (or Antwerp.)

Write to me now, David. I feel lonely. Let me hear your 'authentic accents' or I shall begin to think that after all you're just someone that I invented – a character out of one of my unsuccessful novels. Oh dangerous game. I feel a shocking *tendresse* about you this afternoon, I can't think why. Oh most improper! Altogether I feel thoroughly intoxicated with being alive & with thinking and with balancing on knife edges, and I do wish, dear David, that you were here & that we could talk and talk and talk.

love, I.

UNRRA
c/o British Military
Mission to Belgium
FPO BAOR
September 16th, 1945

PUT THIS FULL
ADDRESS ON ⟶
THE ENVELOPE

David, a letter from you at last thank heavens. I was beginning to think your 'plane had hit a mountain or something. Poor Muluk – I often think about her & wonder how it all seemed to her & reflect on how we are all born to sorrow. Poor child. I hope you were kind to her. I hope she will recover.

Since writing you will have received a short lecture from me on the Existentialist school of novelists. I have meanwhile decided that my comparison with the Julien Sorel[91] era was superficial. These French boys of today have a much deeper & more metaphysical sort of ague.[92] When I've read some more & know more what it's all about I'll send you over one or two. They aren't yet to be had in London, or weren't when I left.

Your London mood is much as I suspected it might be. I'm sorry about the lack of people, though. Have you not been to see Carol? And what news is there of John Willett? How do your parents seem after this long time? What are your sisters doing now? I'm not dreaming, am I, when I think that you have

---

[91] see n 89.

[92] A fever (such as from malaria) marked by paroxysms of chills, fever, or sweating.

sisters?[93] I vaguely recall meeting them on that Boxing Day in 1938 which now seems itself the essence of a dream.

I went to Antwerp on Saturday & watched ships by the docks & saw the Cathedral by moonlight & followed a brass band round the middle of the town about 11pm. and ended up in a café drinking cognac by myself. (I am still stunned with admiration of this wonderful continental habit of having no licensing hours.) Yesterday I went by car to Ostend with one of our people who was going on leave, and to seek for some lost luggage of mine (which I didn't find.) Ostend was more unlike Belfast & more charmingly like some Cornish fishing village than I had expected. The blue & red fishing boats are crowded in 'basins' right in the middle of the town & the quays are strewn with nets. On the way back I spent the afternoon in Bruges, which has a sort of picturesque concentrated Flemish beauty which is almost unbearable. What towers & pinnacles! My God, those people knew how to build. And Bruges is full of waterways, so that these wonderful creations are joined by mediaeval bridges, and reflected in still waters & troubled by swans until one just wants to cry & endure it no longer. I also saw the Memlings at Bruges, which are exquisite & beautifully housed. It was too late to linger in Ghent, & I just battered on the door of the cathedral which was closed, blast it, but is a most noble thing outside, one of the finest I've yet seen.

Now I was so glad to get away from London & from my myriad friends there & from the remains of old entanglements & bitternesses. I thought, how wonderful to be somewhere where no one knows me. Yet here already I stifle with loneliness & with wanting somebody to be intelligent & tender with me! It's no nostalgia

---

[93] DH had 2 sisters, one of whom, Barbara Robbins, in 1998 vividly recalled IM's visit on Boxing Day 1938, possibly the last time IM and DH met pre-war.

for my London friends, much as I adore them. But I wish you were here. Even writing to you is a relief from all sorts of things. Yes, one day soon I shall be able to tell you the Story of my Life, which will be even more of a relief. Not so eventful, but dismal & bitter the way lives tend to become. One wants to be pitied? One wants, more, to be judged. So all that is something you will have to put up with one day before long.

Breughel's 'Fall of Icarus' is in the gallery here – a picture I love. It's one of the most poetic of great pictures. I have bought a large reproduction for many hundred francs & hung it in my office where it distracts me from the horrors of UNRRA.

I haven't yet thought it diplomatic to broach the possibility of a trip to England. The prospects aren't too hopeful. But I'll keep watching & seize whatever chance may turn up. Meanwhile give me news of who you see & what you do. Goodbye for the moment, my dear. I'll write again soon.

All my love to you.

I.

GIVE THE WHOLE ADDRESS – C/O BRITISH MISSION ALONE ISN'T STRICTLY ENOUGH. $\longrightarrow$

UNRRA
c/o British Military
Mission to Belgium
FPO BAOR
October 4th, 1945

Dearest David, your letter written in the Flying Scotsman[94] is now with me. It's strange to think of you wondering round all my old haunts in London – and many other haunts, I daresay, that I never dreamed of. You are probably able to get infinitely more out of

---

[94] Express passenger service running between London and Edinburgh since 1862

the literary pub life than I ever got. I just ran away from it in the end. One of the many disadvantages of femininity, of course, is that it's more difficult to cope with that sort of society & appear neither a whore nor a bluestocking. Also, in the end, it seemed to me that the percentage of really intelligent conversation was rather small. Soho is so damnably full of people with some talent & sensibility, but not much solid ferro-concrete intelligence – and (blue stocking after all, perhaps) I find as I grow older that I do require from people, if I'm really to enjoy their company, plenty of the good old Oxford & Cambridge clearness of thought & expression. And oh the nauseating vanity of so many of those Bohemians! I liked a lot of them very well. Tambi, for instance, is a darling & has beautiful hair.[95] But relationships were always stormy. People turned out so often to be childish & malicious. Finally I decided I was wasting my time & ceased frequenting the pubs & started staying at home & reading or else chatting with colder more civilised sort of chaps & was much happier. But maybe I was just unlucky in the individuals I met, & as I say it's all more tricky for a woman. What a croaking raven I am, enough of this!

I shall be amused to hear news of Carol. Lucy Klatschko is working at the Ministry of Agriculture in Soho Square, under her own home, & would be delighted to see you. I met Lucy quite a lot in my later London period & found her as adorable as ever.

I mentioned the idea of leave in England to my chief, but find

[95] Meary James Thurairajah Tambimuttu (1915-1983) aka Tambi was a Tamil poet, editor and critic who arrived penniless in London from Ceylon in 1938, haunted the pubs and clubs of Fitzrovia and was befriended by T.S. Eliot. Tambi published the immensely influential bi-monthly *Poetry London* in which IM tried unsuccessfully to get a poem published (*Life*, ch 7).

that there is a rule that overseas staff cannot have leave within three months of their arrival overseas! My chief goes on leave himself for a fortnight from Saturday, & during his absence the likelihood of a duty visit is nil. After he comes back, maybe. Stars continue adverse, but I've not given up hope.

I'm amused to hear that your new boss is Edwin Muir.[96] I connect him, though not very clearly, with all sorts of things – literature, & some Polish friends of mine in London, & Kafka's mistress. I forget exactly what the latter story was – that the Muirs took her in after Kafka's death, or something. What would there be left to do in the world after having been Kafka's mistress?

Which reminds that I have discovered a wonderful novelist – more or less everything that the modern novelist should be, and a woman, bless her! Simone de Beauvoir, Jean Paul Sartre's mistress & full of his philosophy. However, I'll tell you no more about her now, as you must be fed up with these cries of enthusiasm about the French.

I can't think why BC[97] should send you to Scotland. A consolation prize, after Iran, or so that you could tell the Czechs about the Scots? More talk later, when I'm in a more coherent mood. *Au revoir, cheri.*

I.

PS. I can't place the Black Horse.[98] Where is it?

---

[96] Edwin Muir b. Orkney (1887-1959) poet, novelist and noted translator esp. of Franz Kafka. Muir lived briefly in Prague in the early 1920s and by 1945 was Director of the British Council in Prague.

[97] BC: the British Council, with whom DH worked for much of his life.

[98] The Black Horse, Fitzroy, The Swiss and Wellington and Wheatsheaf, were well-known for their literary-bohemian ambience, and formed part of a familiar Fitzrovian pub crawl (see *Life* ch 6).

UNRRA
c/o British Military
Mission to Belgium
FPO BAOR
October 10th, 1945

Cheri, I apologise about the excessive chatter about these French chaps. It's just that I'm feeling excited about these people, and there's hardly anyone here I can talk to, and you're one of the few of my friends whom it's still a positive pleasure to write to. When I was younger, I remember, I loved writing long letters to all sorts of people – a kind of exhibitionism I daresay (which my letters of today aren't free of, I daresay too.) – but now I only <u>want</u> to write when I can feel a genuine sense of communication. I feel that with you. Writing to you is much more like talking to you, & getting your letters like hearing your voice. Most of the other letters I get are just bits of paper where the personality has dried up with the ink. All your charm & horridness comes across quite fresh!

Existentialism, which is being acclaimed as the new philosophy of France & the philosophy of this age (acclaimed, by its adherents that is, – fairly numerous among French intellectuals) is a group of theories descended from Kierkegaard, via Jaspers & Heidigger [*sic*], & now incarnated in Jean-Paul Sartre (non Catholic variety) & Gabriel Marcel[99] (Catholic variety) and others. It's anti-metaphysical, & phenomenalist in flavour – concerned with the concrete puzzle of personal existence, rather than with general theories about the universe. In general, I suppose, it's a theory of the self, the relation between selves, & the self's attitude

[99] For Kierkegaard see n 80. Karl Jaspers (1883-1969) German psychiatrist, philosopher, theologian; on work of the French philosopher J-P Sartre (1905-80) IM would soon write her first book; Gabriel Marcel (1889-1973) French philosopher and playwright.

to death. I won't try to expound, as I haven't read the texts. What excites me more than the philosophy itself is the extra-ordinary bunch of good novelists which it is inspiring.

(I did not intend to write anything like the above paragraph, which just shews how one's pen runs away, & gets out of control.) The novel I cited to you was a bad example – far too romanesque. Most of these boys, if they're not straightforwardly realist, have learnt a big lesson from Kafka.

My sweet, you will undoubtedly quarrel with Tambi – everyone does. One has to develop a special sort of shock-proof relationship to cope with those Soho people. Bernard Spencer I can't place, though the name's familiar. I don't think I've ever read his poetry.[100] Darling, how I wish too I were in London to wander about with you & drink mild & bitters & talk. Also, no doubt, to go to bed with you, if you were interested. I'm sorry you find the English so bad on love. Your generalisations seemed to reflect a brief but intensive survey. I daresay I should fall equally below the standard.

There's another half paragraph that I didn't intend to write. Shall I tear it up & start another page? No. After all what does it matter. You may as well have another armful of my more oblique gaucheries. I can't think why I feel so fastidious & on edge. Perhaps because it's very very late at night & I'm in that state of tense wakefulness that verges on absolute collapse into sleep. I feel the usual imbecile tenderness about you, *ça va sans dire*.[101] Heigh ho. (yawn.)

De Gaulle was in Brussels today, & from the...........

[*Rest of letter missing*]

---

[100] The poet Bernard Spencer (1909-63) had worked like DH in Cairo for the British Council.

[101] That goes without saying.

Brussels
October 20th, 1945

My dear, your letter surprised me – it also gladdened & relieved me in an odd way, & reduced me to tears, (as your letters used to, though more bitterly, in the old days.) You still have this way of moving me in depths of myself where no one else ever seems to come. I was foolish of course to throw in so casually a reference to something which will someday be a serious question between us. Part of the reason was – well, the history from my side. I still have a sort of lingering inferiority complex where you are concerned. I really did love you rather a lot when I was 19, with all the absolute devotion of my extreme youth. It was the first time I'd ever felt a truly <u>physical</u> passion for anyone (you were, a historical detail you might like to know, the first man who ever kissed me; it was one evening in 124 Walton Street.) – that in addition to a great tenderness & romanticism. And when, later, you dropped me, & made a few unpleasant remarks, that tore me a good deal. There was the desolation of losing you and also (since I was young & proud & set a high value on myself) the sting of having so shamelessly offered myself & been rejected. I cursed myself afterwards for having spoken & written so indiscreetly [*sic*] – I felt I'd behaved with a complete lack of restraint & dignity. Anyhow, I got it into my head that any display of affection or emotion on my part would be greeted by a snub from you. This idea was confirmed once or twice in the earlier stages of our correspondence. You used to be rather a cruel & insolent young brute, David. Sometime the only adequate reply would have been a slap in the face. Yet as you were unfortunately far away! and as I didn't want to weigh down my letters with curses, I let it pass & kept a habit of caution. I freely admit of course that in my extreme youth (and maybe later on, too) I must very often have 'asked for it.'

Well, I still have this feeling of wariness when I write to you.

This feeling that I mustn't 'give myself away' – that if I do, you will snub me – that I may respond savagely – & that something may get broken. What is there though, in the beaten way of friendship, to 'give away' now, since obviously I don't feel the same about you as I did when I was 19? I'm not the same person, neither are you. I suppose I must have said, implicitly or explicitly, in these letters most of the things I feel about you. The height & depth of our friendship & its increasing importance. But I am still shy of making gestures. It's not easy, here, to distinguish between a decent moderation & prudence, (as between two intelligent complicated beings) and a sort of fringe of sheer insincerity. You understand me.

I was desolated & furious at not being in London when you returned. Then, when you wrote from London, I was furious again to think of you slipping so easily (it seemed) into the company of people I despised, such as Tambimuttu & Co. Perhaps after all I am still rather a prude. More cynically speaking, I was just rather cross & jealous. It all emphasised your unlikeness to me: the perhaps disastrous fact that you are a wild 'bad' character & that I am a more sober 'goody goody' character – & that maybe we wouldn't be able to go on liking each other face to face half as much as we do in letters. I don't really believe that, but one must coolly acknowledge that such things are possible. Anyway, the result of all this was that things are possible. Anyway, the result of all this was that I was sufficiently lacking in sincerity to try to match my tone to the casual careless tone which you sometimes use – which of course was wrong, since it was something quite <u>different</u> that was in question. I'm sorry.

Yes, it's not simple, darling, I know – I know you have two faces, a dark one & a bright one. Some of what I've said may sound a bit priggish & critical (well – after all – one may exempt one's acquaintances from criticism, but one's friends get treated more as one treats oneself.) – but you know without my telling you, how much everything that is wild in you is bound up with the things I love most in you. And the appearance, the 'style', is nothing anyway – it's in one's actual relations to people that the test occurs – and there I know I have done things I could weep with shame about. The rest is little – froth on the surface. I love you as you are, at odds with yourself. <u>You</u> should be wary too, for all sorts of reasons. I have far more of the bitch in me than you've probably ever realised. (This in spite of what I said about being prudish – there's a most pernicious sense in which the two aren't altogether contradictory!) You are right about the importance of the physical aspect; we must be prepared to begin our relation in a way from the beginning again when we meet. (This is a confused paragraph, but there is a train of thought!)

Darling, don't say too much in reply to this. I am so afraid that we may somehow entangle ourselves in words. We mustn't get into the habit of writing emotional letters. I'm sorry I shocked you, but I'm glad it <u>was</u> a shock! You know I don't feel casual about the future of our relationship.

Since writing this I have heard that I may have to leave Brussels before long – for Germany, or maybe for London. There's no peace or security in this organisation! It's pretty certainly impossible in any case that I shall see you before you leave London. A 'duty' visit is out of the question now, since my chief, who might have arranged it, is being sent straight to Frankfurt – whither I may have to go & join him – but God knows. It will be 1946 and Prague before we meet, I think.

This news makes me feel suddenly very homeless & unreal. Be patient with me, David. We must take things coolly & easily. You are very important to me.

Much love.

I.

UNRRA
c/o British Mil. Mission to Belgium
BAOR
November 3rd, 1945

Dear David, damn and blast you for not writing for so long. Please let me have an immediate account of what's going on. It occurs to me that you are due to leave London in a few days. Give me your Prague address, if you know it yet. It's odd to think of your shifting about the world like this. Your letters <u>look</u> just the same. Now I suppose when you're in Prague we shall be back to the old regime of letters taking 3 weeks to arrive. Write any way before you leave London for the more dubious Slav postal services. I hope you are not annoyed with me because of some *bêtise*.[102]

Recent UNRRA upheavals have left me with so little work to do here that it seems unlikely that I shall stay much longer in Brussels. My chief, now posted to Frankfurt, is passing through on Tuesday & I shall know then whether I'm to go to Germany. I don't mind where I go, so long as it isn't back to London. You will be gone, & there is no sort of life in England that I want to go back to. Germany will be unhappy & cold – but may be interesting. I should like to meet some Germans. The quasi-monastic quasi-degenerate atmosphere of Army messes is amusing too – provided there are one or two pleasant people to be cynical with. It would be nice to do some <u>work</u> for UNRRA – & I think there is plenty in Germany. And I have no objection to drinking NAAFI's cheap gin[103] in as many European towns as possible before going grimly back to Real Life & seeing my failures & incapacities without trimmings.

---

[102] Foolishness.

[103] The Navy, Army and Air Force Institutes (NAAFI) ran recreational establishments and sold goods to servicemen and their families.

Meanwhile Brussels continues wonderful & full of surprises. Last week I had a great experience. I met Jean Paul Sartre. He was in Brussels to lecture on existentialism, & I was introduced to him at a small gathering after the lecture, & met him again at a long café seance the following day. His talk is ruthlessly gorgeously lucid – & I begin to like his ideas more & more. He's accused by many of being a corruptor of the youth (*philosophe pernicieux, mauvais maître*[104] as an article that I read this morning started) – he's certainly excessively obsessed, in his novels, with the more horrid aspects of sex. But his writing and talking on morals – will, liberty, choice – is hard & lucid & invigorating. It's the <u>real thing</u> – so exciting, & so sobering, to meet at last – after turning away in despair from the shallow stupid milk & water 'ethics' of English 'moralists' like Ross & Pritchard I wish I knew more of German philosophy. Have you read Nietzsche & Schopenhauer & those boys? I begin to think that, as far as ethics is concerned, their great big mistakes are worth infinitely more than the colourless finicky liberalism of our Rosses & Cook Wilsons.[105]

Yesterday, another joy, I heard Charles Trenet sing.[106] (A farewell recital before going to <u>America</u> of all places.) What a madman! There's something magical about almost any tolerable song. And <u>here</u> what a crazy wedding of words & music! It was wonderful.

I wonder what you've been doing & who seeing in the last part of your leave. I got a letter the other day from Leo Pliatzky (Do you remember him?) who is now back at Oxford & who mentions

---

[104] Pernicious philosopher; bad instructor/ example.

[105] For Ross and Pritchard see Pt2, n 9 . IM had had to read *Statement and Inference* by John Cook Wilson (1849-1915) when studying Greats: his work has not stood the test of time.

[106] Charles Trenet (1913-2001) French singer and song-writer – 'La Mer' and 'Douce France' among his celebrated songs.

as in & around Oxford once more the following: Tom Oliver, Bob Morrison, Stuart Schultz, Ron Bellamy, Pat Thompson, Hugh Clegg, Colin Judd – some of whom you may remember. Did you go down to Oxford – or would it have been too melancholy?

Good luck in Prague. I hope Edwin Muir turns out to be as charming as the reports say. Write to me soon, darling, please.

All my love to you. I.

UNRRA
c/o British Mil. Mission to Belgium
BAOR
November 6th, 1945

Darling, you're [*sic*] failure to reply to my letter has reduced me to a state of ridiculous panic. This simply mustn't be. Please write at once, even if it's only to tell me I'm impossible. I'm always rather impetuous & foolish on paper. And off it too. You <u>must</u> be patient with me. I care for you rather a lot.

UNRRA
c/o British Mil. Mission to Belgium
BAOR
Sunday, November 6th, 1945

Your letter of November 2 has at last arrived. I was beginning to be really very angry with you, my dear, for not replying – & rather angry with myself for minding so much. You will have received by now another short lecture on Jean Paul Sartre (what a bore I am) & a letter expressing panic which I now kick myself for having written. Reflecting on my other letter I thought afterwards I'd said one or two foolish things. Anyway, never mind. Thank you for the photo. I find I'd quite forgotten what you looked like. My 'pleasantly selective memory', to which you once referred me, retained only a general impression of black hair & mockery. Here, you look as if you were attending a lecture on the Right & the Good. You look a nice sort of chap though & I wish I could meet you. Have you any inside information on how soon the general public might be able to visit Prague? I've always wanted to study those baroque styles.

I'm glad you saw Alastine.[107] I'm sorry it hit you like that, but of course it would. It was far better to see her. Re her feelings, I don't see why you should imagine that you are the only one who can behave how you don't feel. I hope the pain has worn off a bit by now.

This point you asked me to elaborate – I find it rather difficult. Vague generalisations don't help much, & the various illustrative stories would take a long time to tell, & would probably sound just like penny dreadfuls[108] at the end of it all. There are certain subtle treasons which are hard to describe. In general I notice a tendency to want to be loved, & not engage myself in return – that, plus a really dangerous lack of decision & willpower where other people's feelings are concerned. A sort of paralysis, maybe, before the picture of myself which I see in someone who loves me. Mortal sin; hell, not purgatory. The real crash as far as my self-esteem & general psychological security was concerned was this Hungarian story, which I think I mentioned to you in a letter at the time. Recently I tried to tell you the whole of this story on paper, but I was so sickened at the results that I tore it up. It was all rather dramatic & the mixture of *s'accuse* & *s'excuse*[109]

---

[107] Alastine's husband George wrote on 8/11/2001: DH turned up on the doorstep, unannounced, one 'summer's afternoon'. He and DH barely exchanged a word but his wife insisted on going out with DH, without George, but pushing their baby son in his pram. The outing was brief and Alastine showed no sign of upset. Yet in 1998 DH's name induced in Alastine both visible distress and sudden silence: she recalled DH in terms of abhorrence.

[108] A lurid nineteenth-century fictional magazine.

[109] cf. *Qui s'excuse s'accuse*: 'he who apologises, accuses himself'.

was nauseating. It's a quadrilateral tale that would make rather a good psychological novel. The outline, it won't make sense in outline, but anyway, it started when I went to live with a young man whom I didn't love but whom I was sorry for because he was in love with me, & because he had a complex about women, (because of a homosexual past) & because he was likely to be sent abroad any moment. This was one Michael Foot of Oxford, whom you may remember. In the midst of this, the brilliant & darling Pip Bosanquet[110] came to lodge at Seaforth, who was then breaking off her relations with an economics don at Balliol, called Thomas Balogh, a horribly clever Hungarian Jew. I met Thomas, fell terribly in love, & he with me, & thus involved Michael in some rather hideous sufferings – in the course of which I somehow managed to avert my eyes and be, most of the time, insanely happy with Thomas. That is until I began to realise that Thomas was the devil incarnate & that I must tear myself away, although I adored him more & more madly every day. Pip, whom I love too, more than I ever thought I could love any woman, fell in love with Michael, most successfully salvaged what was left after my behaviour & married him, and they are now living happily at Oxford. She has the philosophy post at Somerville which I was after too, but she deserves it anyway, as she is much better at philosophy than I am, & will be a real Susan Stebbing[111] one day. Thomas & I continued to tear each others guts out for some six months & then parted. The whole process took about 18 months & left me in a state of utter despair & self-hatred. I can't really describe what happened without explaining the characters

---

[110] MRD Foot (b.1919), later SOE historian; Philippa Foot (b.1920) Oxford philosopher.

[111] Stebbing (1885-1943) British analytical philosopher. IM worked at HM Treasury with Stebbing's neice Peggy Pyke-Lees.

of the people concerned – & it would take too long. Michael – terribly tense and tangled emotionally, very intelligent, honest & good. Pip – very tender & adorable, yet morally tough & subtle, & with lots of will & self-control – Thomas, well Thomas is hard to describe – age 38, very brilliant & attractive & (without really realising it himself) quite unscrupulous. Self deception to infinity. Myself – oh insanely in love & utterly devoid of will power. It was my first introduction to complete passionate love. It was also my first introduction to hate. Michael hated me for deceiving him & then for seeming indifferent. Pip hated me for making Michael suffer. I hated Michael because he spoilt my celestial relation with Thomas. Later, I hated Thomas diabolically because he was the devil & was making me into a devil too. Above all I loathed & despised myself for being what I was & for not being able to end a situation which was torture for all of us. Pip & I continued to live together at Seaforth almost till the end – it was fantastic – we wept almost continually. I saw my relation to her gradually being destroyed, by my own fault, yet I did nothing to save it. She behaved wonderfully throughout. My God, I did love her. Since then Thomas has married a hunting & shooting woman with lots of money,[112] who is thoroughly extroverted & probably will never realise that he is Satan. I am told they are very happy. Pip still writes me long affectionate letters – but there are some things which no friendship can survive. I still feel sick when I think of her & Michael – & they must feel the same when they think of me.

I seem to have written something down after all. There are two other men I should mention, not because they come into the story directly, but because I rather loved, & lost them both, about

---

[112] Pen Tower, then Gatty, then Balogh.

the same time, when I was looking round for support. One was Frank Thompson, whom I mentioned to you, who was British liaison officer with the partisans in Bulgaria & whom the Germans captured & shot. The other is Donald MacKinnon, whose name you may know, who was my philosophy tutor, also Pip's. Donald is rather like Bernanos' country priest[113] – he carries his love for people & his mistrust of himself almost to the edge of insanity. Yet he is lucid and unsentimental & tough & really good in the strong brave way which is real goodness, & not self-love with a twist. He's also, incidentally, a philosopher of the first quality. I think I'll always be a bit in love with Donald, in a Mary Magdalen[*sic*]-Christ sort of way. After meeting him one really understands how the impact of one personality could change one's entire view of the universe, & how those people at Galilee got up & followed without any hesitation. I learnt all sorts of things from Donald. Then a moment came when his wife began to imagine (wrongly, I am sure) that he was falling in love with me. As a result, he broke off our relationship. Suddenly & completely – & since then (two years ago) I haven't seen or heard from him, except for one note asking me not to come to a philosophical meeting which he was going to attend. He must have known from Pip & from things that I had told him before about Michael, the outline of the events that followed – but during all that hideous time, he didn't say one word or make one gesture – which, for someone like him must have needed a great strength & courage, for which I admire & love him. I hope this makes some sense to you. Not I mean because he's in love with me – he isn't – but because he must have known his intervention could have been decisive.

I didn't mean to say this sort of thing when I started, but now

---

[113] Bernanos: *Journal d'un curé de campagne* (1936).

I'm glad I've said it – for these people & these events are part of me. There are lots of other people, of course, & lots of other men, before & since, & some of them important, but not so much. Your existence helped a good deal in an odd way. Yet everything was so poisoned at that time that I had the feeling that I was deceiving you too. I remember once sitting down to write to you in Thomas's cottage at Dorchester where we used to spend idyllic weekends, and feeling somehow a bloody imposter & wishing I could really talk to you, & not being able to. Not that I have any 'duty' to tell you about my love affaires – but I would like you to know me.

I daresay you won't ever get this letter, as you'll have gone to Prague before it comes. Let me know your Prague address, & write to me soon. Brussels is as lovely as ever, but I've very little work to do & with the winter coming on I've a bad conscience. It might be better to get into Germany where, even if there's no work, I shall be a lot colder & more uncomfortable, which may ease my conscience! I evidently have a strain of Nemisism,[114] as a result of my parents being too lenient in early youth. Looking at that photograph of you makes me remember my childhood & how I used to feel weak at the knees. What a fantastic frightening irrational world one lives in. Be patient with me always, David. I do love you rather a lot. I'll write again soon & bore you with more observations on Sartre & Camus & Jouhandeau.[115] I'll also tell you about a novel which I've begun to write. Let me know your moves. It's pouring with rain & I must go out to tea with some Belgians. Damn.

Love. I.

---

[114] Nemesis means retribution, fate or doom. Nemisism is IM's coinage indicating her fear she has a habit of courting disaster.

[115] Marcel Jouhandeau (1888-1979) French writer.

Brussels

Tuesday, November 13th

In the midst of a very complicated Jules Berry film last night,[116] in which everyone talked *argot*[117] & I gave up trying to follow, it suddenly occurred to me that it might now be possible to come over & see you. Today all has gone according to plan, including our admirably business-like 'phone call, & I have arranged to leave Brussels on Thursday morning – so I may see you sometime on Friday. I'll try to telephone at some reasonable hour. I gather though there may be delays at Ostend, so don't be surprised if I don't show up till Saturday or Sunday. Your letter of the 7th & the 9th arrived just after I'd phoned you.

   Au revoir, mon prince.

   I.

UNRRA

c/o British Mil. Mission to Belgium

BAOR

November 6th, 1945

Dear heart, here I am in Brussels, after the usual travel horrors[118]. I eventually got on a boat about 5 o'clock yesterday, & reached B. at 2pm today. Since then I have been turned out of my hotel, got myself into another & better one, & called at UNRRA HQ to talk about my future (where I found awaiting me alas only one

---

[116] Jules Berry (1883-1951), prolific French actor and director.

[117] Idiomatic slang.

[118] IM left Brussels on Thursday 16 November to meet up with David Hicks in London for two momentous weeks, their first time together since – roughly – Christmas 1938, months before the war had begun. This time in London, she told another friend, was 'a tornado... ten days that positively shook the world'. During this visit she and David decided to marry and she also re-read Frank's letters which made her feel 'very unhappy and very proud'.

out of date letter from you containing your brief observations on Nietzsche!) The idea at the moment seems to be that I should go to an UNRRA transit camp in Holland till I am reassigned to Germany or Austria. But all that may be changed on Monday when I go to Antwerp to see my proper chief. God knows.

I feel happy go lucky about it. Anywhere, in dear bad Europe, so long as there is a postal service to Prague. (And I can take *Etre et le Néant*[119] along with me!) I feel quite unprecedentedly autonomous (which is odd, as I'm now engaged to surrender my autonomy, in certain respects at least. Paradox! Ho! Hunt it down! 'Whose service is perfect freedom' etc.)

Let me say, quick, now, & get it over, that of course, if you meet someone else in Prague, or if you decide you like the Jewesses too much, or if you just decide I am not quite right for you after all, don't feel yourself tied up, dearest, but speak at once, which will be much better & avoid miseries later. I fully realise how we have, in a way, been 'framed' – just by circumstances. It would have been so dreadful if we had not fallen in love, after that build up. But don't let the heavy hand of Destiny push you etc unless you really want etc. Sorry, darling, to talk thus too much, but I must just say this & then shut up. Realising that perhaps with eg Lucy there was a sort of joy – & not with me – I don't know. I want to be perfect for you. Yet one must first face all the puzzles & paradoxes, not to brood on them, but to choose firmly with them all in sight & knowing what one is doing. And let me say that I think I have the general idea of what a curious sort of bastard you are, but that I do want to marry you (fully realising how often we should annoy each other) and I want to bear your children.

Which things having been said, let us change the subject. (God! How much I want a letter from you. This letter business is

---

[119] Sartre's 1943 book of philosophy: *Being and Nothingness*.

going to be ghastly, with me trailing round the continent, & you shut in behind those Bohemian mountains or whatever & letters taking months. And that photograph, which isn't at all like you & just mocks me with its powerful non-resemblance!) This man William Faulkner is excellent. Bless the Belgians for having told me about him! Whatever minor deity it is that is allowed to do me minor good turns arranged that, amid the dozen or so detective stories on the shelf in the Purfleet transit camp there should be a copy of Faulkner's *Sanctuary*! This I read, after I'd finished *Absalom*. A very nasty powerful tragic pathetic piece, with fewer purple patches. F. has it in for chaste college girls with short skirts. (Quite right too!) He sharpens my zest for writing, that man. (Which reminds me of another thing for which *je t'en veux!*[120] You let me go away without telling you *anything* about what I've been writing & what I'm intending to write. Even where there was a large typescript under your nose you refused to rise. Of course I wanted to shew you, imbecile, I just wanted you to press me!)

I suppose I must go to bed. I scarcely slept last night & today has been a nagging sort of day. I don't want to stop talking to you though. Your parents' question about my sense of humour rather haunts me! Not the sort of thing one can ever <u>discuss</u> though, without getting convicted at once. Odd how humble I feel vis à vis you. In all other relations the years of homage have given me a certain confidence or even arrogance. With you I am entirely *deroutée.*[121]

At Purfleet I kept thinking of Muluk & of that heart-breaking letter you shewed me. How incomprehensible it all is – the way we cross each other & suffer.

---

[120] I need you.

[121] Roughly: 'I feel entirely puzzled by you'.

I must stop talking now, for the moment.

Write to me, you, blue eyed David, & if you can find a photo of another of your faces, do send it. Oh darling, good night, all my love to you.

I.

PS Keep on writing c/o Belgian Mission for the present. I'll let you have the new address as soon as I know it.

> 31 UNRRA Administrative Base
> BAOR
> December 3rd, 1945

Darling, I am leaving Brussels in a day or two for Haaren, in Holland, where we have a hell of a transit camp & administrative base & whence I shall be reassigned heaven knows when to heaven knows where. Note the new address. Letters will be forwarded from B. if any arrive after I've gone. No word from you yet, but never mind. What a life! How do these people expect me to master Sartre, & write my novel, if they shift me around like this?

In a book of Sartre which I was reading yesterday, commenting (justly) on the difference between love-in-presence & love-in-absence, he said that love is arrested in the absence of the beloved, no longer seems 'inexhaustible' (as the person is inexhaustible), & soon becomes schematised. Ye-e-es – but this needs qualification. Proust says somewhere 'What we receive in the presence of the beloved object is a 'negative', which we develop later alone.' There is something in that too. Reflecting on all this I wondered, eerily, how much one is really <u>present</u>, even to people one loves. This thing of realising the <u>present</u> is so important. I connected these thoughts suddenly with what you wrote me in the letter you never sent about mountains & rivers & sleeping under the sky. Very little of <u>that</u> has ever given me a really joyous sense of the present. It has more often been books, or connecting two thoughts together, – occasional moments with people, & rarely, moments by the sea. But I remember sitting on a hillside in Scotland this summer & looking at a wonderful view & feeling damn miserable & completely somewhere else. However, if you had been there it would probably have been quite different.

That remark of SK's[122] about not taking the laws of our actions from others. Thinking it over, I think it very profound & not to be dismissed by reference to psychological laws & so on. Properly understood I think it's shattering. It's the sort of truth that underlies a novel like *The Possessed*.

All this sounds like notes for an essay. Sorry! I am in a terrible rush with departure arrangements. I saw Ernest Collet today, & *Horizon*[123] have already sent him a month's consignment. What wonderful business-men they are! He has just come back from Paris, & says he thinks he can get me translation rights for Raymond Queneau's novels!

I have not yet had time to examine this startling idea. (I suggested it vaguely to Ernest before I left.) Up against it now, I doubt my capacities. Doubt if anything will come of it. Queneau wants to see me, & that certainly can't be managed at the moment.[124] The question of Tournai has not come up again, I'm glad to say.

Dear, what a horrid letter. I do love you, though. Write often, please. What Czecho news?

All my love, David.   I.

---

[122] Evidently DH has been quoting Soren Kierkegaard.

[123] see n 86.

[124] IM met Queneau in Austria on 18 Feb 1946.

encore à Bruxelles.
lundi soir.

December 3rd, 1945

Sweetheart, what a strange life. I believe I wrote you some Thoughts
this afternoon, in note form too. Too bad. Never mind. This
evening I just feel gloomily & blankly in need of you. I can't
think <u>why</u> I feel like this about you. A form of insanity I suppose. How well I remember shaking my head in uncomprehend-
ing amazement when chaps wrote this sort of letter to me. Even
in my dreams I'm conscious of you all the time – I mean, even
when you don't appear in person in the dream, my dream self is
David-conscious. I wake up quite exhausted! It's odd – I've never
been quite so transcendentally conscious of anyone before! Apropos [*sic*] of Tournai, by the way, in case there was any ambiguity
in my last letter, the answer is of course No when the question
arises. I've no desire just <u>yet</u> to be unfaithful to you! I'll let you
know when that happens. You too please. I wonder will you often
want other women when we're married? (I can't get used to these
phrases. It's still a bit of a hippogriff[125] I'm afraid. Yesterday I
referred to you in a conversation as my 'fiançé' & gave myself a
dreadful shock!) I don't think I should take that very calmly. However, we shall see. I might evolve a technique. Or have a panel of
philosophy professors myself.

What I really want now is not to talk any more, but to run my
fingers through your hair & hold you very closely. But as it is, I
suppose I'll have to go on talking. Our letter world seems <u>now</u>
very poor. Yet one writes, it's better than nothing. I keep thinking
of poor Muluk.

I had another talk with Ernest on the Queneau question. The
only thing to be done, since I can't get to Paris would be to have

---

[125] See n 46.

a shot at translating first & worry about the formalities afterward. More sensible, anyway, since I daresay I would find Q. beyond me when it came to it. <u>Your</u> help would be valuable. I'm not sure that my obscene vocabulary is large enough in English.[126] (Not that Q. is as bad as Sartre in this respect. To translate S. one would have to be a positive scientist in pornography.) I haven't any Q. with me, & he's out of stock at Brussels, so the question doesn't immediately arise.

At Haaren I shall be housed in a monastery, miles from anywhere, (a <u>real</u> monastery, metaphor *dans le coin*) with lots of other unemployed UNRRA. A perfect madhouse scene. I hope they let me alone to be mad in my own corner in my own way.

Darling, *quelle vie absurde*! We are both as mad as hatters & isn't it wonderful? I long to hear news of Prague. Does it stand on a large river & if so which? I suppose I could buy a map, couldn't I. *Dearly beloved, good night.*

I.

Only just still in Brussels
31 UNRRA Administrative Base
BAOR
December 4th, 1945

David darling, your letter of Nov. 30 has just come (blast you for not writing earlier) with the news of your departure. My God! with these bloody air letters crawling along we'll be farther apart than ever before, damn these contrary deities. You'll probably have missed my letters to London saying that I am leaving Brussels for Haaren in Holland, where there is a big UNRRA boarding

---

[126] IM translated Queneau's novel *Pierrot mon ami* during 1946. The publisher John Lehman turned this down and commissioned Julian Maclaren-Ross to translate the novel instead.

school (in a monastery, out in the wilds!) where I shall wait, with hundreds of other nervy unemployed UNRRANS until my fate is fixed. Note the new address above. Letters will be forwarded from Brussels, so never mind if you've been writing to me there. My London address by the way, in case of accidents, is 4 Eastbourne Road, Chiswick W.4. as you may or may not have written down somewhere. God! what a life.

One becomes such a dipsomaniac[127] for affection & tendresse in these circumstances, at least I do. I wasn't able to wring as much as I wanted out of your letter, but no doubt that was because you were in a hurry or because I'm rather *desolée*[128] anyway at this departure from Brussels & my dear literary pals & fellow *Sartristes.*[129] (Last night I dreamt I met Simone de Beauvoir. Her first play is now running magnificently in Paris. What a woman!) All of which reminds me, & I give you due notice, that I propose to hang around a lot in Paris in the next ten years or so. One of the advantages of marrying you, as I see it, is that we shall do quite a lot of wandering in Europe. And I want to see that Med people talk about. Where the money will come from is another matter. We'd both better think about the Best Seller angle. I suppose too that I'd better continue to have a job, for the next year or two anyhow, (that may of course turn out to be indispensable to our being together, if there's a ban on unemployed wives in Praha[130].) and maybe for longer. *Mais nous verrons.*[131]

Sweetheart, I miss you miserably. My life seemed full <u>before</u> but now there is a great void in it where you aren't. Your pres-

---

[127] Alcoholic, but here meaning 'addict'.

[128] Sad, regretful, devastated.

[129] Followers/admirers of Sartre.

[130] 'Prague' in Czech language.

[131] But we'll see.

ence gave me so much that was vivid & live & unpredictable. If you don't write <u>very</u> often I shall be furious with you. I am going out now to try to mail this to Czecho from an APO. I hope it'll prove possible! Six months complete silence would be a trial to a talkative pair like us. (At least, I'm very talkative on paper.)

Darling extraordinary egocentric impossible David, I do love you. Warning: I may not be able to mail <u>anything</u> from Haaren, as postal facilities will be of the simplest. So don't panic (as if you ever would!) if there's a longish silence after this letter. I hope there won't be. If necessary I'll write via your or my people in London.

Au revoir, my honey
   I.

31 UNRRA Administrative Base
BAOR
December 6th, 1945

Sweetheart, by now you'll have been several days in Prague, how odd – I try hard to picture it, but nothing very clear emerges. A panorama of buildings vaguely baroque, some mountains in the background (alright, incorrect) & David in the foreground. I've forgotten what you look like again, how tiresome. I get periods of terribly yearning for you. And God knows how long it'll be now before I get a letter. You should have written again before leaving London. *Salaud!*[132]

As for me, I am now in Holland, at a spot between Tilburg & 'S-Hertogenbosch, at an enormous monastery, with hundreds of other UNRRA chaps & girls. Considering how ghastly this set-up <u>might</u> be, it's really not too bad. There is central heating, the food

---

[132] You bastard!

is alright, general organisation is decent, & there is a bar. Since I'm likely to be here for a week or two anyhow I'm going to do the latest UNRRA Field Training Course – five days of lectures afternoon & morning. This will be boring in patches, as I know most of it, but may be amusing too. In the long interims I shall read & I hope I'll be collected enough to write too. (I've a room to myself, thank God, furnished with a bed & a radiator. At this moment I am sitting on the bed with feet on the radiator.) I still don't know where I go from here, but *je m'en fiche*.[133] It's likely to be Germany or Austria.

It's nice, living in a monastery. One wing has been left to the monks & one sees their black robes flapping in the distance – & the corridors are filled with pictures of old boys who became cardinals. I haunt the chapel, which is probably out of bounds to us chaps, & get drunk on incense. I ask myself to what extent you have an essentially religious nature. What a damfool question. But then you see I think I <u>have</u>! These germs in the blood must be confessed to. What is the defining characteristic of a religious nature anyway? A certain sense of sin combined with a certain sense of beauty? Something like that, selon Murdoch. However I speak without reflection. I'm really thinking about <u>you</u> & the odd mixture you are of the Bloom & the Stephen. I wish you'd enlighten me, sometime.

There is so much to <u>do</u> this winter. (I hope to God I'll have more <u>time</u> when I'm married than I have now. To have more time, is in fact one of my matrimonial aims!) I want to read 'Etre et le Néant'. I want to write this novel. And I'd also like to translate some Queneau. Alas, this programme won't get half covered. For the novel, by the way, which is concerned partly with a young man who makes a dream picture of a woman he has known, writes her

---

[133] I don't care.

into a novel, & then meets her again after a long interval, my visit to London gave me a certain amount of 'copy' – maybe I can use it even if you can't! My vein is turgid & tragical anyway. Oh heaven this effort <u>not</u> to say things – to suppress the adjective, to shorten the sentence, to streamline the paragraph. Creating, for me, is a mad effort to keep the door sufficiently <u>shut</u> so that only the perfect shape I want emerges. Only it doesn't emerge – only monsters, with lots of legs & superfluous eyes.

I thirst for news of you & Prague. Please tell me everything. What your work is, where you live, how you feel, what Prague looks like, whether Edwin Muir is pleasant, whether you have a piano, what the chances are of my ever getting in.

I'll write again in a day or two.
Much love to you, dearest.
I.

31 UNRRA Administrative Base
BAOR
December 7th, 1945

Darling, I withdraw my imprecations; your letter of Dec 1st, written from London before you left, has now been forwarded from Brussels. But, sweetness, what a picture you paint! Maybe it was the 'flu or Dr Armstrong Influenza Mixture. The cynical & disillusioned David, having lived through his gay & sparkling youth, the wanton lips, the flowers, the wine etc, now finds himself upon the verge of his tragic era. Gloom encircles him. Nothing left to him but Iris. All becomes weighty & serious & dark. No more lighthearted friendships. No more laughter in drink. Poor darling. Would you like a nice wreath of chrysanthemums?

Alright, maybe it was the 'flu; but it gave me a mild shock & then made me laugh like hell! Dearest, do you mind if we go on being young for a little while yet? I don't care about the cynical woman, but I should hate to forgo the flowers & the wine & the laughter in & out of drink. You may have sown what you consider to be a decent crop of wild oats, but I certainly haven't finished sowing mine. I was rather relying on you for a certain amount of cooperation in this process. With you, I was proposing to begin my *jeunesse dorée*[134] in real earnest. (Darling, I <u>don't</u> want to be just the tragic theme in your life, your incarnated death wish! Surely you don't really see me as the beginning of the darkness?

I see you so <u>very</u> differently. After the years of my own timidity & partly living – after the people sober & withdrawn from life – after the various visions of marriage as equals security & Settling Down and a large income and a house in Bucks & no more madness – you are the great wide sea & peril & a high wind. Europe, & long talks in cafés & dancing together & getting drunk together, & long evenings at home too, writing things, & criticising each others' things, & quarrelling, & having crazy friends & crazy new ideas, & reading books & seeing pictures, & new cities, & making love, & a littler later having splendid children & bringing them up beautifully. Darling, if I'm the theme, development, & the coda, let me tell you that my mood is definitely allegro!

You talk of Muluk. I know. What can one do? If there was any fault, it's now well in the past. There's nothing to do now, I suppose, except write soothingly without awakening any hopes. (<u>Terribly</u> difficult, that.) It's a pity one can't believe that lighting candles or something does some good, or prayer – this reminds me that I propose to take a D. Phil. Sometime. So that's another thing we can save up for, as well as sending the boys to Winchester. You had better produce some novels suitable to be made

---

[134] Gilded youth.

into film scripts. The Peter Raffaty story, it occurs to me, might well make a film! <u>That's</u> how to get money. I shall <u>never</u> manage it. My novels are too full of <u>thought</u>.) Leo[135] reports a party held in 1 Pusey St, which included Peter Shinney (undecided between Athens & the Ashmolean) Lionel Munby, & Graham Hill. All very odd to think on. I'd like to go to Ox. next leave & see the boys & girls.

Dearie, I hope these letters are reaching you. I have no confidence in the UNRRA postal officials on whom, in this Dutch desert, I have to rely.

Au revoir, my darling. I hope the sight of Prague has revived a little of your joie de vivre! I'll write again very soon.

All my love, David.

I.

Holland
Decemer 9th, 1945

Dearest, just a note to say that on Tuesday I am leaving here for Salzburg. I am delighted, of course, I shan't be so <u>very</u> far from you, (as we reckon distances in our starcrossed experience – tho' I don't suppose any slipping to & from will be possible. I don't yet know my military address in Austria, but I'll send it as soon as I get there. I hope letters will be easier from now on. (I haven't yet had any of your Czech letters, & I don't suppose you've had any of my Dutch ones.)

I am going by road, stopping one night in Cologne & one night in, I think, Darmstadt. Let me have John Willet's Vienna address, by the way, if you have it. I don't suppose I'll ever be in Vienna, but if I ever am I'd like to look him up.

---

[135] Leo Pliatzky – see Pt 2 n 13.

I'll write a real letter later from Austria. Darling, I feel happier these days than I ever remember being.

All my love to you.

I.

UNRRA USFA
Salzburg
APO 777 US Army
December 15th, 1945

Darling, this is an experiment to see if these airmail letters arrive quicker. An APO chap told me it made no difference at all, but maybe he was wrong. God knows however when I'll ever get your reply with the information. On Monday I see the UNRRA personnel department here, who will probably push me on to some other part of Austria. I don't mind. I breathe this wonderful air & look at the sun on mountain peaks behind mountain peaks – & what does it matter, so long as I stay in Austria & can go on looking at mountains or walking along their edges? Oh David, what a gem of a city Salzburg is though. It's bedraggled & poor & dirty with the war & the melting snow – but so lovely, with the swift river in the centre, & the mediaeval castle up above, & the dozens of fine arrogant baroque churches, & the ecclesiastical squares with ironwork doorways, & the chaps wearing tyrolean hats & carrying rucksacks, & the endless sun-slashed mountains all around. I'm just drunk with it. One well-placed bomb has blasted the cathedral, but there's hardly any other war damage. My German is dreadful I find. I must work at it. Oh darling darling what an odd life. When ever shall I see you again? Keep on writing (& so will I) – we shall get the letters some day!

Much love I.

UNRRA
Salzburg
December 17th, 1945

Dearest, I would give Gross Glockner & the Koenigsee just now for a letter from you – but alas it will probably be weeks before I get one.

Yesterday I went skiing, 6000 feet up over Zell am See – henceforth you may consider me a convert to mountains, snow, exercise & the open air life. I shall take every chance I can to ski. Oh David, what a sensation! What a lot of things in earth & heaven were never dreamt of in my philosophy![136] The blazing sun on the snow, the air, the sunburnt faces, the sounds that carry for miles, the sea of mountain peaks all round.... Yes. How far shall we be in Prague from such things, & please may we go to winter sports next winter?

Today was fantastic. I went with 4 UNRRA chaps & a guide to Hitler's house at Berchtesgaden. There is this huge wonderful villa, with its incredibly lovely view over the mountains, & near it the chalets of Goering, & of Mussolini, & the enormous SS barracks that house the 2000 troops that guarded Hitler. The whole place wrecked & blasted, since the raids of last February – & the whole place entirely desolate & deserted. We saw only one American soldier in the distance while we were there. We wandered about by ourselves & explored the houses. The whole region was completely silent. The only sound we heard all the time we were there was the bells of a woodsleigh passing along the road. All completely silent & deserted & covered in snow & marked with the names of Yankee soldiers. It was such a fitting & beautiful anticlimax!

---

[136] *Hamlet* I v.

Tomorrow I am going on a tour of the lakes near Salzburg. And on Wednesday, my darling, I am going to <u>Innsbruck</u>, where I shall be stationed. I'm to be communications officer there – liaison with the French Army (I. is in the French zone). It will [be] tricky & I hope amusing. Food is dreadful I gather – but mountains will make up for vitamin deficiencies. [*Written along side of page*: Salzburg will forward letters – so keep on writing there – I'll let you have my new address as soon as possible.]

The worst thing is the mail situation which is <u>very</u> bad. God knows whether & when my letters will reach you henceforth, or yours me. Be prepared for a long gap. David, this is bloody, isn't it, this separation. Not a word from you since you left England. Where are all those letters? In what dismal cul de sac in Vienna or where? Keep on writing, darling, & the dam will break somewhere. I will do the same.

My dearest, I miss you constantly, with a sort of physical pain. I love you, & I'm conscious of you all the time. I long for next year, & for the trials & the high winds of our life together! In expectation of that, I greet you joyously!

Darling, farewell for the moment, & my love, my love.

I.

c/o UNRRA Central H.Q.
Vienna. C.M.F.
December 20th, 1945

David darling, here I am at last in the wilds of the Tyrol. My God Innsbruck is lovely! There is a great thaw on at the moment & the lower slopes of the mountains are green – & then above are the black & grey & white summits & the clouds. The mountains are much nearer & higher than at Salzburg. The town is beautiful – thoroughly mediaeval & twisted & condensed & full of arches & courtyards & baroque buildings & an admirable river.

It's an odd set-up. This is the HQ of the French Zone of Austria, & all UNRRA's business must be done via the French military. That was why I was sent here, because I'm French-speaking. The UNRRA office is bilingual, with French as basic, then German & English – and our Displaced Persons speak only Russian or Polish – so the atmosphere is divinely polyglot. There are only 4 DP camps in this zone, & admirably run, I gather. The personnel are thoroughly international & very charming. My chief is a French colonel of <u>devastating</u> sex appeal, age 60 or so, for whom I fell right from the start! There <u>are</u> drawbacks of course. We depend on France for supplies, & the food is scanty & bad. Also the communal life… We breakfast ensemble at 8.30 in the mess, start work at 9, lunch together at 1, knock off at 6, drink in the French officers' club till 7.30, & dine ensemble – & private life begins about half past 8. (Wine *ad lib* at lunch & dinner is a consolation!) I am billeted in a pleasant hotel in the middle of the town. My job also is not too satisfactory – rather jack-of-all-trades, which I don't care for. However Austria has now been recognised as a United Nation, & will receive full UNRRA help, so there will be expansions & new job possibilities in the immediate future. It's all extremely interesting & I'm glad to be here – *la France, les montagnes…* what more could the heart desire?

One of the first people I met in the office, incidentally, was a Persian princess, called Djemboulate (sp?) who claimed to know you! I was overjoyed & nearly embraced her, to her surprise! She says if you don't remember her, you will probably remember some characters called Arnini, Mohammah & Tamara, and Mocharaf – also Persian blue bloods of some kind. She, poor thing, went to German [*sic*] to search for her husband & after living in great poverty in some Austrian village, got into one of our DP camps after the liberation, & is now waiting for transport back to Persia. She has a daughter of 5 – & her husband eventually turned out to be in Australia. Being surrounded by these <u>real</u> hard luck stories makes one shut up about the food & the cigarette shortage.

Dearest, I wonder when I shall <u>ever</u> get a letter from you? I wonder even if you are getting these letters, as the address is so vague. A British colleague (the only other British woman in the zone) tells me she has received only two letters from her husband since October, & she knows that he writes at least once a week. This terrified me. But no I won't fret about it. This is just one more trial & we've put up with so many trials, we can cope with this one. If necessary I'll try later writing via England – asking my parents or yours to repost the letters. That might be quicker! What a situation! Note the c/o Vienna address, by the way – that is supposed to be better than the US Army one.

Oh David, having you is like having a keel to my boat after rocking about uncertainly & turning turtle in every storm! You are very close – & yet at the same time you are very strange & far. It's very odd, how my blood darkens & my heart beats at the thought of you. Damned irrational!

Looking at marble clouds & plaster cherubs in these churches I dream of Prague & feel nearer to you. Darling, remember me. May the gods keep you.

All my tenderness & love.
 I.

      c/o UNRRA Central H.Q.
        Vienna. C.M.F.
       December 31st, 1945

Dearest, I quite intended this letter to be a letter to somebody else – a worthy Somervillian to whom I have been owing correspondence for months – but here I am writing to you instead! Perhaps it is the mixture of cognac & red wine we had at lunch (the one <u>good</u> feature of our messing arrangements) that leaves me with so little control over my pen that I immediately do what I want to do, regardless of my intention when I wrote the address. Oh darling, still no letter from you. It seems an eternity since I heard you speak & sometimes now our days in London seem like a wonderful dream that I dreamed. Thinking it this way & that way & over & under & considering too all the mean motives of ambition & worldiness & avarice which alas one contains in oneself as well as the beautiful ones, I still feel quite sure our decision was right. Oh I long for you David. Though I forsee [*sic*] the difficulties so well too – yet I know my best self will survive with you. With you it will be life & strength & the vivid world. I still have nightmares that you don't love me or that you don't love me enough (it sometimes seems to me impossible that you should. You know me so little. I feel that I know you much better than you know me. You were so incurious! That frightened me.) but I go cheerfully on as one goes on in the face of a wind when one is going home.

It's foolish how one clings to any sort of little thing which is connected with the beloved! I chat with the Princess about Teheran. I ask for news of John Willett from our folks from Vienna. I reread your two letters sent to me in Belgium (a high unsatisfactory pair, if I may say so. Darling, I am <u>insatiable</u>. Do I bore you? And only one of them, now I think of it, was written since my pilgrimage. More than a month, just living on one letter.) God damn it David, it probably is the cognac. I feel so melted at the moment, I could just cry for you. Damn & blast you, you unreliable Hebrophile. I positively love you. Occasionally I meet a Czech DP & we talk about Prague & I am as ready to weep as he is, as if it were my home town. Other times, I wonder if you're really getting my letters, or whether the address isn't inadequate. Yet I'm happy, & more content than I can every remember being. I'm writing a lot. Yesterday to my surprise one of my minor characters produced a long speech lasting some 30 pages, involving the past lives of the other characters & necessitating a lot of tiresome changes in what I had already written. Yet I think lately

I was complaining to you about their lack of spirit! One is never content. It's like children – either they're dull & lifeless or else they give you no peace – I'd much rather have the latter, for all its inconveniences. Trouble is, I get to love my characters too much – with the bad ones, I see so clearly just why they're like that, & that it isn't really their fault – & they become positively lovable & ruin all my plans.

Sometimes I feel a sort of savagery about you & I want to shake you in the same sort of way that I sometimes want to shake myself. It's odd how close you seem to me – considering our dissimilarities. I wonder if I shall always find it hard to get on with your friends? I look back with surprise on the sea of shyness which over-whelmed me in London. I hadn't felt like that with people for years. Perhaps it was part of this terror with which you sometimes inspire me. You, I know, will always charm my friends.

David darling, I yearn for you, your hair, your eyes, your hands. I am incomplete now without you. I wonder, can you manage me, with my needs & demands – my great arrogance & my great yearning to submit? I feel now that you & I together can compass the universe.

Oh my dear, write often & one day I shall start getting your letters.

Any chance of your getting into Austria in the spring?

Here the sun is shining on the snow – a blue & gold & black landscape. How very very odd life is.

My love to you, sweetheart.

    I.

                             c/o UNRRA Central H.Q.
                                     Vienna. C.M.F.
                                 January 5th, 1946

Dearest, still no letter from you, but I feel sure I am just <u>going</u> to get one (a first batch of letters from England got through yesterday) – & this makes me oddly reluctant to write. I <u>do</u> long to hear your voice again…

All oddly peaceful here. I feel at home in this place & with these people as I've not felt in years. We are living, for the moment, in a hotel on the mountain side, 1000 feet above Innsbruck, & from my window I can see mountain peaks in Italy. We go to work by mountain railway! Little did I think etc when I was slaving in Great Portland Street! A *télèpherique,*[137] leaving from the door, takes us up in 10 minutes to the snowfields, where the skiing & sunbathing is [*sic*] splendid: I begin to enjoy this desert island life. I like the UNRRA people very much – it's an exceedingly communal existence, but works excellently. (Too much to eat & drink at present! A car goes over the Brenner once a week to bring us our wine ration from Italy. And did I tell you? We have changed over from French Army rations to US Army rations. From penury to paradise! Instead of black bread & ersatz coffee we live on grapefruit & condensed milk & meat *ad lib*. <u>Extremely</u> immoral in the midst of a population <u>really</u> short of food.) I've had a chance to run round the camps in a jeep too, which has been most interesting, though sobering.

Oh darling, darling, this time seems as long as the whole six years without you! I keep remembering your gestures & your voice… My feeling for you is something very rich & deep lying across my whole life. I feel fainting with tenderness but quite without words today! Yet words are so damned important now that we're living on paper again. I shall want words from you – & words & words! Write all that you think, sweetheart, *y compris*[138] the doubts & terrors. Write all that you think & feel.

---

[137] Cable car.
[138] Including.

I'm nodding with sleep, after an afternoon of mountain air & skiing. My most darling David, all my love & blessing.

Goodnight.

I.

c/o UNRRA Central H.Q.
Vienna. C.M.F.
January 13th, 1946

Dearest, at <u>last</u> a letter from you has arrived – your Prague letter dated 15th December. You bloody swine, what were you doing between December 5th & 15th? Or was there no bag, or some other trivial excuse? God! How I've been longing for that letter, mooning around in the snow wondering if you ever really existed. I'm delighted that you liked Buber,[139] & you quoted all the right things! One can think & think about that book. I wish I'd brought my copy here, silly ass. I think though that you're wrong *vis à vis* chaps like Buber & SK, to let yourself be annoyed by vocabulary & the unsatisfactoriness of explanations. What the hell, darling – are you still looking for a Complete Philosophy? These chaps are offering you a lot of poetry & very profound thought set in a certain outmoded/unacceptable philosophical setting – take the thought & the poetry and never mind the rest. It's an infantile hangover from the days when you thought you understood dialectical materialism.

I liked your too meagre description of Prague. What sort of life are chaps living there now? Is there music, drama, any sort of intellectual life? Is the city damaged? Do the trams run? Please send me some picture postcards of the place. I want to know what I'm in for. I hope they jolly well get the central heating going

---

[139] Martin Buber (1878-1965) infuential Austrian – later Israeli – thinker.

before next winter. How is your Czech progressing? Is it dreadfully difficult? What are other BC people like? Details of Edwin Muir, for instance. How often do these damn bags go? I want to know what sort of ration to expect. I'm sorry about the cigarette & drink shortage – I'm afraid I'm not in any position here to send you comforts. I gather from the end of your letter that you have music, even if beer & mountains are lacking.

Here life has fallen into a quiet blissful routine. We rise at 7.30 & have breakfast, we catch the 8.30 *funiculaire*[140] down the mountain. (Did I tell you we have requisitioned a <u>divine</u> hotel, picture of it enclosed, right up on the mountain, 1000 feet over Innsbruck, with a view of peaks & peaks away into Italy?) We work, we catch *funiculaires* up & down at lunch time, & again at 6.o'clock. Dinner at 7. At weekends one walks or skis or just looks in dumb joy at the view. When the liquor ration comes in we have orgies & drink ourselves nearly insensible. It's the perfect hermit life. I am reading & writing a lot, skiing a certain amount, & spending a good deal of time just looking out of my window & feeling like a goddess. Darling, I'm really happy & serene for the first time in years.

I notice in you & your letters a certain lack of interest in or curiosity about <u>me</u>. I suspect that you are more concerned about my effect on you than about me myself. You self centred blighter. Actually, I am quite an interesting person. Sometime, later on, I must try to attract your attention. I liked your description of your love for me as an act of faith! Of course it is, on both sides, rather a leap in the dark, since we've seen so little of each other. Are you frightened? I am sometimes, but not deeply. One must live. To refuse this would be to refuse life.

I didn't altogether understand what you said about the

---

[140] Cable car.

demonic David. 'Ever new subjugation.' I can't yet make out how much you are likely to want to dominate me. I think I should be sorry if you didn't want to! I see our relation as a very fruitful struggle. I was amused that you compared yourself to Buber's cat. I hope you didn't too seriously mean that you find speech relationships hard. To me, talk with someone I love is so essential – in fact it is <u>the</u> thing, & all physical things somehow merge with it.

Reading a French book of essays on the novel, it struck me that your & my conceptions of the novel are probably radically different. Take this remark for instance (made by a cove called Henri Rambaud) *'L'ordre du roman n'est pas purement celui de l'oeuvre d'art, avec sa recherche de la perfection formelle, mais bien d'abord celui de la création, avec cette prodigalité, ce gaspillage, ce mepris de la parcimonie qui eclate dans l'univers comme la signature d'une force inépuisable'.*[141] I think I disagree with this interesting statement – while I think you would probably agree. In my own work I <u>do</u> seek formal perfection & economy. I am not at all a *raconteur* – whereas you have the makings of an excellent one. I approach the thing (probably too) intellectually, trying to express certain definite ideas. For you, I imagine, the act is more vivid, unreflective, careless, a sort of song in praise of experience which is quite mixed up with experience. Another remark made by the same cove, incidentally, which I find <u>admirable i</u>s: *'Il faut reconnâitre au principe de son* (the novelist's) *oeuvre la composition de deux elements distincts. L'un sans doute, vient bien du dehors, c'est tout ce qu'il emprunte, inévitablement, à son experience, incidents de sa vie, contacts avec les êtres, et le reste; mais l'autre n'a sa*

---

[141] 'The purpose of the novel isn't just to be an artwork straining for formal perfection, but first and foremost that of a creation with the sort of prodigality, wastefulness, contempt for stinginess which bursts upon the world like the mark of an inexhaustible force'.

source qu'en lui, dans sa nature et dans ses décisions souveraines. Et des deux, avec les maîtres, c'est toujours le second qui, de bien loin, compte le plus.[142] Another thing which occurred to me lately, after sad experiences on two fronts, is that writing a novel is after all rather like learning to ski! One may know the theory perfectly, watch the experts with attention, study the line of the slope, have a clear idea of what one is going to do – but when one is well started & has a good speed one loses all control & ends up by turning a somersault or going in quite the wrong direction! (The snow is all hard & icy at the moment – I can't do <u>anything</u> on skis this weekend.)

I agree that my definition of a religious nature was not good (I think it [*sic*] withdrew it later) but yours is much worse. 'Faith in dogma' is not a necessary part of it, though I daresay a sort of humility & submission is. Anyhow never mind the definition. I have it & you haven't & I shall have to go to mass in the Cathedral all by myself. But don't you love the smell of incense? Another book you must read is Bernanos 'Diary of a Country Priest.' By the way, can you get books in Prague, & in what languages? Is there much of an English or French colony?

Sometimes I feel vaguely restless, point of view sex, & rather like kissing *n'importe qui*.[143] However I've done nothing about that so far. I feel a very deep & fundamental peace, because of you. Oh darling, how I wish you were here, to quarrel with, to make love with – David, please write as often as you can – I so desperately want your letters.

---

[142] 'Two distinct elements connected with the novelist's labour of creation need recognising. One unquestionably comes from outside: everything that it unavoidably borrows from her experience, incidents from her life, contact with others, and so forth; but the other has its source only inside her, within her nature and her independent decisions. And of these two, where masters (of art) are concerned, its always the second which, by far, counts for most.'

[143] Anybody.

Evening on my mountains. A few lights here & there in the town. I must stop. Don't forget the picture postcards. I'd send you some too, only I haven't yet found a shop that sells them in this absolutely destitute place.

Oh sweetheart, all my love, all my love –

    I.

c/o UNRRA Central H.Q.
Vienna. C.M.F.
January 19th, 1946

My darling, at last two more letters, one your epic about the journey (begun on Dec 3rd) & the other your letter of Dec. 29 from Prague about Bratislava. (These posts are quite insane.) Poor David, I hope you're not suffering too acute agonies in that palace on the Danube. Your remark about eating the local food sends shivers through me. What a grotesque existence we're both living now. Oh darling, I <u>do</u> wish you luck with the Slovakian Electricity Company & the Bratislava Water Board! Yes, I'm sorry it's not to be Prague, but I'm sure B. is an excellent city too & I've always wanted to live on the banks of the Danube. What is the <u>mountain</u> situation? As far as the lack of theatres, cinemas, art exhibitions & other frills of civilisation is concerned, I find I can be extremely happy here without them, & see no reason why I shouldn't manage as much in Bratislava, with your company thrown in. (Letters by the way <u>should</u> be much quicker now – though God knows. The UNRRA postal system is unpredictable.) I like the sound of your female comrade. But NO DON'T fall in love with her. Missing the Muirs is sad too. Look, send me some postcards of this Slovakian burg. I can't even think where it is (will study the map tomorrow.) God! Just reading over that first page of your letter my imagination reels. We here, with the American Army next door & the French all round cannot get a couple of tables

& chairs for our office. What you will manage to achieve, all by yourselves beside the Danube, I just can't think! (How wide is the river there?) Don't run away from responsibility you idiot! You never know, they might raise your salary eventually! You are going to have a wife with expensive tastes. (Kierkegaard at two guineas a volume, & so on. Any chance of my getting a job down there? I suppose there are no English-speaking shows in the town apart from you & the Embassy. And I doubt whether my literary activities will be much benefit to the common exchequer. I still find it difficult to see how exactly it will take me, this business of being a wife. Whether I shall really get interested in cooking & tidying the house & so on, or whether I shall have a bright snappy job of some kind & drag you out to restaurants to eat (if there ever are any) or whether I shall selfishly busy myself in books, dreamily emerging when you return home to make you some ghastly undercooked meal. Darling, what <u>risks</u> you're running! For heavens sake, stand no nonsense of any kind from me, it would be fatal (this seriously.) Children, I think a bit later when Europe is more organised & one can get these fancy foods that children eat these days & generally exist without eternally queuing or scrounging. (A look at the Austrians here has given one an insight into the ghastliness of this shortage of <u>everything</u> that seems to be so general outside of Brussels. It's a full time job for these people to get enough food & clothes to go on living at all normally.)

I'm having German lessons now & managing to stammer a little German with Chambermaids & odd D.P.s – but my *Wortschatz*[144] is still very small. What tongues do they speak in Bratislava? Is Slovakian different from Czech? Don't go learning any outlandish dialect, will you? It's bad enough learning Czech instead of the pure fountain of Russian. (Oh wonderful wonder-

---

[144] Vocabulary.

ful language! Our Russian speaking Persian princess has a small but beautiful voice & often sings us songs in Russian. She is soon going back to Teheran, by the way. Her emotion on this subject overflows the office, naturally enough.)

Darling, there's something I miss in your letters. A sort of personal impact. It's not your fault, it's probably impossible to give me just what I want, language isn't constructed that way. A deep irrational desire to be dominated, to be held – together with a savage joyous disinclination to submit easily. I wonder if that makes sense, doubt it. Oh my darling, I do long to see you. Your physical presence twists something in me always. Sorry, try to understand this.

I am fed up with my novel, for the moment. My efforts to 'expel myself' from the characters & give them an independent life has resulted in their becoming thoroughly tiresome & unreal. For the central character, who is supposed to be a rather charming dreamy though ineffectual youth, I am developing a passionate hatred, & am almost ready to change the structure of the thing just so that he shall jolly well <u>not</u> triumph over his difficulties in the end. Yet it means a lot nevertheless to have these people about me & to think about them as I walk along a road & wonder what exactly they will do when the next crisis comes upon them. Thank God for feeling independent & not depending on cinemas & dances & cigarettes & booze (or even ballet) as most of the people here do & get nervy when they can't get 'em. Booze actually we've had too damn much of lately. Someone had a birthday last week, we had an allnight blind. Bottles of Scotch appeared magically on all sides. I confess that I <u>did</u> fall very gladly into the arms of a handsome young French driver, but it wasn't in the nature of a conscious act. Don't worry.)

Oh my angel, write & write & write. I can't have too many letters from you. And send me a postcard or two of that Danube.

It's better to address letters direct & not through the F.O?

David, what are the chances of my being able to live with you, with or without a job, by early summer? I'll write again in a day or two.

My love. I.

Innsbruck

January 22nd, 1946

Angel, just a note to catch the courier. Life rolls peacefully. Wonderful rushes up the mountain in the jeep for lunch. Blue skies & our mountains. Rilke. Looking at a map I see Bratislava is very interestingly placed. Vienna is rather a <u>long</u> train ride off, & Budapest even farther, but it's a good spot – what a vortex of tongues & races it must be. And oh my dear is it beautiful? I begin to get a taste for *mittel-europaische*[145] civilisations, said she knowing nothing whatever about them... (At least I am reading a book on the Destiny of Austria & realising how little I know of these enchanting regions, historically or any other way.)

Heard the *Wiener Sängerknaben*[146] in Innsbruck last night – most exquisite voices but could have been more polished & they sang too damn much Joe Strauss. It looks like the Austrians are prouder of Strauss than they are of Mozart. Some lovely motets to begin with. Huge enthusiastic audience.

No books to be had in this burg. (Luckily I am well provided) – but I picked up a copy of 'Fontaine' the other day which reminded me of this superb remark of Gabriel Marcel – '*On se condamne à exister avec la même espece de réalité qu'on attribue à l'autrui.*'[147] What a train of thought one could start from these!

---

[145] Central European.

[146] Vienna Boys Choir.

Much love, dearest – write often –
    I.

c/o UNRRA Central H.Q.
Vienna. C.M.F.
January 25th, 1946

Darling, after a day which seems to have been interminable I sit down (4 am) to write to you, once again under the influence of drink, I regret to say.

Much emotion in this last day or two. On Wednesday I was involved in a midnight dash to the Brenner in pursuit of a D.P. Yugoslav driver who, having smashed up an UNRRA truck, was afraid to return to HQ & tried to make a dash for Italy via the Brenner, carrying a loaded pistol with him, the poor fool. The French arrested him at the frontier & I, being the only French speaker in the office when the crisis occurred, had to cope with complicated phone calls & eventually go up to investigate in a jeep. We brought him back to Innsbruck & he sat behind us in the jeep & cried all the way. Thereafter, a great battle with the hard cynical swine at HQ whose only reaction was 'put him in the cooler' and a cynical laugh. God! So few people in this great relief organisation can make any imaginative effort to understand what the displaced person problem really is. <u>All</u> these D.P.'s [*sic*] are either apathetic or inclined to be thugs or crooks – they've had to be to survive. This boy – age 24 – a King Peter partisan – God knows how he's lived these last five years. And when he does something hysterical all our HQ gentleman can think of is getting him the maximum penalty, just because they're riled at an UNRRA truck being smashed! I haven't felt such misery &

---

[147] 'We condemn ourselves to live by the same style of reality as we ascribe to others'.

fury for a long time. The charge of 'stealing a car' (quite false) was eventually dropped, & he is now in jug, awaiting trial on charge of carrying firearms – & will probably end up being shot willy nilly back to Yugoslavia to be slaughtered by Tito's men. What a sickening world. These sort of incidents suddenly make one realise how <u>irrevocably</u> broken so many lives have been by this war. Nothing nothing nothing ahead for these people. What can one do?

I went dancing tonight, with some of the worst HQ offenders, & got thoroughly drunk on Slivowitz, the local beverage. A contradictory paradoxical life. Yet self mutilation does no good. If it did I'd gladly cut off a few fingers in the mood I am now.

Oh darling, be there & steady me. You must understand.

And I do love you, in the depths as in the heights.

I.

c/o UNRRA Central H.Q.
Vienna. C.M.F.
January 27th, 1946

Pig dog, another courier has come, bringing no letter from you! I've had precisely three letters from you since you reached Czecho – & I must have written you about 50 – however it <u>may</u> all be the fault of the postal system & not of you. I shall be expecting a large batch of highly personal & informative letters in the immediate future.

Our little community is still rather strained & emotional after the row we had about the Yugoslav boy (I wrote an account I believe in some disgracefully drunken moment). The French, having more sense than I'd expected, are not going to pursue the firearms charge – however instead they are handing him to the Yugoslav authorities to be repatriated – which is probably the last thing he wants. All a bloody business. There's nothing more one can do now.

I went for a long mountain walk this morning (the snow's too hard & icy for skiing, at least I think so) & this afternoon tried to write with notable unsuccess. My characters seem to me a lot of silly spoilt nervy pseudo intellectuals without any real joy or any real Angst in them. What I hoped would be a rich enamelled surface à la Raymond Queneau or Samuel Beckett (know those boys?) looks a pretty facile tinselly sort of glitter to my coldly judging eye. Fed up, I returned to the *Briefe an einen jungen Dichter*,[148] for some good sobering moral advice. Oh superb, wonderful Rilke, how wise you are, & how I adore you, as I'm sure that wretched boy adored you, putting away his ghastly poems in a drawer! *Und wenn aus dieser Wendung nach innen, aus dieser Versenkung in die eigene Welt Verse Kommen, dann werden sie nicht daran denken, jemanden zu fragen ob es gute Verse sind…. Ein Kunstwerk ist gut, wenn es aus Notwendigkeit entstand. In dieser Art seines Ursprungs liegt sein Urteil; es gibt kein anderes.*[149]

A very blue evening over my mountains & my valley & the great bell of the Cathedral rings for the angelus. How will I ever leave these mountains, even to marry you? How leave this absolutely celestial solitude & silence? I have such an intoxicating sense of <u>real</u> liberty & independence at last. Perhaps you'll have to come & fetch me with a bridle & a bit. Yet you are already a part of this sense of liberty. Darling, sometimes it looks so very

---

[148] Rilke's *Letters To A Young Poet* are ten marvellous letters written to 19-year-old Franz Kappus – referred to by IM as 'that wretched boy' – about to enter the German military. He approached Rilke for a critique of his poetry and for guidance. Rilke was only 27 when the first letter was written. The resulting five-year correspondence is a much-loved manual concerning what is needed to be an artist and an adult. Stephen Mitchell's translation used here.

[149] 'And if out of this turning-within, out of this immersion in your own world, poems come, then you will not think of asking anyone whether they are good or not… A work of art is good if it has arisen out of necessity. That is the only way one can judge it; there is no other.'

perilous ahead – because we know each other so little – yet it looks splendid too. A rough sea to dive into. You said once I would have to be hard with you. Yes. And you too with me. We shall manage it.

I saw last night a German coloured film of Storm's 'Immensee'.[150] Colour admirable full of subtlety & much superior to any English or Hollywood efforts. It was a simple, sugary, nicely restrained & unspectacular version of the tale. Do you know it? Reinhard [*sic*] reminds me a bit of you – as Costals used to remind me of you, only now I realise you are much more sentimental than Costals. Reinhard probably somnambulated[151] into any number of people. Fortunately I haven't the patient submissive temperament of Elizabeth!

I'm LONGING to know what sort of a place Bratislava is. Postcards, please. Isn't it quite a port, or was? What does Hungary smell like, now you're on the verge of it? What a position, if one could only really sense the clashes & crosscurrents! I suppose German is spoken quite a lot?

Darling, blessings on your dark hair & blue eyes. Write! I tire of soliliquising.

All, all my love to you.

I.

PS I'm still writing to the Prague address, as you see – I'm afraid the B. postal people may never have heard of the B.C. Let me have an address *quam celerrime.*[152]

c/o UNRRA Central H.Q.

---

[150] The novella by Theodor Storm (1849) was filmed in colour in 1943 by Veit Harlan, who studied under the wing of Max Reinhardt and who also made the notorious Nazi propaganda film *Jew Suss*. His first wife was Jewish and perished with her family in Auschwitz. Costals unidentified.

[151] Sleep-walked.

[152] As fast as possible (see n 3).

Vienna. C.M.F.

January 28th, 1946

Sweetheart, just an experiment to see if the Bratislava postal authorities <u>have</u> heard of the British Council. I have been sending my letters via Prague up to now for which you may be cursing me but after all it's probably your fault for not writing oftener & giving me better instructions.

This confusing country seems to be flying straight into spring, tho' we haven't really had a winter yet. Blazing sunshine all the time, snow at 1500 m. or so, but very hard & frozen & bad for skiing.

I feel hungry for political news. Papers are so late & irregular here. The situation everywhere looks pretty bad (I was going to say the situation in China, but why pick on China?) – alas for UNO. Everyone is starting out so much more cynically this time. I wish I could see something of Austrian politics, but my German is so bad & our position here so delicate anyway, it's impossible. What impression have you got of the present Czech government? What sort of town is Bratislava politically? It is an interesting spot to be. What's the transport to Vienna like, assuming one could cross the frontier, & how long does it take? Yes, I know this isn't a real letter at all, nevertheless let mestate categorically that I love you.

I.

c/o UNRRA Central H.Q.

Vienna. C.M.F.

February 4th, 1946

Darling, a fine romance with no letters![153] Another week has gone by & nothing from you – <u>not</u> your fault I know, but damn these

---

[153] cf. Jerome Kern's song 'A fine romance with no kisses' (*Swing Time* 1936).

posts. The last letter I had from you was dated 29th Dec! I am going to address this to Bratislava come what may & hope it reaches you.

Here the *Sonnen-paradies* business[154] is really getting started. I spent a wonderful long afternoon yesterday skiing in the blazing sun, with sleeves rolled up. My skiing begins to take shape a little & I'm becoming ambitious & no longer look with dizzy amaze at the perpendicular slopes down which the experts fly, but with appreciative interest & aspiration! My turns are still a bit unpredictable & I don't think I'll start on any major ski runs for a while – but its all more & more exhilarating. And a damn waste of time!

I've had one or two patches of nerves lately. It's this confined life. The opinions even of people for whom one has little respect get an exaggerated importance. I get hypersensitive & worry if I'm 'left out' of anything, just like I did at school – all very infantile & interesting to observe. Also the complete non-existence of any sustained private life, & the fact that one is watched & commented on the whole time – this is especially so for us four women here, being in such a minority – gets on one's nerves. However, the chaps are a <u>nice</u> lot of chaps & kind & decent even if not particularly sensitive or intellectual. I like them all, & we have a good camaraderie on the whole, only I do have these spells of nerves when some idiotic thing wounds me. All very stupid. I wish some of your letters would arrive & balance me again!

Another cause of depression is my novel which I have decided is really very bad, almost to the point of chucking it, which I hate to do. I don't think I <u>will</u> chuck it actually, but I've very little hope of reclaiming it. The characters are tiresome & unreal, the situ-

---

[154] Sun-paradise.

ation is strained & the force & poetry which might have saved it are drying up. I wish I could get <u>out</u> the things which I feel inside me. Perhaps I never will. See Costals' patronising comments on Solange's father, a man who lived his whole life without ever expressing himself, & what an enfer. I feel thoroughly incoherent at present & can't even talk about the thing. I hope <u>you</u> are writing hard – or if not writing, thinking & creating something. We can't both be defeated on this front. There aren't many people I could get any vicarious satisfaction from the literary successes of (see, I can't even write an English sentence!) but I certainly could get a lot of satisfaction from yours – not 'best seller' sense, *bien entendu*, but the creation of something good.

After frenzied & unsuccessful efforts to finish a chapter I'm thoroughly tired of before I start I return with blushes & shame to Rilke & hear his serene quiet voice: *Kunstwerke sind von einer unendlichen Einsamkeit.[…] Da gibt kein Messen mit der Zeit, da gibt kein Jahr, und zehn Jahr [sic] sind nichts. Künstler sein heisst: nicht rechnen und zählen; reifen wie der Baum, der seine Säfte nicht drängt und getrost in den Stürmen des Frühlings steht ohne die Angst, das dahinter kein Sommer kommen könnte. Er kommt doch….. Geduld ist alles.*[155]

Darling, how much I expect from you. Infinite things. Sometime I'm afraid & feel that I will be a very difficult person to be married to – nervy & selfish & ambitious. You must be patient, & if it isn't too much to ask (& who can I ask it of, if not you?) try to understand me. I wish I knew you better. I'm so often frightened because I feel I don't know you.

I have a photograph of Rodin's 'La Cathedrale' – two hands

---

[155] 'Works of art are of an infinite solitude…In this there is no measuring with time, a year doesn't matter, and ten years are nothing. Being an artist means: not numbering and counting, but ripening like a tree, which doesn't force its sap, and stands confidently in the storms of spring, not afraid that afterward summer may not come. It does come. … patience is everything.'

lifted together, palms facing & fingers a little touching – Do you know it? – a sort of yearning aspiring shaping gesture. Marriage should be like that.

Kind friends have sent me books from home, but nothing that particularly nourishes me: Sean O'Casey, DH Lawrence's poems, & Sidney Keyes.[156] Oh for a draught of Kierkegaard! Talking of which, I quoted to an intelligent friend in London this remark of Simone de Beauvoir (Sartre's mistress) '*Il nous faut savoir que nous ne créons jamais pour autrui que des points de départ et pourtant les vouloir pour nous comme des fins.*'[157] She now writes back that it means nothing to her, & that others of my friends to whom she has quoted it are equally blank! I hope you find it a bit striking & intelligible? Such things are shocks, their non comprehension I mean.

Write to me & go on writing, my David. Send postcards of Bratislava. Send your love. And send lots & lots of talk. My darling, I yearn for your voice.

My love to you.

I.

c/o UNRRA Central H.Q.
Vienna. C.M.F.
February 9th, 1946

Sweetheart, still no letter from you, since one dated in December! Sorry to harp on this, but it does make a difference to life. Not your fault I know – but oh, do do what you can to push those let-

---

[156] O'Casey (1880-1964) Irish playwright, from a Protestant and shabby genteel North Dublin background similar to that of IM's mother; Keyes, see n 54.

[157] We must realise that for others we only ever make starting-points, while for ourselves wanting them as ends.

ters round by the quickest way. I still have no news of Bratislava or your job or the Danube or you or anything.

This weekend I am spending at Landeck, a town some 150 km west along the Inn Valley, where there is an UNRRA camp & where two of my friends are working, one as Camp Director & the other as Welfare Officer. A blinding snowstorm this morning up on our mountain – changing to rain as we came down into the town – I'm hoping for sun further along the valley. This will be my first weekend away from the Family Circle since Christmas & I shall <u>much</u> appreciate it! I like our chaps here a lot, but the close quarters of so many highly various personalities is a strain at times.

My greatest consolation here is a pair of Parisian boys, age about 24, who speak only French (& lovely Argot at that), who spent most of their war in the Maquis (having escaped from POW camps), *croix de guerre*, very wild & mad & bad, & regarded by the English & Yanks here as a damn nuisance – which they probably are. Oh David, how can I describe these two to you? I wish I could 'photograph' them – their gestures, their voices, their expressions. They give me the same sort of joy that one gets from watching squirrels or birds at play – a pure ecstatic tenderness! Their devotion to each other is so charming too. (Do you remember the two Arab boys in the 'Seven Pillars',[158] who were such a nuisance to everyone?) They are always exceedingly gay, yet very human & gentle. (I am now coming back to my old way of dividing humanity into the people who have hearts & the people who are heartless. These two are definitely of the warm-hearted. There is also with us a girl, a French typist, very correct French *Jeune Fille*, but very gay & charming (also + heart), & I spend a lot of time with these three, just chattering, or learning

---

[158] T.E. Lawrence: *Seven Pillars of Wisdom* (1922).

songs. (André & Pierre know more French songs than anyone I've yet met. Helène & I coax these songs out of them at the rate of one or two a week.)

Such things are very important. The balance of people is easily upset. A fresh personality can put us all off our feed for days. God! David, how much I need *tendresse* from people, & gentleness, the possibility of liking & being liked with real warmth. I was so extremely protected in London from this point of view – there was a whole great background of people whom I loved & who loved me & who were always glad to see me. Such people exist here too, but fewer of course & in this narrow life one depends on them more. I wish I were one of these ruthless toughs – no of course I don't, but I don't like this tendency-to-suffer (there's some German word I daresay, *Opferfähigskeits-tendenz* or something perhaps!)

Talking of which, I continue to read the wise & beloved Rilke (in intervals of Max Brod's 'Kafka' – interesting chap Brod, rather unexpected – know anything about him?) What chaps these Germans are for abstract nouns. I remember the other night coming to the end of a very long admonitory sentence, containing a dozen or so of these nouns, all relating to control of one's emotions & artistic sensibilities, & the last two words, when I reached them, breathless, were 'zur Ewigkeit'[159] – thus, with a last magnificent gesture, raising the whole thing to the nth power! What a man.

The Landeck supply officer has just rolled in & offered me a lift to Landeck in his lorry if I leave at once. *Au revoir, cheri – je ta'aime – je t'embrasse*[160]

    I.

---

[159] To infinity.

[160] I love and embrace you.

c/o UNRRA Central H.Q.
Vienna. C.M.F.
February 12th, 1946

Dearest, a letter from you <u>did</u> arrive yesterday – dated December 14th! It came with a batch, all dated about that time, that had gone astray, probably sent to the China Mission or UNRRA Iceland. I nearly wept, it was almost worse than nothing. Darling, where <u>are</u> all your letters going to? You must have written to me once or twice since December 28th!

I feel very cut off from people at present, *y compris* you.[161] Many *ennuis*[162] at the office. You remember the two French boys I spoke of in a previous letter? To my intense sorrow & desolation, they have decided to quit – they say the English (apart from me) don't like them & that they're stifling here – too much sitting, not enough rolling. All true. I see they <u>have</u> to go. Like caged birds, one must free them – but oh how sad when they fly away forever. These two have such *joie de vivre*, they've been very good for me. I'd better confess too that I have been to bed once with André – he is the more beautiful Italianate one, the younger of the two. A fully conscious act, which I do not regret at all, unless it upsets you, & please don't let it.

Everyone here is in a nervous condition at present. Whenever I enter the dining room now I have a nervous crisis about where I'm to sit for fear of hurting someone's feelings! I daresay your little communities suffer the same electrical storms from time to time. Shifts in the emotional balance of power upset the whole office for days. I find myself less & less in sympathy with the upper strata & more & more with the lower. My main pals now are not the Assistant Directors, but the drivers & the telephonist &

---

[161] Including you.
[162] Troubles/cares.

the Transport Officer, who are a little (only a little) less useful point of view culture, but oh so much more satisfactory point of view humanity. There's no one here at all anyway who has any sort of intellectual finish or even general knowledge. I am reading Brod's book on Kafka, & almost everyone has seen me reading it & asked 'Who is Kafka?' & that goes for the Directors & Assistant directors too, the ignorant bastards. *Au revoir*, my dear, my dear – I long for your letters –

My love I.

c/o UNRRA Central H.Q.
Vienna. C.M.F.
Monday, February 18th, 1946

My dear, your letter of 21st January has just come. A shock, yes. It's hard to know what to say. It's frightening how people can deceive themselves & how quickly their moods can change, from very deep too. Yet it did seem stable, in spite of our panics. Thank you for having had the guts to write so frankly (even lyrically, if I may say so.) What do I suggest? Well, I suggest we quietly call it off as far as you and I are concerned. There seems little choice – and in my saner moments I do see that it would have been risky. I don't seem to have a real gift for making you happy, & others have it, that's that. Further, I'd suggest that you <u>don't</u> marry this Dornford Yates heroine[163] without considerable reflection & lapse of time. For heavens sake don't tie yourself up in a moment of exaltation to someone you'll gradually find out to be not intelligent enough or not profound enough for you. Remember that you've just nearly made one mistake – don't go & make another.

---

[163] see n 49.

Take it coolly & gently. If you do <u>so</u> much want to get married, why not consider old Muluk who <u>would</u> be faithful to you and <u>did</u> make you happy? I feel afraid for you, miserable in Bratislava & being pressed for decisions. Don't make them. Also, don't fret at all about me. I see the wisdom of our conclusion & I'm not shattered by it.

I hope you got my letters addressed to B C Bratislava – not that it matters, since letters from me must be simply an occasion of embarrassment now. You must have been miserable in this interval waiting for my answer. Well, darling don't be miserable any more. Concentrate on being <u>prudent</u>. Do write to me please & tell me what's happening & be as frank as you can. And don't worry about me because I am perfectly alright & only wishing you not to be a fool & wreck your chances of happiness. You are a splendid creature David & lots of splendid women will want to marry you, so don't throw yourself away on someone unworthy. I care very much about your being happy.

All my love, & write soon.

I.

Postscript

Bratislava
Stefanikova 8a
May 28th, 1946

My dearest Iris,

I had your querulous letter of 16 April a long time ago and immediately began to answer it, but for three weeks have not had one single period long enough at a stretch to do the job properly.

My dear, of course I know how you have felt about this business, and of course I realised how unsatisfactory my other letter must seem. But it was at that time impossible to do more than merely express a pious wish to see you again.

You are right in most of what you say. I don't want to prolong my justification. One thing I dislike about you is your way of compelling self-examination: it's a disagreeable trait, though perhaps unconscious, because self-examination induces self-contempt. You may be right that my two letters showed ego-centricity, but it was the ego-centricity of humiliation. I was, as a matter of fact, regarding you throughout as happily released from a burden, and contemplating with compassion the fate of anyone who ultimately undertook me. No doubt you'll agree with that. For this reason it would have seemed irrelevant to try to decide on the form your emotional turmoil might for the time being take. I could without difficulty have imagined a dozen different forms, through each of which I have no doubt you passed in turn, or you are more superhuman than even I give you credit for. But why do you think I ought to have chosen any one of these states and written a letter calculated to assuage it? I presumed that however I framed my original announcement you would dislike it: the fault is in the facts, not in their literary cocoon. And the facts are such as to be in the long run more of a burden to me than to you. No intention to undervalue your feelings, but you do remain a whole person, with your ability to spring intact, whereas I am doubtful if I shall ever become one. No decision is ever taken but is broken a dozen times. The word 'love' is no more than a macabre joke, meaning not even capacity to use, but only capacity to harm. The joke is that I really do love the people I harm, and they are many: I respect them, sob with pity for them, long for them, send them gifts, neglect, despise, but never forget them. What good does all this do? Only harm. But I am harmed most myself. I decline yearly in my own esteem.

And yet – how much am I to listen to all these voices: yours, my mother's, the harmonious voices of the moral world? How much am I to judge myself by these standards? For the voices run contrary: if I follow one and marry a woman I have promised to marry, I offend another by marrying a woman whom I cannot make happy. There is no voice I can follow but my own, and if it vacillates, *tant pis*, it is all I have as guide. I was wrong, there is no doubt of it, to speak to you so surely. But I didn't know. It was the fault of a tender heart, not a ruthless one.

My Molly has a good deal more spine and intelligence than I at first gave her credit for. In April we spent a fortnight ski-ing in the Tatry, which gave us a chance to know each other better. I learned good things, she on the whole bad. Nevertheless she still wants me to marry her, and it may happen very soon. I am all prepared for it. We have many tastes in common, and she is a compliant character. Perhaps nothing very vital would come from this marriage, one can't really tell. At least a domestic atmosphere.

Is that what you wanted to know? Now why don't you say, as Ali did, 'I could have done very well without you, my boy.'

I like you enormously, better than anyone I can think of. But was

much worried at the thought of being married to you. Probably the same with anyone else, but it seemed more terrifying in your case. Brain, will and womb, you are formidable: you used to write you wanted to be subdued, but I couldn't picture it somehow, I believed you, of course, my girl, I believed you wanted it. But didn't fancy myself being chap enough to do it. We see the world very differently.

In London this summer? Well, I expected to get some leave, why not. But leave may be cut down again so much that it wouldnt' be worth while going home. I am sick of being buggered about in this way, but *que faire.*

We have just had the elections here. They were completely fair. In Slovakia there was a good deal of hooliganism on the part of the Communists. In Bohemia and Moravia the Bolshis have 40%, which I suppose is a majority. In Slovakia they have 30% and the Democrats – i.e. the reactionaries, collaborators and smooth boys 60%. So it is rather an easy set-up as between the two ends of the Republic, and I don't suppose our own position will be improved thereby.

We have started our institute here, a fine big building hopelessly understaffed and underequipped but gaining popularity and standing.

Well, be a bit more friendly, can't you?

David Hicks and Molly Purchase, wedding July 1946, courtesy Julia Lysaght

In case of difficulty in purchasing any Short Books
title through normal channels, please contact
BOOKPOST Tel: 01624 836000
Fax: 01624 837033
email: bookshop@enterprise.net
www.bookpost.co.uk
Please quote ref. 'Short Books

W.4

Faintly
the mazes of
the moment !
...some throat &
sky whispers
gentle, & low,
...raw) but I hope
...dan. I...it
But I wish
...k on it.
...t of. _____ ...is

Put this full
address on
the envelope →

c/o

UNRRA
C/o British Militar
Mission to Belgii
    FPO
    BAOR.

...ay.   + Sept. LS

David, a letter f
thank heavens. I was b
your 'plane had hit a
something. Poor Muluk
about her & wonder ho
to her & reflect on ho
born to sorrow. Poor chil
were kind to her. I h
recover.

...w bloody to miss
all's well & that
home. Write to

...t judge yet
...nces are of gettin
you go again.

Since ...wri